The Politics of Leisure Policy

Second Edition

Ian P. Henry

Professor of Leisure Policy and Management
Loughborough University

palgrave

First edition 1993
Second edition 2001

Published by
PALGRAVE
Houndmills, Basingstoke, Hampshire RG21 6XS
Companies and representatives throughout the world

ISBN 0–333–94854–8 hardback
ISBN 0–333–94853–X paperback

This book is printed on paper suitable for recycling and made from
fully managed and sustained forest sources.

A catalogue record for this book is available from the British Library.

Library of Congress Cataloging-In-Publication Data
Henry, Ian P., 1951-
    The politics of leisure policy/ Ian Henry.– 2nd ed.
        p. cm. – (Public policy and politics)
    Includes bibliographical references and index.
    ISBN 0–333–94854–8 (cloth)
    1. Leisure–Government policy–Europe. I. Title. II. Series.

GV73 .H46 2001
306.4′812′094–dc21

2001032747

10   9   8   7   6   5   4   3   2   1
10   09   08   07   06   05   04   03   02   01

Copy-edited and typeset by Povey–Edmondson
Tavistock and Rochdale, England

Printed in China

Public Policy and Politics

Series Editors: Colin Fudge and Robin Hambleton

Public policy-making in western democracies is confronted by new pressures. Central values relating to the role of the state, the role of markets and the role of citizenship are now all contested and the consensus built up around the Keynesian welfare state is under challenge. New social movements are entering the political arena: electronic technologies are transforming the nature of employment: changes in demographic structure are creating heightened demands for public services; unforeseen social and health problems are emerging; and, most disturbing, social and economic inequalities are increasing in many countries.

How governments – at international, national and local levels – respond to this developing agenda is the central focus of the Public Policy and Politics series. Aimed at a student, professional, practitioner and academic readership, it aims to provide up-to-date, comprehensive and authoritative analyses of public policy-making in practice.

The series is international and interdisciplinary in scope, and bridges theory and practice by relating the substance of policy to the politics of the policy-making process.

Public Policy and Politics

Series Editors: Colin Fudge and Robin Hambleton

PUBLISHED

Rob Atkinson and Graham Moon, *Urban Politics in Britain: The City, the State and the Market*

Danny Burns, Robin Hambleton and Paul Hoggett, *The Politics of Decentralisation: Revitalising Local Democracy*

Stephen Glaister, June Burnham, Handley M. G. Stevens and Tony Travers, *Transport Policy in Britain*

Christopher Ham, *Health Policy in Britain: The Politics and Organisation of the National Health Service* (fourth edition)

Ian Henry, *The Politics of Leisure Policy* (second edition)

Peter Malpass and Alan Murie, *Housing Policy and Practice* (fifth edition)

Robin Means and Randall Smith, *Community Care: Policy and Practice* (second edition)

Gerry Stoker, *The Politics of Local Government* (second edition)

Kieron Walsh, *Public Services and Market Mechanisms: Competition, Contracting and the New Public Management*

FORTHCOMING

Tony Green and Geoff Whitty, *The Changing Politics of Education: Education Policy in Contemporary Britain*

Robin Hambleton, *Reinventing Local Governance*

Public Policy and Politics

Series Standing Order

ISBN 0–333–71705–8 hardcover

ISBN 0–333–69349–3 paperback

(outside North America only)

You can receive future titles in this series as they are published. To place a standing order please contact your bookseller or, in the case of difficulty, write to us at the address below with your name and address, the title of the series and an ISBN quoted above.

Customer Services Department, Macmillan Distribution Ltd
Houndmills, Basingstoke, Hampshire RG21 6XS, England

To our parents
George and Agnes Henry
and
Fred and Edith Dodd

Contents

List of Tables and Figures

Tables

Figures

Preface

Writing the second edition of this book has allowed me to draw on not only the professional experiences and debates with colleagues, students and friends relating to the politics and policy of leisure, but also to reflect on commentary and criticism of the arguments laid out in the first edition. Although I stand by the frameworks adopted to explain developments in this field which were developed in the first edition, nevertheless I have benefited from discussion and been able to refine and in some cases redefine aspects of the argument to accommodate policy developments in the 1990s. Interaction with colleagues and students has certainly enriched my understanding and informed analysis and I am pleased to be able to acknowledge my debts in this respect.

Many of the ideas and the structure of the original version of this book grew out of discussion and joint work undertaken with Peter Bramham on state policy. Peter's imagination, disciplinary rigour and modesty made our collaboration professionally and personally very fruitful, while his dry sense of humour made it invariably good fun. I was fortunate to work with a group of colleagues at Ilkley with Peter for much of the 1980s, which included Les Haywood, Frank Kew John Spink and John Capenerhurst who continued to provide a source of constructive criticism in the 1990s despite our too infrequent meetings. In addition, discussion with the wider leisure studies community have proved helpful and I am particularly indebted to Fred Coalter and Chris Gratton who have commented in a variety of ways on the earlier texts.

For the period since the last edition was published I have been able to draw on local resources at Loughborough University, in the Department of Physical Education, Sports Science and Recreation Management, more specifically in the Institute of Sport and Leisure Policy. The generosity and stimulation from colleagues and research students has been a major benefit. In particular I am grateful for having had the opportunity to work alongside the late Professor Sue Glyptis whose quiet professionalism was an inspiration. Other colleagues, Tess Kay, Michael Collins, Eleni Theodoraki, Lisa Kikulis, Guy Jackson, Joe Maguire, Emma Poulton and, more

xiv   *Preface*

recently, Leigh Robinson and Barrie Houlihan have provided an excellent critical network, while (former) research students as a whole contributed greatly to the development of my education in relation to policy in this area. I should mention in particular Jean Yule, Pantelis Nassis, Jae Bok Lee, Lionel Arnaud, Juan-Luis Paramio Salcines, Nic Matthews and David Denyer with whom I have worked on related topics. Discussions with David and Juan, both of whom worked on aspects of policy in Sheffield, contributed to my detailed understanding of the city context which forms a part of the discussion in the penultimate chapter of the book.

In addition to resources 'at home' I have benefited enormously from working with colleagues in European networks. The group which ran the MA in European Leisure Studies (PELS) from the Universities of Loughborough, Deusto, Tilburg and the Flemish Free University in Brussels, Eric Corijn, Roberto San Salvador, Hugo van der Poel, Ana Goytia, Hans Mommaas, Theo Beckers and Greg Richards, and the rich diversity of the students on the programme, fostered a global/local perspective on policy issues. I was also fortunate enough to work with Jean Camy of the University of Lyon I, and Christine Dulac of the University of Aix-Marseille II on local policy initiatives in France, and though this material is not directly rehearsed here, it provided rich insights into urban entrepreneurialism and social regulation in two major French cities.

I am also grateful to a number of people in UK local government who gave of their time in interviews and discussion, many of whom cannot be mentioned here because they were party to confidential interviews. I am able to single out Gordon Bates, former Chief Officer for Recreation and the Arts of Middlesbrough and President of the Institute of Leisure and Amenity Management. His analysis of change in local government is invariably astute and represents an excellent example of the critical thinking of the 'reflexive practitioner'. He has been an excellent sounding board and a real stimulus over an extended period.

Finally, and most significantly I come to my own family, my wife Carol and our two sons Alasdair and James, whose irreverent but unfailing support provides a sense of perspective and makes such things worthwhile.

Loughborough   IAN P. HENRY

Guide to Reading the Book

The aim of this book is to provide an analysis of leisure policy and practice in the context of changing political, economic and social conditions. It seeks not simply to describe the development of leisure policy but to account for its forms and chronology by reference to the theoretical debates concerning the nature of the state in Britain and its roles in the field of leisure. While the politics of welfare rendered the provision of consumption services problematic in the 1980s and early 1990s, the role of leisure in terms of its production function (as an income generator in its own right, and as a stimulus to other forms of the investment), and as source of identity rendered leisure policy significant in new ways. As a result of this, the rationale for state involvement in leisure changed subtly over time, and when New Labour came to power in 1997 it was faced with the problematic of re-establishing a social agenda while effectively accepting the market-led approach fostered by its predecessors.

The book is selective in its treatment of leisure policy. Its major concerns are policy for sport and active recreation, and the arts and culture. It also deals with tourism but is restricted in its treatment of state policing of leisure behaviour and of media policy. These are significant limitations, particularly when one acknowledges that watching television, for example, is excluded while it constitutes a major leisure pursuit for the majority of the population. Nevertheless despite the fact that leisure is a disparate phenomenon incorporating a wide range of constituent areas of activity, the need to sustain focused discussion warranted some circumscription.

An historical account of the state's role in leisure over the period since the industrial revolution is presented in Chapter 1. The discussion highlights the fact that even in apparently 'non-interventionist' phases the state has intervened heavily to shape or curtail leisure behaviour. The incremental development of leisure policy up to the post-war period of expansion of the welfare state is outlined in this chapter and the major themes are summarised in Table 1.1 at the end of the chapter.

Chapter 2 takes the chronology of policy development a stage further, but focuses explicitly on the relationship between political ideologies and leisure policy. The major political ideologies are rehearsed and their implications for leisure policy drawn out. Specific attention is given to the attempts by New Labour to define an ideological position. Ideologies of gender and race are also considered together with their implications for leisure policy. Again the structure of the arguments developed is summarised in Tables 2.1 to 2.3 at the end of the chapter.

The focus of Chapter 3 is the contemporary situation in respect of central government leisure policy and the contribution which theories of the state can make to an understanding of why and how government policies have developed. Competing theories of the state are outlined and their adequacy as explanatory frameworks in respect of leisure policy in contemporary Britain considered.

Much of the responsibility for the detailed formulation and implementation of leisure policy has traditionally resided with local government. Local–central relations provided the battleground on which many of the ideological and organisational struggles between the New Right and their opponents took place in the 1980s and early 1990s. As the neo-liberal economics of Thatcherism sought to squeeze local expenditure and to exact further efficiency, so it undermined local autonomy. The situation inherited by local government in the 1990s therefore fostered the role of leisure as a potential contributor to local economies. Chapter 4 considers the implications of this heritage for local government leisure services under the Conservative and Labour administrations of the 1990s and into the new century, while the following chapter considers the impact of such changes on the professionalisation of leisure services. The notion of the 'leisure professional' emerged at the beginning of the 1970s, at a time when the dominant concept was one of the welfare semi-profession. Chapter 5 outlines the adaptation of public sector professionalism in leisure services to the economic imperatives of the contemporary period, and the emergence of new managerialism in the leisure field.

Chapter 6 provides an analysis of the relationship between the commercial and voluntary sector counterparts of the public sector in leisure. In particular, it seeks to explain the impact of changes in the public and private spheres of leisure on the increasingly polarised social structure of contemporary Britain.

Chapter 7 outlines regulation theory as a useful vehicle for conceptualising the shift in public policy in leisure which has taken place over the period since the mid-1970s. Regulation theory introduces the notion of a shift from one form of economic organisation to another, from Fordism to post-, neo-, or after-Fordism. The chapter argues that although this shift may not have been complete, the social relations which government sought to develop up to the late 1990s were designed to complement such a shift. Table 7.1 seeks to summarise the argument on which the chapter is based. A case study of leisure policy change in Sheffield is employed to illustrate the shift from Fordist to post-Fordist approaches to leisure policy-making in contemporary Britain.

The final chapter of the book seeks both to illustrate the strategic relations at play in the state's role in leisure policy at the local and national levels, and to focus in particular on the transnational context of policy intervention in leisure by the European Union.

The chapters of the book have been written with a view to sustaining both coherence and progression of the central argument, while individual chapters might be regarded as providing relatively self-contained treatments of the chapter topics. This should allow the reader either to read selectively or to read the text as a unified whole.

1 The Politics of Leisure and Policy

Introduction

At the beginning of the 1960s, following the post-war period of major growth, Daniel Bell (1960) felt able to declare *The End of Ideology*, by which he referred to the political consensus organised around social democratic politics and institutions. The battle between the political left and right appeared to Bell and many others to have become obsolete. Three decades later, Fukuyama (1990) was asking whether we were at *The End of History*, by which he also meant to signal the end of political debate between left and right but this time with consensus organised around a neo-liberal political paradigm. The mistaken nature of Bell's claims (the publishing of his book was followed by the rapid politicisation of the public sphere, particularly in the UK, with the resurgence of a radical left and the emergence of Thatcherism) should serve to warn us of the dangers of assuming the permanence of another paradigm.

In Britain in the closing years of the century, a New Labour government had been elected and was searching desperately for the means with which to define its political position and to differentiate itself in ideological and policy terms from the political opposition and from its 'socialist' past. The struggle for political definition and legitimacy across the closing decades of the century provides the context for the central theme of this book which is to explain the emergence, shaping and implications of leisure policy at the beginning of the new millennium.

A brief sketch of the emergence and development of leisure studies as an academic field might portray it in terms of four broad waves of theory. The first, in the 1970s, is what might be seen as an emerging pluralist orthodoxy, perhaps most articulately argued by Ken Roberts (1978). The second wave, evident in the 1980s, provided a series of radical critiques of the pluralist account, focusing on social divisions and inequalities in structural terms, with neo-Weberian accounts (Coalter, with Duffield, and Long,

1

1987), neo-Marxist accounts (Clarke and Critcher, 1985; Hargreaves, 1986), feminist accounts (Deem, 1986; Green, Hebron and Woodward, 1990; Wimbush and Talbot, 1988), and socialist policy programmes (Whannel, 1983) challenging that pluralist orthodoxy. In the 1990s a third wave in leisure studies emerged associated with the in-roads which postmodernism has made into social theory. While 'mainstream' social theorists began to turn their attention seriously to culture, leisure and lifestyle (Baudrillard, 1988; Lash and Urry, 1994; Urry, 1990), some leisure theorists actively embraced destructured and relativised postmodern perspectives (Rojek, 1994) which contrasted with the structured certainties of the radical critiques of the previous decade. Alongside, and in part as a reaction to, postmodern perspectives, a fourth wave is discernible. Holistic approaches, theoretical traditions which sought to explain the increasingly globalised nature of the experience and the governance of leisure, have gained some ground. Accounts of globalisation of culture (Robertson, 1992) and of sport (Maguire, 1995) reflect such a trend. These four 'waves' provide some of the intellectual backdrop to understanding the context of contemporary leisure policy.

The delivery of leisure services, where this has been the responsibility of government, has largely been the role of local government, and it is local government which over the last three decades has arguably been the tier of government most subject to ideological, financial and political pressures. Yet it is in this area that sustained analysis of the state and leisure is most lacking. The major empirical analyses of local government of the 1970s (Blackie, Coppock, and Duffield, 1979; Dower, Rapoport, Strelitz, and Kew, 1979; Lewes and Mennell, 1976; Travis and Veal, 1979) not surprisingly lack any developed framework for the analysis of the politics of leisure, assuming a largely unarticulated pluralist perspective. However in the 1980s, in part because of funding difficulties (a function of tensions within the political system), research into public sector leisure politics was limited. The analysis by Coalter *et al.* (1987) of the rationale for public sector investment in leisure provides an exception. However this study was required to concentrate on the rationales rehearsed by political actors rather than on an analysis of actors' interests, or of policy processes and outcomes, and the radical critiques of leisure referred to earlier are relatively absent from the analysis of local government leisure policy in this period.

Some discussion of the impact of Compulsory Competitive Tendering (CCT) as a policy, either consciously or by implication, provides critical discussion of the (negative) redistributive effects of CCT in leisure (Centre for Leisure and Tourism Studies, 1992; Centre for Leisure Research, 1993), and to this has been added the literature on Best Value launched by the Labour government (Nicholls, 1999; Williams, 1999). This tends to be technocratic in its focus rather than fostering political analysis *per se*. In the 1990s, although postmodernism has in other fields triggered interest, for example in Foucauldian critiques of power, there is a virtual absence of such studies in leisure policy. Concern with globalisation and governance has, however, provided some impetus to discussions of local governance of leisure (Henry, 1999). Nevertheless, the picture which emerges is one of relative neglect of leisure policy studies at the level of local government which go beyond the technocratic concerns of commentary on such initiatives as CCT, quality assurance, or Best Value. This book seeks to redress that balance and much of what follows relates directly to the local government context.

Although the politics of leisure became more intense and adversarial in the last three decades of the twentieth century, this does not imply that political struggle was absent in earlier periods of growth and stabilisation of the welfare state, or, indeed, throughout the period of industrialisation in modern Britain. The overt use of leisure as a political instrument is even illustrated clearly in the publication of the *King's Book of Sports* of Charles 1, which sought to reinforce alliances between aristocracy and the 'common people' in opposition to the embryonic, puritan-led middle classes (Hill, 1964). This declaration articulated the monarch's support for certain popular recreations which the puritan movement had sought to suppress. Thus, leisure as a tool of social policy, or as a vehicle for the promotion of certain interests, is not a new phenomenon. It will therefore be one of the concerns of this chapter to provide an account of the evolution of leisure politics and policy in industrialising Britain in the period since the beginning of the nineteenth century. Such an historical account provides the opportunity to identify the trajectory of leisure policy over time and to explore the historical antecedents of contemporary political struggles.

Before embarking on this review, it is important to clarify the ways in which key terms are to be used in this analysis. The concept of policy employed here follows the injunction that it should 'include all actions of governments, not just stated intentions ... as well as an understanding of why governments sometimes choose to do nothing about a particular question' (Goldsmith, 1980: 22). Analysis of public policy which deals solely with the policy statements or intentions of politicians or officials will fail to address a number of important questions relating to, for example, the unintended consequences of policies adopted, the policies rejected, the process of selection of policy options for consideration, and the related question of 'non-decisions'. We therefore seek to incorporate analysis of policy content, policy determination (including non-decisions), and policy implementation and outcomes within this study.

Lowi (1972) outlines four types or categories of public policy; *distributive policies* – benefiting all or most citizens indiscriminately; *redistributive policies* – generally favouring a segment of the population at the cost of other segments; *constituent policies* – which define procedures in a democratic society such as election laws; and, finally, *regulative policies* – controlling the behaviour of members of the community. Leisure policies take predominantly one of three forms. They may be intended to be distributive, as for example in the funding of sports to foster morale through national success, or redistributive, in leisure provision aimed at particular groups or geographical areas, such as leisure for the unemployed or for areas of special need. Finally, they may be regulative, in for instance, the banning of the use of recreational drugs. Regulative policies, the policing of leisure, obviously relate to a key element of the state's activity in fostering or controlling leisure practices. Analysis of this aspect of the state's involvement in leisure traditionally received considerable attention from neo-Marxist commentators, such as the influential Centre for Contemporary Cultural Studies (Hall and Jefferson, 1976) and other radical critics (Hebdige, 1988). However the primary focus of this text will be the distributive and redistributive leisure policies of government, and the interests served by such policies.

Some preliminary remarks in respect of definition of the term 'leisure' may also be useful. It is not intended here to enter into what has become a relatively sterile definitional debate, but rather to underline why such debates are sterile, and to highlight certain implications for theorising the nature of leisure policy. The leisure studies literature abounds with attempts to define the essential features of leisure (cf. Kaplan, 1975; Murphy, 1981; Neulinger, 1974; Parker, 1971; Roberts, 1978; Shivers, 1981) which invariably report the difficulty of providing definitions that incorporate all that is 'leisure' while excluding all that is not. Leisure is defined in terms of 'residual time', or of its 'function' (typically in opposition to work), in terms of its 'content' (leisure activities), or as an 'ideal state of mind'. Many of these authors follow the approach of Kaplan in adopting a composite definition which incorporates aspects of the time/function/content/state of mind approaches.

> Leisure ... consists of relatively self-determined activity/experience that falls into one's economically free-time roles, that is seen as leisure by participants, that is psychologically pleasant in anticipation or recollection, that potentially covers the whole range of commitment and intensity, that contains characteristic norms and constraints, and that provides opportunities for recreation, personal growth, and service to others. (Kaplan, 1975: 26)

Clearly virtually no application of the term leisure incorporates all elements of this definition, and therefore the constituent elements of the definition cannot be said to constitute necessary conditions for the application of the term leisure. However, such elements can be regarded as sufficient conditions for the application of the term. In Wittgenstein's terms, there is a 'family resemblance' between the various applications of the term, rather than a single set of traits common to all that is leisure (Wittgenstein, 1970)

There are perhaps three major implications of this explanation of the nature of meaning for our use of the term leisure in the context of this book. The first is a recognition that leisure policy will imply slightly different emphases in different contexts, and that we should therefore specify the family of applications of the term we wish to adopt. Thus leisure policy may be associated with policies for free time, for passive or active recreations (in sport, the arts, popular culture, or informal recreation), with policies aimed at compensating for the alienation of work (or of unemployment), or at fostering personal fulfilment through non-work activities. The second implication is that there may well be overlap with the application of other terms such as 'education' or 'education policy' in certain contexts, but our definitions should not seek to exclude all that is not leisure. Finally it should be recognised that different theoretical positions imply emphasis on different family features of the same term. Thus structuralist Marxist explanations emphasise the key feature of leisure as its function in providing relief from the alienation of work or non-work. Feminists, on the other hand, point to the legitimating functions of such definitions which imply a necessary relationship between paid work and leisure, while conservative theorists, arguing for the separation of cultural life from the material concerns of existence, stress the notion of leisure as non-utilitarian activity, or as a state of mind. Such treatments of the concept of leisure must inevitably be partial.

Leisure politics and policy in industrialising Britain

There are a number of reasons why it is appropriate to begin a brief historical overview of the politics of leisure policy at the end of the eighteenth century, a point at which the process of industrialisation and attendant urbanisation had clearly got underway. For some writers, leisure as a distinctive category of social activity is a product of industrialisation itself, the very separation of work and non-work being a function of work time and work discipline (Clarke and Critcher, 1985; Murphy, 1981; Myerscough, 1974). Other writers stress the separation of the production of cultural forms from their consumption in the nineteenth century as the logic of capitalism becomes applied to leisure markets, represented in an urbanised and concentrated population (Bailey, 1987). Perhaps the most compelling reason in the context of our concern with contemporary leisure politics is the argument that the shift from rural-agrarian, to urban-industrial, society is in some ways analogous to the shifts in economic and social organisation which have occurred in the restructuring of social, political and economic relations in Britain in the period since the late 1960s. Change at the turn of the eighteenth century and at the latter stages of the twentieth century may be explained differently by liberal historians and post-industrial theorists on the one hand, and neo-Marxist historians and radical political economists on the other, but there is some agreement in both camps that such change was, and is, fundamental.

In the account which follows we will detail the politics of leisure policy as falling into eight distinct periods since the late eighteenth century. The chronology of these periods is not exact, the dominant tendencies of one period may have echoes, or forerunners, in contiguous periods but the nature of leisure policy, and the political debates which surround such policy, can be best understood by reference to the nature of the rationales for state intervention in leisure. The commentary in the current chapter will be restricted to the period up to the mid-1970s, with a more detailed discussion of the central state's role in leisure in contemporary Britain located in chapter 3, following a discussion of the nature of contemporary political ideologies and their implications for leisure policy.

1780–1840: the state and regulative leisure policies: the suppression of popular recreations

Although the primary concern of this text is with distributive and redistributive leisure policies, the importance of state attempts to control popular recreations during this period cannot be denied. The concern of the landed gentry and the emerging industrial middle class represented in Parliament and in the local magistracy, was with social stability. The political revolutions of the American War of Independence and the French Revolution were fresh memories at a time when the economic and social fabric of society was being reconstituted. Advances in agrarian production, and associated enclosure of common land provided push factors, reducing rural populations, while the development of industrial technology pro-vided a pull factor in the form of employment in new urban-based factory production. The industrial and agrarian revolutions together generated a volatile demography which, it was feared, might provide a breeding ground for political militancy and working-class revolt, particularly since such changes brought together, often in brutish and insanitary conditions, large masses of people in numbers which had never before been experienced (Thompson, 1967).

Given the fear of instability, discipline for the new urban masses was seen as crucial, and it was perhaps in their recreational lives that such groups illustrated least control. Folk football, the gathering of large crowds for spectator 'events' such as prize fighting, racing, public executions, fairs and wakes, animal baiting and the like were not simply brutish and unruly, they were also occasions of con-siderable damage and potential disorder (Cunningham, 1980; Holt,

1989). However concern with recreational behaviour was not only related to worries about social disorder, it was also a matter of concern to industrial interests which regarded the instilling of work discipline as essential to the obtaining of a reasonable return on investment (Thompson, 1967). While agrarian production had relied on seasonal patterns of work with extended periods of effort, particularly at harvest time, followed by traditional feasts and holiday periods, industrial production was ruled by the 24-hour clock. In order to maximise production machines had to be in operation as far as possible around the clock and this meant that workers had to be available for labour at the appointed hour. Absenteeism and drunkenness at work were seen as the result of uncontrolled revelry and resulted in loss of profit in factories which depended on a workforce to be regularly available, compliant, and alert. Thus control of recreation was regarded as essential to the maintenance of levels of production.

Contemporary thinking about the role of the state at the beginning of the nineteenth century was reflected in the tenets of Adam Smith, whose book *The Wealth of Nations*, published in 1776, had gone through ten editions by the turn of the century. Smith's liberal economics provided a rationale for a non-interventionist state, arguing that the 'invisible hand' of the market would provide the most efficient allocator of private and public goods. Social policy was also to be minimalist, restricted to easing any obstruction to market forces. The offering of relief to the poor under the Elizabethan Poor Law and the Speenhamland System was seen as such an obstruction, and the adoption of the Poor Law Amendment Act of 1834 provides the best example of the new minimalist approach to social policy. This legislation sought to make the 'workhouse test' of social need a criterion of state aid. Conditions of work, and discipline in the poorhouse were to be so stringent that any individual willingly accepting a place could truly be said to be destitute. Work in the poor house was also to be remunerated at below the level of any other form of employment to ensure that those in receipt of poor relief would not stay willingly in this situation, and that wage levels would not be 'unduly' affected (i.e. in an upward direction; (Fraser, 1984).

Leisure policy in this period could not, however, be described as non-interventionist, since both the national legislature and the local magistracy, sought to intervene heavily in the leisure lives of the population. They sought to control mass gatherings of potentially volatile crowds and to curtail leisure forms (particularly those relating to drink) which were seen as a threat to order or to industrial production. Licensing of Beer Houses was introduced in 1820 in an attempt to combat the deleterious effects of drink. Folk football was suppressed, partly by enclosure of common land and partly by the efforts of local magistrates, with the Highways Act 1835 making street football illegal. The Suppression of Blood Sports Act 1833 banned those cruel animal sports pursued by the working class, and imported into urban settings from their rural origins. Animal baiting, throwing at cocks, the holding of public cock-fights, were all banned, though the hunting, shooting and fishing of the middle classes were left intact, providing good evidence of the selective nature of the establishment's opprobrium for cruel sports (Malcolmson, 1973) Local authorities and police forces clamped down (with varying degrees of intensity and success) on pugilism, gambling, prostitution, illegal drinking, and some traditional fairs and wakes. For some middle-class reformers this was clearly part of a civilising mission, with groups such as the Lords Day Observance Society, and the Temperance Movement having also significant working-class adherents, although the Royal Society for the Prevention of Cruelty to Animals which failed to condemn middle-class blood sports retained a predominantly middle-class membership (Harrison, 1967, 1971).

Despite the selective suppression of popular recreations by the state, some commentators argue that these activities were remarkably resilient and survived, albeit hid from public view (Cunningham, 1980). It seems likely that pugilism, wrestling, animal baiting and the 'worship of St. Monday' (the unofficial extension of the weekend absence from work) and other recreational forms survived in part with the commercial patronage of the publican (replacing the patronage of the rural gentry) as they developed commercial sponsorship of such leisure forms as a means of increasing volume of sales of alcohol. Thus, although large scale investment in leisure was unusual and largely unsuccessful before the middle of the nineteenth century (Vamplew, 1988), nevertheless such investment by the publican as a small scale entrepreneur gathered pace, particularly after 1820 when the real value of industrial wages began to rise as did the proportion of the working population in industrial employment.

The erosion of laissez-faire philosophies:
state support for middle-class philanthropy
and reform (c. 1840–1900)

The drawing of chronological boundaries in cultural histories is rarely an exact science and the suppression of popular recreations continued well into the middle of the century, with the legislation specifically banning public cock-fighting in 1849, and betting shops in 1854. Nevertheless the mid-century period marks the beginnings of a more positive approach to state intervention in the fields of social policy in general, and leisure policy in particular.

Concern relating to working-class recreation had abated for a number of reasons. Firstly, the spectacular growth of urban populations (by 1851 half the population were urban dwellers) had made it clear that a failure on the part of the state to check the worst excesses of capitalism would generate health and sanitation problems for all sectors of the population, and would do little to enhance the work potential of the workforce. In addition, fears relating to political instability had to some extent been allayed by the mid-century. 1848, the year of European revolutions, left Britain relatively unscathed, generating confidence in the 'responsible' nature of the political aspirations (or apathy) of the working classes (Thompson, 1963). Nevertheless, the Chartist activities of the 1840s and the organisation of elements of the 'labour aristocracy' into an embryonic union movement warned against complacency on the part of the establishment. Without some form of prophylactic legislation, the seeds of urban and industrial discontent might well germinate into something altogether more serious.

Although in the earlier part of the century state intervention had been restricted largely to regulative policies, the growing confidence of government manifested itself by the middle of the century in legislation such as the Factories Acts of 1847 and 1867, which sought to protect, initially, women and children, and subsequently a wider range of workers, from excessive hours of work and dangerous and unhealthy working conditions. State influence on the physical development of the city and state activity in relation to health and sanitation were also increased following Chadwick's Commission, and the three subsequent Public Health Acts of 1848, 1872 and 1875, together with the 1866 Sanitation Act (Bruce, 1968).

In the sphere of education the shift in political thinking across the period is clearly indicated. Whitbread's 1807 Bill for the introduction of education for pauper children, and Brougham's Bill of 1820 to introduce a compulsory parochial education system were both defeated. The nature of the associated parliamentary debates indicate a fear that education of labouring or pauper children would simply give them ideas above their station. However when the Whig Chancellor, Althorp, succeeded in securing £33 000 as an annual grant to fund an education inspectorate to oversee the existing, patchy framework of education provision and the development of training for apprentice teachers, the government had embarked on a programme of intervention in the sphere of education which was to lead to the introduction and control of universal education provision in Forster's 1870 Education Act.

Thus, progressive state intervention was clearly established across a range of activities in the social, political, and economic spheres. Leisure policy would be no exception in this respect, though here the state sought largely to foster the philanthropic or self-improvement rationales of middle- and working-class individuals and groups involved in promoting what came to be known as 'rational recreation'.

The support of middle-class philanthropists for rational recreation was, in part, a recognition that the suppression of popular recreations had not been entirely successful, and that their replacement by wholesome leisure forms might prove a more effective 'civilising' strategy (Bailey, 1987). The Church of England, through Sunday School recreation programmes, sought to provide alternative attractions to the more dissolute leisure forms centred on the public house, with day trips, educational visits and so on. The provision of public parks, often on land donated by middle-class benefactors, and the development of mechanics' institutes, public libraries and museums, also constituted attempts by middle-class reformers to tame popular recreations. The newly codified games of rugby and football were promoted, influenced by the 'muscular Christian' movement, as a means of propagating appropriate values of self-discipline, teamwork and subordination of individual interests to the greater good of the team. Wholesome development of the body complemented the wholesome development of the mind in the 'improving' recreations promoted not only by middle-class reformers, but also by elements of the respectable working class.

Marxist analysis might seek to define this middle-class paternalism as simply an extension, but in more subtle form, of 'social control' attempted in the suppression of popular recreations in the early part of the century (Donajgrodsky, 1977). However, such a reading of history fails to acknowledge the fact that working-class groups successfully resisted certain forms of paternalism, while selectively accepting others. A considerable number of football clubs for example, including many still in the Football League, which were originally founded in the context of religious groups, soon exerted their independence. Similarly, the Reverend Henry Solly's attempts to sustain a teetotal Working Men's Clubs organisation resulted in his being ousted from the national executive of that organisation (Bailey, 1987). Furthermore, where attempts were made to exclude working-class people from participation in a sport, they could be resisted. This was the case for example with the Amateur Athletics Association's exclusion from competition of those involved in physical labour (on the grounds that the nature of their work gave them an unfair physical advantage), and also with the Rugby Union's refusal to permit 'broken time' payments. These barriers proved ineffectual in the face of determined working-class opposition. Organisations either gave way, as the Amateur Athletics Association did, or rival organisations were established as was the case with the breakaway Rugby League. Clearly some exclusionary practices continued, but equally working people were able to assert their will in many instances. Finally, where middle-class provision simply did not appeal to working-class tastes (for example when the Mechanics' Institutes failed in Manchester, or in the case of Temperance experiments with alcohol-free pubs) this had to be modified or it simply withered from underuse. The problem with the claims about social control is that they tend to portray the working-class population as passively accepting the wishes of a dominant middle class, and fail to account for the successful resistance of the working class to the imposition of unwelcome leisure forms.

Since the state's legislative efforts, and those of middle-class (and even working-class) reformers, were aimed at the sphere of public life, the position of women and their leisure needs have proved difficult to investigate. They are rarely recorded in formal histories. Feminists suggest this is a reflection of the gendered interests of those who were in a position to construct contemporary accounts, and of those who now research history, though feminist 'herstories' began to emerge in the 1990s (Alexander, 1990; Hall, 1990). However, in part, it also reflects the difficulties of conducting a life in the public sphere for women and their consequent problems in establishing a collective identity and undertaking collective action, when public roles were subordinated to domestic roles.

During this period, the state's role was rather less one of direct provision for leisure, than one of fostering the enlightened paternalism of voluntary bodies. The Museums Act 1849, the Public Libraries Act 1850 and the Recreation Grounds Act 1852, sought to allow the use of public funds in order that local authorities could capitalise on gifts of land, exhibits or books from benefactors. The Public Health Acts were complemented by the provision of recreation grounds in the city as 'clean air' zones, and the Public Baths and Washhouses Act 1846 which was not so much inspired by a concern for promoting swimming, as it was with the fostering of working-class hygiene through bathing. Physical education was introduced into the curriculum in the Education Act 1870 but this simply took the form of military drill. In summary, the health, discipline and cultural improvement rationales which inspired state initiatives clearly reflected the thinking of the rational recreation and muscular Christian movements.

As Myerscough (1974) points out the disposable income of the working class and their free time increased significantly in real terms across the second half of the nineteenth century. This attracted investment in leisure and related industries in the commercial sector of a considerable order. Bailey (1987), for example, traces the growing market concentration in the music-hall business, while Harrison (1971) identifies similar traits in the brewing industry. The concentration of capital was almost inevitable where large-scale investment decisions had to be made, as with the building of piers (Walvin, 1978). However, this process was by no means universal in all sectors of the leisure industries, as Walton's analysis of tourist provision in Blackpool illustrates (Walton, 1975). Indeed, Bailey is able to claim that despite the attempts of the early century to reform working-class recreation, and the subsequent activities inspired by rational recreation, that the commercial sector, in providing other distracting leisure opportunities which satisfied working-class demand, was actually successful in taming working-class recreational habits where others had failed. With the establishment of the urban male franchise in 1867, extended to rural workers in 1884, there is evidence that the establishment had come to trust the workforce to act responsibly, and that the need to exert control over male popular recreations was no longer an issue by the end of the century.

Laying the foundations of the Welfare State (c. 1900–39)

While the role of government in the second half of the nineteenth century involved aspects of political, industrial and social reform, the aim, in social policy terms at least, was to mediate rather than reform the effects of urban industrial capitalism. It was only with the advent of a Liberal government in 1905, with the support of the embryonic Labour Party (the Labour Representation Committee), and after 20 years of Conservative rule, that a genuine embracing of social reforms as both desirable and necessary, became evident. The Unemployed Workmen's Act 1905, the introduction of school meals in 1907, and of old age pensions in 1908, provide evidence of a mild departure from the 'individualist' philosophy of self-help, and a recognition that social and economic difficulties could not simply be explained away as the result of the inadequacies of the individuals or groups concerned.

However, though measures such as these might prefigure the growth of the welfare state in the post-Second World War period, the introduction of such measures did not represent a wholehearted acceptance of welfare principles. The introduction of school meals, for example, was prompted by fears for the physical development of the nation's working class and their subsequent fitness for military service (Howkins and Lowerson, 1979). Furthermore, after the brief post-war boom of 1918–20 and the introduction of legislation such as the Unemployment Insurance Act 1920, a number of regressive measures were introduced as it was judged that the country could not afford even such mild welfare programmes. The school leaving age was dropped from 14 to 13, dole payments reduced, and a means test introduced by Ramsay McDonald's National Government.

Nevertheless the principle of state involvement in the economic and welfare areas was well established and the steps taken to limit intervention were inspired by concern over what the economy could sustain, rather than resulting from any objection in principle to the notion of state involvement. As the first steps in welfare state provision were being developed in a limited and incremental way, so leisure initiatives taken by the state also began to emerge. The Town Planning Act 1909 which itself marked a significant stage in the state's willingness to intervene in spatial development, adopted recreational open space as one of the significant categories of land use for recording purposes (Travis and Veal, 1979). The Forestry Commission was inaugurated in 1917 as the first governmental body to have a statutory duty to provide for recreation. Following pressures exerted through mass trespasses the government also legislated to allow access to areas of land in private ownership, in the Access to the Mountains Act 1939 (though this was ineffectual since access agreements were to be a matter of voluntary initiative). Nevertheless, in the Physical Training and Recreation Act 1937, the state not only provided for physical recreation through permissive legislation, but also provided £2 million, an enormous sum in real terms, to promote this initiative. The legislation was certainly predominantly motivated by a concern about the impact of un-employment, especially on the young, and about the use of leisure by political organisations, fascist youth movements in continental Europe, and the British Workers' Sports Federation at home (Evans, 1974). It was also stimulated by Britain's deteriorating position in international sporting competition. Nevertheless the parliamentary debate of the Bill indicates that for one leading socialist politician at least, it evoked a recognition of the need for a new rationale for leisure provision:

> I think the desire for playing is justification in itself for playing; there is no need to seek the justification of national well being for playing, because your own well being is a sufficient justification. The idea that you must borrow some justification for playing is one of the worst legacies of the Puritan Revolution ... This idea that you must get all girls and boys in rows, like chocolate soldiers, and make them go through evolutions, is a miserable substitute for giving them sufficient playgrounds in which they can play games in their own way. (Aneurin Bevan quoted in McIntosh, 1963: 108)

While the second half of the nineteenth century had seen the development of state support for voluntary initiative in the leisure field, the first half of the twentieth century was to be noted for the 'incorporation' of voluntary organisations through legislation such as the National Trust Act 1907, and the Physical Training and Recreation Act. Major organisations such as the National Trust, the National Playing Fields Association, the Central Council for Physical Training and Recreation, and the British Worker's Sports Federation were national in scope. The last of these was less well established on a national level but was regarded as too 'radical' to warrant incorporation by the establishment (Jones, 1986). Nevertheless the Federation was a leading influence in the mass trespasses organised in the Peak District, which resulted in the 1939 Access to the Mountains legislation.

State involvement in the media also began in the interwar years with the formation of the British Broadcasting Corporation out of the commercial British Broadcasting Company in 1926. Its first Director General, John Reith, shaped its policy, central to which was the aim of elevation (rather than reflection) of cultural tastes. The cultural elitism inherent in this stance continued until the postwar period when three radio services were inaugurated, the Light Programme, the Home Service and the Third Programme, which were seen as broadly reflecting the cultural predilections of the working, middle, and upper classes (Glover, 1984).

The maturing of the Welfare State, 1945–76

If the foundations of the Welfare State had been laid in the various measures of welfare reform between the two wars, the programme of reforms which constitute the welfare state in modern Britain are largely the product of the post-war Labour government of Clement Attlee. However, though Labour implemented much of the reform, there was an evident interventionist strand to Conservative thinking in the immediate post-war period, even in respect of leisure, as Julian Amery's post-war pamphlet indicates:

> Last but not least, in any scheme of social policy comes the problem of the right opportunities for leisure. To guide and elevate the pleasure of the people, to enrich their lives as well as to increase their livelihood is surely not outside the duties of an enlightened state. (Amery, 1946)

Indeed the 1944 Education Act had been steered by a Conservative minister, Rab Butler, serving in the wartime coalition government.

Nevertheless the extension of compulsory schooling, was complemented by a series of measures, including the development of the
National Health Service launched in 1948, the Family Allowances
Act 1945, the Distribution of Industries Act 1945, the National
Insurance Act 1946 and the introduction of 'blue print planning' in
the Town and Country Planning Act 1947, together with a series of
lesser measures which constituted, in policy intention at least, a
reformist programme.

The surprise defeat of the Conservatives under Churchill in 1945
is taken by political commentators to have resulted from the
'inspection effect', which reflected the concern of those who had
been called on to make sacrifices during the war years to take stock
of the kind of society for which they had been asked to make such
sacrifices. State intervention had been made respectable by the
experience of wartime government; it had been essential during
the war years and had proved successful. However, though the
general review of the welfare system may have been inspired by
reformist thinking, the nature of state intervention in leisure in the
post-war period was rather different. The establishment of the Arts
Council in 1946, the National Parks Commission in 1949, and the
Wolfenden Report which led to the establishment of the (advisory)
Sports Council in 1965, were not inspired solely, or even primarily,
by a concern to provide equality of opportunity through direct state
provision.

The Arts Council was the successor to the Committee for
Entertainment, Music and the Arts (CEMA), which was set up in
1939 initially funded by a charity, the Pilgrim Trust, and subsequently funded from 1940 by government. The aim of this body was
to provide for the high and popular arts in order to foster public
morale. The experience gained with CEMA which promoted more
than 6000 concerts during the war years, demonstrated that there
could be a popular demand for the arts, that there was a paucity of
facilities in which to stage arts events, and that by providing funding
for professional artists standards of performance could be raised.

There was general agreement across the political parties that the
arts should be supported, and the Arts Council received its Royal
Charter in 1946. The concerns of the Council were to promote
professional rather than amateur art, to limit itself to promotion of
high arts, to concentrate on excellence rather than participation, and

to involve itself in only very limited direct provision, stimulating provision by others through grant aid. A corollary of its decision to focus on excellence was the concentration on arts provision in London, which, it was held, could generate the critical mass of audience and artists required to achieve and support international quality performance. By the early 1960s the regional offices inherited from CEMA had been closed down and London-based companies were able to account for more than half of the Arts Council of Great Britain's budget (Braden, 1977; Clark, 1980). Government's concern with the arts was therefore rather less reformist, in the sense of reducing inequalities through state provision, than it was 'conservationist', or even 'paternalist' in attempting to maintain and improve standards of provision in high cultural forms. There was some attempt at the 'democratisation of culture', improving access to the high arts (for some) through subsidy of such cultural forms, but there was little credence given to 'cultural democracy', allowing groups to promote and foster their own cultural forms. The pre-war elitist cultural policy of Reith's BBC was thus reproduced in the activities of the post-war Arts Council.

Similarly, the National Parks and Access to the Countryside Act 1949 was as much concerned with conservation matters and the protection of industrial interests in the countryside as it was with promoting recreation (Shoard, 1980). The Act was not designed to achieve wide-ranging access for urban populations to countryside, but rather was concerned with the preservation and management of remote areas of landscape subject to increasing recreational pressures. The Act designated nine National Parks which still remain, with land predominantly (78%) in private hands.

Even the establishment of a Sports Council, advocated in the Wolfenden Report, was not justified by reference to sport and recreation as intrinsically worthwhile, and therefore to be positively promoted for all. Rather the rationale for state involvement was founded on extrinsic factors, such as Britain's failing reputation in international sporting competition, and, on the domestic scene, a concern with the emergence of youth sub-cultures and the presumed moral qualities inherent in sporting activity which might provide a useful antidote to counter anti-social tendencies on the part of the young.

In effect the rationale for state intervention in leisure had not changed significantly from that underpinning the Physical Training and Recreation Act 1937. It was essentially inspired by a form of traditional pluralism, in that state intervention or subsidy was justified by reference to the externalities which might be achieved by support for leisure. In the pre-war period the concern with sport had been in part motivated by worries related to unemployed youth and the dangers of alternative uses of recreation by fascist movements intent on attracting the young. In the post-war period, the Wolfenden Report was also in part promoted because of worries about youth, but on this occasion the affluent youth which were a product of post-war economic growth. Young people had been given discretionary time and income, and this was associated in popular consciousness with the emergence of youth sub-cultures and associated 'anti-social' behaviour.

As with sport, promotion of the countryside and of the arts were also motivated to a considerable degree by extrinsic factors, the need to conserve the environment and protect economic activity, and the need to preserve 'Britain's' cultural heritage (usually referred to at this stage in unitary, homogeneous terms). This is a form of traditional pluralism because competing interest groups are seen as meeting their own interests through the market or through voluntary associations, and state intervention was only to be justified where externalities accrue or where there are market imperfections or disbenefits generated by the operation of the unrestricted, 'free' market. Traditional pluralism is to be contrasted with 'welfare reformism', which far from justifying state involvement on the grounds of some extrinsic gain, promotes the rights of the individual to have access to leisure opportunities for their own sake. Welfare reformism seeks to modify the market in terms of social goods, and it was not until the late 1960s and early 1970s that such reformist thinking became evident in government policy.

The Labour government of 1964–70 was of considerable significance in the leisure context in that it introduced a number of leisure policy initiatives which set the tone for the 1970s, with its expansion of state intervention in leisure. Harold Wilson had declared the theme of his government to be that of modernisation in his 'white heat of technology' speech, and leisure was the most 'modern' of public sector service areas in which to promote opportunities. In the 1959 election campaign, both Conservative and Labour Parties had published policy documents relating to leisure (Kerr, Ashton, and Carless, 1959; Labour Party, 1959). Both parties expressed support for the establishment of a Sports Advisory Council, and the Conservatives when in power did appoint a Minister for Sport, Quintin Hogg. Hogg, however, was inimical to any extension of state involvement in sport (Coalter *et al.*, 1987) and it was left to the incoming Labour government to establish the Council in 1965. Initially the Council was simply an arm of government, but was given quasi-autonomous status in 1971 by the Heath administration which succeeded Wilson's government because it wished to insulate the Council from political control (Coalter *et al.*, 1987). Since the government continues to be the paymaster for the Sports Council, policy autonomy has never been clear cut, and accusations that quangos are merely tools of government policy have increasingly been made in recent years. The Sports Council modified the policy slogan recommended by the Wolfenden Committee from 'recreation for all' to 'sport for all', though its initial strategy was one of focusing predominantly on excellence, rather than participation (Coghlan with Webb, 1990).

The welfare reformist rationale can perhaps be identified most clearly by the mid-1970s when, following the reorganisation of local government and a massive increase in leisure investment by the new authorities, the Labour government drew up its White Paper *Sport and Recreation* identifying recreation as 'one of the community's everyday needs', thus granting leisure services the status of a welfare right as "part of the general fabric of social services" (Department of Environment, 1975). Ironically this recognition of access to sport and recreation as a right came at the very time when Britain's economic problems were becoming clearly evident. The oil crisis of the early 1970s, the floating of major currencies and the devaluation of sterling, the world recession and the costs of Britain's entry into the EEC, together conspired to reinforce and highlight the structural weaknesses of the British economy, and to generate severe balance of payments problems. Indeed, the effects of Britain's trading deficit resulted in the Labour government seeking a loan from the International Monetary Fund in 1976 which was granted on condition that attempts be made to reduce public spending.

The Wilson Administration of 1964–70 had a marked effect on areas of leisure policy other than sport. It produced White Papers on the arts, and on countryside recreation, both of which evidenced welfare reformist thinking. When Jenny Lee became Labour Minister for the Arts in 1964, she immediately set about reviewing the direction of arts policy. Although the subsequent policy document *A Policy for the Arts: The First Steps* stopped short of advocating cultural democracy, it widened the range of arts to be supported by the Arts Council, modifying its Royal Charter, and decentralised decision-making and expenditure away from London, setting up separate Arts Councils for Scotland and Wales and fostering the development of Regional Arts Associations.

Nevertheless, even though liberalisation of arts policy merely meant wider access to a greater range of established art forms, this change in policy was built upon in the 1970s with the advent of Arts Council funding for community arts. The community arts movement, though fragmented, advocated a strong form of cultural democracy (Kelly, 1984) and though the Council continued to spend the major part of its grant on the four major national companies, and its support for community arts was a small experimental programme over a restricted period (1975–77), the debates around community arts raised important social, aesthetic and political issues. For some, Arts Council funding of community arts was justified by the argument that it might lead people on to participation or appreciation of the high arts. For others community arts were seen as expressions of popular culture to be valued in their own right as expressing the cultural proclivities of a wider social group than the cultural elite, the guardians of high culture in the form of Arts Council decision-makers. A debate was provoked between traditionalists who argued that aesthetic criteria alone should be employed to judge the adequacy of community arts products, and those who argued that the social significance of the products and the processes of community arts production were much more important than traditional aesthetic criteria. This latter group advocated cultural democracy rather than democratisation of culture: that is, that the aim of arts policy should be to promote opportunities for cultural self-expression for all cultural groups, rather than merely promoting particular, traditional, products of high culture. The issue was finally defused at the end of the period of experimental funding by the decision that community arts should be dealt with and funded at the level of the Regional Arts Associations. Nevertheless, the debate between welfare reformists in the form of the cultural democracy movement and traditional pluralism, in the form of those promoting the democratisation of culture, had been opened up.

The Wilson government also published the 1967 White Paper *Leisure in the Countryside*, which outlined the basis for the 1968 Countryside Act. This piece of legislation widened the remit of the National Parks Commission, renaming it the Countryside Commission and adding responsibilities beyond the designated National Parks. The new Countryside Commission, unlike the Arts and Sports Councils, did not become a quango until 1982, coming directly under the aegis of (what was to become) the Department of the Environment. One of its new key roles was to foster the establishment of provision for countryside recreation, particularly of country parks, through grant aid to local authorities and other potential providers. This extension of provision was partly reformist in its inspiration in that the advent of country parks was designed, in part, to make countryside recreation opportunities more readily available to less affluent, and geographically dispersed, populations which had not had easy access to the remote National Parks. However, there was also an environmental conservation concern, in that overuse of ecologically and economically sensitive areas within the Parks had become an important issue.

Although the leisure White Papers, and the establishment of the new leisure bodies, provided evidence of the willingness of Labour governments to expand support for public sector leisure provision, and to recognise leisure 'needs' as constituting fundamental social needs, nevertheless the vast expansion of facilities and services which occurred in the 1970s was largely a product of local government support. Local government was reorganised in most parts of Britain in 1974 (the London Boroughs having been reorganised in 1964), and though there was no change in the legal requirements facing local government in respect of leisure services, there was a relatively widespread expansion of provision in this new service area. Most leisure provision is made under permissive legislation in England and Wales, with mandatory provision limited to the provision of libraries, physical recreation opportunities for young people and allotments (Travis and Veal, 1979).

Local government provision in the 1970s was fuelled by a number of factors, perhaps the most important of which was a corporate management ideology which underpinned the design of the whole system (Bains, 1972; Redcliff-Maud, 1969). Large-scale local government units were constructed, particularly in the metropolitan areas, in the belief that economies of scale could be achieved in the addressing of considerable local social and economic problems. As part of this corporate management process, large-scale local government departments were constructed in the majority of authorities, with previously separate functions such as parks and amenity horticulture, swimming pools, sports centres (of which the first had only opened in Harlow in 1964), community centres, and in some metropolitan districts, libraries and arts centres (Travis and Veal, 1979). In addition to the economies of scale of organisational size, and the local tax base, it was assumed that large scale local government would attract talented professionals and politicians who would not have been drawn by the parochial concerns, fragmented responsibilities and restricted career opportunities of the old system. Thus the professionalisation of a range of service areas in local government including personal social services, educational management and leisure services was accelerated through the process of local government reorganisation. By the end of the 1970s the professional bodies of the constituent elements of leisure services in local government, the Institute of Parks Administration, the Association of Recreation Management and the Recreation Managers Association, had amalgamated to form a single body (of the major leisure professional bodies, leaving only the Institute of Baths and Recreation Management standing alone), and began constructing their own unified syllabus leading to examination to accord 'professional' membership status. This follows the classic professionalisation patterns of the liberal welfare professions (Coalter, 1990; Johnson, 1969).

The growth in facilities for sport and physical recreation in particular over the 1970s was impressive. In 1972 there were 30 municipal sports centres, and less than 500 indoor swimming pools in operation in England. By 1978 this had increased to 350 sports centres and more than 850 pools (Sports Council, 1983). However, a series of research reports by the Sports Council and the Arts Council indicated that the provision of facilities alone did not, of itself, eliminate recreational disadvantage. Male, white, middle-class individuals with access to private transport, were invariably over-represented among users of the new sports centres (Collins, 1979; Gregory, 1979; Grimshaw and Prescott-Clarke, 1978). Similarly, audiences for the publicly funded arts, although reflecting less of a gender and age bias, nevertheless replicated other features of the skewed user profiles of sports facilities (Arts Council, 1974). Indeed by the time the economic problems of the mid-1970s manifested themselves, the welfare framework of leisure provision was subject to criticism not only by the New Right, as economically unafford-able, but also by elements of the left, particularly those concerned with race and gender, for its failure to redress social inequalities. State intervention inspired by welfare reformism had failed to enhance the life chances of many of those who constituted its primary targets, and, with the advent in 1979 of a Conservative government controlled by the New Right, leisure services, along with other areas of welfare policy, were to be subject to intense scrutiny.

Conclusion

This chapter has sought to sketch the trajectory of (distributive and redistributive) leisure policy across the period since the early stages of industrialisation. Although our concerns here have been limited to the nature of public policy change, parallel shifts in the nature of the commercial and voluntary sectors may be traced across the same period. Table 1.1 highlights both the structure of some of the arguments developed in this chapter in relation to policy develop-ments, and indicates in outline some of the parallels which may be drawn with commercial and voluntary sector practices which will be developed more fully in Chapter 6. The nature of the changing relationships between these sectors becomes central to discussion of contemporary policy change in ensuing chapters.

As we have already indicated, the mid-1970s provides something of a watershed in welfare policy. Economic crisis triggered the resurgence of ideological debate in British politics, which in turn involved a questioning of the legitimate role of the state in civil society. Questions of ideology and legitimacy are central to an understanding of policy change in contemporary Britain. The following chapters will therefore focus on the nature of the ideolo-gical debate in Britain over the last two decades of the century, its implications for leisure policy, its impact on policy development, and the implications such changes hold for theorising the nature of the state in modern Britain. Clearly the local state has been the site of considerable struggle over the period since the mid-1970s, and since this also represents the locus of most policy implementation for leisure, an analysis of its changing role will also be central to our concerns. Chapters 4 and 5, therefore, discuss in detail the nature of policy change at local level, and specifically its impact on professional, political, and 'client' interests by reference to case study material and analysis of local expenditures. Chapter 6 considers parallel developments in the commercial and voluntary sectors. Chapter seven undertakes a synthesis of the major themes identified, focusing discussion of policy development in the context of globalisation processes which dominate the contemporary environment. The final chapter seeks to identify the strategic relations relevant to selected leisure policy decisions at the city, national and the transnational levels.

Table 1.1 Development of leisure sectors over time

Chronology	Illustrative social and economic policies	Illustrative leisure policies	Emphasis in role of state in leisure	Emphasis in role of commercial sector in leisure	Emphasis in role of voluntary sector in leisure
c. 1780–1840 Suppression of popular recreations	Poor Law Amendment Act 1834	Suppression of Bloodsports Act 1833; Enclosure Act 1836	Attempts to control and suppress 'disruptive' leisure forms	Small-scale entrepreneurs (publicans) replace squirearchy as patrons of popular recreations	Formation of organisations to control working class organisations
c. 1840 – c. 1900 Erosion of laissez-faire approach to social/economic policy	Factories Acts 1847, 1867; Education Act 1870	Public Baths and Washhouses Act 1846; Museums Act 1849; Libraries Act 1850, Recreation Grounds Act 1852	State support, particularly for voluntary effort, promoting 'improving' leisure forms	Increasing scale of capital investment e.g. rail, larger music halls, sports stadia, mass production of leisure equipment	Sector reflects paternalism of middle classes but control of leisure organisations (e.g. Working Men's Clubs movement)
c. 1900–c. 1939 Social reforms – laying the foundations of the welfare state	Education Act 1902; Old Age Pensions 1908; National (Health) Insurance 1911; Unemployment Assistance 1934	National Trust Act 1907; Town Planning Act 1909; Forestry Commission founded with recreation role 1919; Physical Recreation and Training Act 1937; Access to the Mountains Act 1939	Increasing recognition of leisure as a legitimate concern of government in its own right	Importation of leisure forms from the US, cinema, music etc. New technology provides leisure equipment e.g. radio, cinema car, motorcycle. New investment attracted by the discretionary income of those in work	Institutionalisation of the voluntary sector with establishment of national organisations and pressure groups e.g. National Trust, Central Council for Physical Recreation and Training, National Playing Fields Association, mass trespass movement

1944–76 growth and maturing of the welfare state	Education Act 1944; Family Allowances 1945; Distribution of Industries Act 1945; National Insurance Act 1946; NHS launched 1948	Arts Council established 1946; National Parks and Access to the Countryside Act 1949; Sports Council founded 1965; Countryside Commission founded 1968, White Paper *Sport and Recreation* 1975	Leisure added to the portfolio of welfare services, 'one of the community's everyday needs'.	Demise of traditional manufacturing industries, growth of service sector. Growth of multi-national investment in UK leisure industries. Major growth areas are home-based leisure and tourism	Growth of voluntary leisure organisations, particularly for the higher socio-economic groups. Break up of working class communities fuels need for formal organisation, especially in 'new' communities
1976–c.1984: New Economic Realism and the re-structuring of the welfare state	1976 onwards pressures on local govt. spending: 1977 White Paper *A Policy for the Inner Cities*	Squeeze on local govt. and Arts Council spending: growth in inner city schemes, 'Football and Community', 'Leisure and Unemployed'; Countryside Commission given quango status and marginalised	Emphasis on leisure expenditure as 'social consumption' gives way to leisure expenditure as 'social expenses'	Concentration of leisure investment in few multinationals, diversification of companies across leisure sector; vertical integration	Restricted corporatism: 'voluntarism' within the state as vol. groups deliver services previously supplied by the state

(continued overleaf)

Table 1.1 *Cont.*

Chronology	Illustrative social and economic policies	Illustrative leisure policies	Emphasis in role of state in leisure	Emphasis in role of commercial sector in leisure	Emphasis in role of voluntary sector in leisure
1985–97 State flexibilisation and disinvestment (the post-Fordist state)	Centralisation of powers to achieve decentralisation or marketisation (i.e., flexibilisation) of provision. Establishment of UDCs, EZ: facilities); abolition of GLC and Met. Counties: community charge and rate/charge capping: Education Act 1988, Citizen's Charter	Reduction of local government budgets; compulsory competitive tendering; local management of schools (control of educational curriculum) GB Sports Council reduced and split into functional division UKSC and ESC. Arts Council reduced in function and funding National Lottery funding largely replacing core grants	Marketisation of service provision; leisure (and tourism) employed as a tool for economic rather than social regeneration; residual provision with leisure as social policy tool in the inner city Promotion of English/British national identity; sporting excellence and youth (education) though core curriculum effectively reduces school timetable for PE	Flexible accumulation strategies adopted by corporate organisations: management buy-outs, divestment, divisional autonomy as a reaction to diseconomies of scale, and lack of flexibility in large-scale organisations	Free market pluralism: Voluntarism 'outwith the state'; voluntary organisations, governing bodies of sport, arts organisations pushed towards sponsorship as alternative to state subsidy

1997–2000+: in search of the responsible market through regulation and partnership.	Minimum wage reintroduced. Britain signs up to Social chapter of the Treaty on European Union	Promotion of economic benefits of sport: support for England World Cup bid; London Olympic bid	Sporting excellence (national identity) and youth (education)	Globalisation strategies seeking partnerships and synergies e.g. inter-penetration of media and professional sports ownership	Lobbying activity at the transnational level e.g. to add sport to the competences of the EU in the Treaty of Amsterdam
	Modernisation of government programme	Restrictions on local government spending remain	Sport and culture as tools of economic regeneration		Growth of Trusts as a means of incorporating the 'third sector' – an extended concept of the voluntary sector
	Budget limits of Conservatives adopted in manifesto pledges up to 2000.	Lottery remains but with disadvantaged areas more firmly targeted	Sport and arts as tools of social inclusion	Extension of commercial sector activity into previously dominantly public sector areas of the market (e.g. health and fitness, indoor tennis)	Funding of voluntary sector through the Lottery
	Devolution to Home Nations and potentially to regions	Sport and social inclusion made a policy issue for UK and EU under Britain's presidency	Reduce bureaucracy, work through third sector, decentralise to the regions		
		Strategic planning for culture (including sport) at regional and local levels	Regulate the excesses of large scale capital (e.g. BSkyB and Manchester Utd. take-over)		

2 Political Ideology and Central Government Leisure Policy

Introduction

In this chapter the account of the historical development of leisure policy of Chapter 1 is linked with the discussion of contemporary policy developments at national and local levels in Chapters 3 and 4 respectively, through a discussion of the nature of political ideologies and their implications for leisure policy. There are two principle reasons for approaching the task in this manner. The first is that, while leisure policy development and innovation in social policy may have been initiated predominantly by Labour governments of the post-war years, such measures were not rescinded by the Conservative governments which succeeded them. The politics of the post-war period up to the early 1970s have been described as the politics of consensus, or pragmatism, a period in which the ideological differences between the parties were marginalised. The emergence of ideological splits within and between the two major parties was a feature of the period since the mid-1970s, and the manifest struggle of New Labour to develop an ideological rationale (a 'third way') underlines the significance of ideological justification of policy for leading players. Although the relationship between ideology and policy goals is not straightforward, nevertheless, there is a real need to clarify the implications of certain ideological positions for leisure policy. For example, in relatively recent times, Thatcherism, associated as it was with the ideology of the New Right, may be said to have had a profound effect on leisure policy. Even after the political demise of Margaret Thatcher herself, the policies introduced under the banner of Thatcherism continued to provide the context for public sector leisure policies, and the Blair government inevitably inherited some of the impacts of Thatcherite thinking on leisure policy. The second reason for prefacing an analysis of contemporary leisure policy in Britain with a discussion of political ideologies and their policy implications is to underline the notion that leisure cannot be insulated from politics.

The significance of leisure as a political issue has traditionally been neglected. The relationship between political values and leisure policy received scant attention in the leisure studies literature until the 1980s (viz. Bramham and Henry, 1985; Coalter *et al.*, 1987; Hargreaves, 1985, 1986; Henry, 1984a, b, c). Furthermore, since then coverage has been sparse, or linked to specific policy issues such as Compulsory Competitive Tendering, and Best Value. However, if politics are concerned with the allocation of scarce resources, then clearly leisure is a political issue, even if only in terms of governmental decisions about the aims, level, and appropriateness of investment in leisure from the public purse, or other related sources such as the National Lottery. Such decisions are at least in part a function of value judgements about the appropriateness of particular leisure forms, and the role and function of the state in social life, that is they are a function of political ideology.

The concept of ideology used here is consistent with that employed in Hall (1982) defined as 'a framework or network of values, concepts, images and propositions which we employ in interpreting and understanding how society works'. In addition, ideologies may also be prescriptive, defining how society should work. This position explicitly rejects the Althusserian notion of ideology as necessarily reflecting a set of illusory relations or false beliefs, or Mannheim's concept of the ideological as that which promotes the status quo. Nevertheless, it should be clear that ideologies do reflect, implicitly or explicitly, sets of interests pertaining to particular groups, politicians, professionals, 'clients', 'consumers', or others. One of the concerns of this book is therefore to identify and evaluate the ways in which such interests are represented or frustrated.

The absence of a developed body of literature on political ideology and leisure policy is reflected in the approach adopted in the remainder of this chapter. The key ideologies of post-war and contemporary British politics are outlined, those of the New Right (liberalism), 'traditional conservatism', socialism, social democracy and New Labour. Commentary is focused on their historical development in post-war Britain, their core values and their implications for social policy. Subsequently a set of leisure policies is identified or 'constructed' which is consistent with each of the ideological positions identified. This forms the basis for the discussion in the following chapters of the politics of contemporary leisure policy in the central and local state in Britain, and in particular of the policy directions and priorities pursued with the advent of the New Labour government since 1997.

Two preliminary points should, however, be emphasised. The first is that although for ease of reference the terms 'left' and 'right' may be used, the relationships between political ideologies are multi-faceted, and cannot be accommodated on a single, simple, unidimensional continuum in the manner advocated by some political theorists. The second issue relates to the terminology employed. The terms 'liberalism' and 'social democracy' are employed rather differently by writers in different traditions. In the context of this chapter they are employed to define, in the case of 'liberalism', the family of values or propositions associated with the New Right, and, in the case of 'social democracy', to define the area of ideological and policy compromise which characterised the period from the immediate post-war years to the mid-1970s. As a consequence, social democracy is not treated as an ideological position in its own right but rather as a compromise between competing ideologies. Furthermore, the labels 'liberal' and 'social democratic' should not be seen as synonymous with values espoused within the Liberal Democratic Party, or its predecessors the Liberal and the Social Democratic Parties. Finally, the sense in which New Labour's approach constitutes a genuine departure from previous ideological formations is a matter subject to scrutiny in the chapters which follow.

Liberalism: the political philosophy of the New Right

Our typology of ideologies begins with a focus on contemporary liberalism, which draws on the intellectual tradition represented in the moral philosophy of Locke and the political economy of Adam Smith. From Locke is derived the notion of society as a set of rational, self-interested individuals who have fundamental, universal rights to life, property and freedom, and who consent to be governed (making a 'contract' with the state) with a minimum of rules, applicable to all, to guarantee those universal rights. Individuals have no special rights (of citizenship) and the state therefore has no role to play in making such provision. Smith, writing in the same epistemological and moral tradition, sees the free market as the vehicle for allowing individuals to maximise their own self-interest, and the role of the state is therefore simply one of ensuring the stability of free markets.

The political philosophies included under the banner of the New Right vary principally in their advocacy of a role for the state. Anarcho-libertarians, such as Rothbard (1978) conclude that if the natural rights of the individual are to be respected, there is no role for the state to play, and that even policing, administration of justice and national defence should be provided by private enterprise (Green, 1987). Nozick, however, while accepting the premises of the anarchist argument, concludes that a minimalist state will be required to guarantee individual rights by 'protection against force, theft, fraud, enforcement of contracts, and so on' (Nozick, 1974: ix). Nevertheless all other public benefits and disbenefits will be dealt with by the private sector. However such radical liberal thinking was not generally evident in the dominant New Right group which emerged in the 1970s and 1980s within the Parliamentary Conservative Party. This group, in forming its political philosophy, drew predominantly on arguments consistent with the economics of Milton Friedman and the 'conservative liberalism' of Friedrich Hayek. Both Friedman (1962) and Hayek (1946, 1976) acknowledge that there is some scope for government intervention in addition to that of maintaining public order for individuals to pursue their private concerns, but such scope is still severely limited.

In order to understand the nature of policy change under Conservative administrations from 1979 to 1997, it is essential to identify the major arguments concerning state involvement in social and economic life which are rehearsed by mainstream writers in the New Right tradition. The adoption of monetarism, the economic philosophy espoused by the liberal administrations on both sides of the Atlantic in the 1980s, reflected a reaction to the failure of state intervention in the 1960s and 1970s to deal with the major problems of western economies, unemployment and inflation. The root cause of these two features, monetarists argue, is the tinkering with the economy for which successive post-war governments (of both parties) were responsible. Monetarists point out that money has been pumped into the economy principally on two pretexts, either to protect uncompetitive industry, or to provide for the disbursement

of benefits from the public purse. In both cases this leads inevitably
to higher rates of inflation, since industrial subsidy or social benefits
are funded ultimately through taxation or the printing of money.
The latter devalues currency and thus induces inflation directly, the
former raises price levels by imposing greater tax burdens on
producers and thereby fuels inflation indirectly. Monetarists, therefore, argue that the only way of making industry competitive is to
control inflation and to allow the market to 'kill off' those areas of
industry which are incapable of competing successfully. This accel-
erates unemployment but unemployment is seen as inevitable in the
long run given the failure to control inflation.

> What recent British governments have tried to do is to keep
> unemployment below the natural rate, and to do so they have had
> to accelerate the rate of inflation – from 2.9% in 1964 to 16% in
> 1974, according to official statistics ... the higher the rate of
> inflation, the more widespread is likely to be the government
> interference in the market. In effect such interference is equivalent
> to increasing the amounts of frictions and obstacles in the labour
> market, and therefore does tend to create a higher level of
> unemployment ... Given the way in which the political and
> economic structure will adapt itself to the rate of inflation, if
> you continue to let inflation accelerate you are going to have
> higher unemployment either way. So you only have a choice
> about which way you want unemployment to come. Do you want
> it to come while you are getting sicker, or do you want it to come
> while you are getting better? (Friedman, 1976: 23–32; quoted in
> Jordan, 1982)

The opposition of the New Right to state intervention in the
economy is not based solely on the claim that it is inefficient. State
intervention is also regarded as unjust. Subsidy for failing industries
is seen as penalising, through taxation, those industries which are
competitive. Similarly, state intervention in terms of subsidised or
free social provision is seen as undermining the self-reliance of the
individual, and creating artificially high demand for such provision.
Furthermore, liberals argue, it is erroneous to suggest that the state
can act in the public interest in promoting either industrial subsidy
or increased social provision. The state cannot act in the public
interest (except in very limited circumstances) firstly because many

of the interests of members of a society are incompatible, and therefore there is a problem in principle of identifying 'the common good' or 'the public interest'; and secondly, even were there no problem in principle, there would still be the practical problem of calculating accurately what collective interests are, in any complex social structure. As a consequence of this argument, Hayek (1976) suggests that the expression 'social justice', which is based on the notion of recognised and sanctioned collective interests, is dangerously misleading and should be expunged from the language.

The key values espoused by the New Right are therefore 'freedom' (of the individual to pursue his or her interests), and 'individual responsibility' (for one's own well-being). For mainstream liberal theorists such as Hayek and Friedman, these values imply a reduced role for the state in the economy and in social provision rather than no role at all, and this, as we shall see, has particular consequences both for the function and form of local government and for the state's role in leisure provision.

Conservatism

Perhaps the key characteristic of conservatism is its resistance to recipes for social change based on utopian ideals, whether these be socialist or liberal in origin. Many of the key arguments of modern conservatism derive from the political philosophy of Hobbes and Burke. For example, the former argues in *Leviathan* (Hobbes, 1968) that loyalty to the monarch under all circumstances is essential because the overthrow of the monarchy may lead to unforeseen anarchy and chaos. Burke, in his *Reflections on the Revolution in France* (Burke, 1969) refines this argument, suggesting that the present set of institutional arrangements represents the lessons of history, and that tradition should therefore be respected in its own right and not simply for fear of change.

It is from the sub-title of *Sybil,* Disraeli's novel which deals with the need to preserve social unity in the industrialising and urbanising society of nineteenth-century England, that we gain the term 'one nation conservatism'. The concerns of Disraeli's political novels, fear of social instability, the responsibilities of the state and of the individual in sustaining social cohesion, are key themes in the writings of twentieth-century commentators such as Gilmour

(1978, 1992), Macmillan (1938), Oakeshott (1976), Pym (1984) and Scruton (1980).

It has been argued that conservatism is not an ideology *per se*, but rather an intuition (Goodwin, 1982) or simply a reactionary response to any ideology of change. However, Scruton's (1980) account of *The Meaning of Conservatism* represents an attempt to develop a systematic explanation of the relationship between the values inherent in the conservative position and the actions (or inaction) which the conservative advocates. In opposition to the core values of liberalism, those of freedom and individual responsibility, Scruton promotes the values of 'tradition', 'allegiance' and 'authority' as the key to social stability.

For the conservative, hierarchies in society are inevitable, they represent the results of historical and present-day struggles, with the more able generally achieving positions of advantage. However, hierarchies are not simply inevitable features of society, they are also desirable in that they allow the most able to gain positions of authority in our society. Authority, nevertheless, brings with it a responsibility for those less fortunate. Those who are brought up to wield authority, and those who achieve positions of authority through their own efforts, must act responsibly and caringly if they are to engender allegiance in others. In the eighteenth century this took the idealised form of a 'caring squirearchy', in the nineteenth century it was evidenced in the responsible and benign industrialist providing for the needs of his workforce. In the twentieth century, for some conservatives (though notably not Roger Scruton) allegiance is engendered by mild Keynesian policies of social reform.

For Scruton the function of government is to preserve civil order, and to bind individuals into the traditional networks of the family the community and the nation. The state should not be used to achieve other ends of providing welfare, promoting individual freedom or controlling the economy. For Pym (1984) Gilmour (1978), and members of the Tory Reform Group of the mid-1980s, however, the ends may have been the same but the means adopted would differ. Gilmour, for example, promotes a Keynesian approach and is willing to accept the modest collectivism, corporatism and elite management of the economy which were a characteristic feature of the Conservative governments of Macmillan and Heath. He opposes the monetarist policies of the New Right on the grounds that they foster divisiveness in society.

if people are not to be seduced by other attractions they must at least feel loyalty to the state. This loyalty will not be deep unless they gain from the state protection and other benefits. Complete economic freedom is not, therefore, an insurance of political freedom. Economic liberalism because of its starkness and its failure to create a sense of community is likely to repel people from the rest of liberalism. (Gilmour, 1978: 118)

Such support for moderate state intervention did not endear 'one nation Conservatives' to the Party leadership under Mrs Thatcher, and Tory 'wets' were therefore increasingly excluded from positions within the Cabinet in the Thatcher governments. John Major's political style was to be rather less adversarial or authoritarian than his predecessor's, and though his rhetoric was occasionally more redolent of 'One Nation' Tory thinking (particularly, as outlined below, in relation to sport), his policy approach represented a similar set of priorities to those adopted under Margaret Thatcher (Evans and Taylor, 1997; Kavanagh, 1994; Ludlam and Smith, 1996).

Socialism

Although the victory of Tony Blair's New Labour Party in 1997 was regarded by commentators as a victory for pragmatism, rather than for socialist ideology (Hay, 1997; Jacques, 1997; Kavanagh, 1997), and although the collapse of socialist systems in Eastern Europe seemed to have signified the demise of socialist thought, an understanding of socialist ideology is of significance both historically in understanding what Labour governments have attempted to achieve and why, but also in understanding some of the tensions within the New Labour Party while in power.

The core values traditionally espoused in the writings of the socialist movement in Britain have been those of equality, freedom and fellowship (or collective responsibility: Geoghegan, 1984; Miller, 1989). There are perhaps two principal differences which encapsulate the contrast between socialism and the liberal tradition. The first relates to the liberal argument that inequalities in society are inevitable and that therefore the socialist aim of ridding society of such inequalities is both unachievable and, in its methods, undesirable, since any such attempt will inevitably cut across the freedom of individuals to pursue their own interests. For socialists however, freedom of the individual is impossible without equality of access to the resources through which the individual may pursue his or her own interests. Secondly, while liberalism argues that the notion of the public interest or public good is severely limited in its application (and applies largely to issues such as law and order which guarantee conditions for the individual to pursue those interests through the market), the notion of collective interests is central to socialist thinking. Thus, whereas the dominant role in the alloc on of welfare for liberals and conservatives is played by the ma t, socialists see private enterprise as generating and satisfying de nd without necessarily meeting the needs of individuals, co munities or classes. Collective action is therefore regarded by s ialists as a necessary corrective to the inequalities generated and p rpetuated in capitalism.

The nature of the collective action to be undertaken by socialists, owever, has traditionally been the subject of debates and divisions n the Labour Party. There are two principal interrelated themes evident in the tensions within British socialism. The first concerns the desirability of the strategy of 'public ownership and control of the means of production, distribution and exchange', the debate between 'fundamentalists' and 'revisionists' and their present day equivalents (Greenleaf, 1983) and is linked to the traditional (structuralist) Marxist adherence to the principle of economic determinism. The second such dimension relates to the role of the state in achievement of socialist goals, specifically whether such goals can be pursued through the state apparatus or whether that apparatus is itself a contributory factor in the inequalities which socialism seeks to counter.

Revisionist, or Fabian, socialism promotes the goal of a socialist society based on mutual cooperation, equality and social justice, to be achieved by incremental reductions of inequalities in a mixed economy. Fundamentalist socialism grows out of a traditional Marxist, class-based analysis of social inequalities which results in the politics of class and class struggle. Both of these forms of socialism share egalitarian goals and an opposition to the free market economics of the right, yet both are founded on very different analyses of society and the economy, and therefore offer contrasting political programmes for the achievement of socialism.

If these are regarded as the major traditional positions in post-war British Labour politics, a third position was identified as emerging in the 1980s, the politics of the New Left, or New Urban Left. The ideology of New Labour, if such implied coherence can be given to this set of values and policy ideas, is arguably not socialist at all, and hence is discussed separately below.

The 'lineage' of revisionist socialism can be traced through the early Fabians, and the incrementalist strategy of Crosland (1956), to the politics of the 'breakaway' Social Democrats of the early 1980s (Owen, 1981; Williams, 1981b). It rejects the class-based analysis of traditional socialism and its programme of large-scale public ownership to be achieved by mobilisation of trades union support, and opts instead for achievement of goals through parliamentary action. Redistribution of wealth and income and the reduction of inequalities in health, education and welfare are to be achieved in a mixed economy through legislative control of capital. The Labour Party (1987) leading Labour politicians (Gould, 1989; Hattersley, 1987) and socialist philosophers (Miller, 1989), in their advocacy of 'market socialism' and Keynesian economic strategies, tended to imply a continuing faith in limited state intervention and the restoration of growth as prerequisite to the extension of social benefits.

The tradition of fundamentalist socialism was dealt a major blow by events in Eastern Europe. This form of socialism encompasses a range of explanations of social and political phenomena which are consonant with the economic determinism of structuralist Marxist accounts of society and the state. According to such accounts, for any reform to provide real benefits for working-class groups it must involve the socialisation of capital, either through struggle in the workplace (in the syndicalist tradition) or through the 'nationalisation' of industries (which may take many forms). The lineage of fundamentalist socialism can be traced through the supporters of Clause IV in the Labour Party constitutional debates of the 1950s (those who opposed the removal of the clause which was seen by some as committing the Party to the dismantling of capitalism), and through the development in the 1960s and early 1970s of radical critiques of Labour governments' compromise with capital (Miliband, 1973). The decline of this group within the Party was evidenced in its failure to prevent the replacement of Clause IV under Tony Blair's leadership in 1996. However, the emergence of the New Urban Left (Gyford, 1985) in the 1970s and 1980s, had already represented a break on the part of many radicals with the economic determinism of traditional Marxist accounts.

The loose coalition of interest groups and movements within the Labour Party, which Gyford identifies as the New Urban Left, has its roots in initiatives such as the Community Development Projects of the 1970s, the student politics of 1968, the women's movement, black organisations, protest groups, opposition to public service cuts, and the radicalisation of public sector professions (Boddy and Fudge, 1984). In these groups reform was sought on social as well as economic issues through political struggle. The New Urban Left was characterised as seeking to promote socialist policies at local level as a reaction to frustration with the failure of post-war Labour governments to achieve socialist goals, and as a resistance to the reductions in state spending of the post-1979 Conservative admin-istrations. The critique of the local state on which the Urban Left drew, was derived from the radical analyses of local government of writers such as Bennington (1976) and Cockburn (1977) and the political commentary of Gramsci (1971) whose concept of hege-mony, domination by consent through intellectual and moral leadership, was employed to explain the separation of political activity from the economic sphere, and to justify attempts at political reform through the local state. The New Urban Left was seen as seeking to undermine the hegemonic domination of capital-ist ideas by providing concrete examples of effective socialism at local level. It is at local level, it was argued, that the state apparatus could be most easily controlled and moulded for socialist purposes because at local level the state could be made more directly accountable to its working-class electorate, through the Labour Party rank and file. Examples of the influence of New Urban Left policies in action were evident in the 1980s in some Labour controlled London Boroughs and Metropolitan Districts, such as Brent, Haringey and Sheffield, and in the work of the subsequently disbanded Greater London Council.

Both traditional Marxist-inspired analysis and that of the New Urban Left were severely critical of post-war Labour governments and their failure to achieve socialist goals. The shortcomings of pre-Blair Labour governments, with their utopian socialist ideological predispositions, were seen as the result of their failure to acknowl-edge that the state remains an instrument of bourgeois domination and to recognise that concessions from the dominant class cannot therefore be obtained simply through legislation. Corporatist management of the economy in the 1960s and 1970s, had drawn trades unions into the management of a capitalist economy in crisis, resulting in the control of wage levels but achieving no socialist advance. Links between the state and the establishment revealed a network of common interests (Miliband, 1973); both the state and the establishment were seen to be anti-socialist (Benn, 1979), and therefore compromise with existing industrial and political structures is invariably doomed to failure. In the circumstances of the 1970s, with the British economy in decline, its currency under pressure and the aftermath of the energy crisis, utopian socialism was seen as no longer viable. This was underlined by the acceptance by the Labour government of the terms of an International Monetary Fund loan in 1976 which meant the imposition of spending limits and the cutting of social programmes. For radical socialist theorists and political activists such as Jordan (1982) and Benn (1982), this sounded the death knell of revisionist policies. With the failure of economic growth, Marxist theorists anticipated the attack on working-class standards of living and on the welfare state, and socialist groups sought to resist that attack predominantly through the mechanism of local government opposition to central government policy.

New Labour: in search of a Third Way

When Tony Blair assumed the leadership of the Labour Party in 1994, following the untimely death of John Smith, he took control of a party that had failed to gain an election victory in four attempts. The unpopularity of the traditional socialist approach, whether in more virulent left-wing form (as with the Bennite 1983 election manifesto) or in the 'softer' form adopted by Neil Kinnock in the 1992 election, meant that replacement of the socialist 'label' became a priority. Blair set about modernising the Party, finally doing away with Clause IV of its constitution on socialising the ownership of production in 1996, which, with a reformed party voting system diluting the influence of the trades unions, reduced the power of the traditional left within the party. Blair even managed to pre-empt Conservative Party scare-mongering among the electorate prior to the 1997 election in respect of Labour's high spending image by adopting the Conservative government's own spending limits in Labour's plans. The retitling of the party as New Labour and the expunging or redefining of the term socialism were other features of a careful repositioning process.

However, while Blair was successful in defining what New Labour was *not* – it was not Old Labour, high spending, anti-market, wedded to class-based politics, nor was it New Conservative, anti-state, and individualist in orientation – it was rather more difficult to specify what New Labour *was*. In effect the Party sought (along with other parties of the centre-left in Europe, and the Democrats in the United States) to establish a new, defining set of values or principles. Often expressed as the search for a third way between the neo-liberal, free market individualism of the New Right, and the statist principles of market regulation and control of the Old Left, New Labour sought to build on the strengths of both market and state without the unquestioned acceptance of the merits of either – the search was, in Wright's terms, for 'a clever state and intelligent markets' (Wright, 1996: 140).

In the run-up to the 1997 election the Blair team began to outline and press home the virtues of a 'stakeholder society'. In speeches on a Far East tour in 1995, Tony Blair began to outline his version of a trust-based capitalism, one in which cooperation and mutual respect (rather than the antagonistic industrial relations of the 1980s or the corporatism of the 1970s) were evident (Blair, 1996). Following the hegemonic dominance of New Right thought over the period since 1979, New Labour finally had begun to muster:

> its own language to set against Thatcherism's litany of market choice and freedom. New Labour's language is of community, solidarity, inclusiveness fairness. It is the language of stake-holding. (Coates, 1999: 357)

For some these represent the new core values of the New Labour government, for others they are rather more a matter of rhetoric than reality, but it is clear that the approach of New Labour owed more to Durkheimian notions of organic solidarity (Durkheim, 1964) than to Marxist notions of class.

Reference to rights (whether for workers, employers or consumers) have been couched by New Labour in terms of obligations, the language of mutual responsibilities owing much to the social philosophy of communitarian thinkers such as Etzioni (1993, 1996) or 'communitarian liberals' such as John Gray (1996, 1997). Thus, although the initial policy moves of the new government after the 1997 election victory reflected a concern to recognise some rights in, for example, the establishment of a minimum wage, and signing up to the social chapter of the Maastricht Treaty, New Labour also sought to place obligations on citizens, such as on those out of work to undertake training in its Welfare to Work programme; or, following Blair's pre-election promise to be tough on crime and tough on the causes of crime, on parents to take control of delinquent children. New Labour's concerns were not with traditional welfare rights but with welfare effectiveness. Tony Blair has argued for a modernisation of the welfare state, and 'the new welfare state must encourage work, not dependency' (*The Guardian*, 1 October 1997: 8).

Stakeholding shows a concern, less with the redistribution of income (in the 1997 election campaign New Labour undertook not to modify top and lower income tax rates for the life of the parliament Baggott, 1999), than with tackling the causes of inequality, and the establishment of the government's Social Exclusion Unit in 1997. The targeting of health and educational inequalities reflects this approach. As Will Hutton expresses it:

> what underpins the fundamental idea of stake-holding is that social and economic inclusion, rather than equality, should be the overriding objective for the contemporary left ... a stakeholder society and a stakeholder economy exist where there is a mutuality of rights and obligations constructed around the notion of economic, social and political inclusions. (Hutton, 1994: 3)

New Labour's prudence in spending in its initial period in power was accompanied (and some would argue rewarded) by economic growth and reducing unemployment. Unlike predecessor Labour governments of the 1960s and 1970s which saw themselves as constrained by globalisation of economies and polities, New Labour sought to embrace the challenge, investing in human capital, through training, education, reskilling and labour flexibilisation to compete effectively in the globalised economy. Ruth Levitas expresses the role of globalisation in New Labour's thinking as reflecting a constraint on people (particularly labour organisations) to act 'responsibly' if the economy is to flourish:

> The rhetoric of the third way thus transforms democratic social-
> ism into a synthesis of stakeholding and communitarianism. But
> it is a synthesis in which individual responsibility is to be enforced
> as obligation through the twin pressures of the global economy
> and the community as policeman. (Levitas, 1998: 127)

Despite ambivalence about European Monetary Union, New Labour has also sought to position itself at the heart of European
Union activity. Nevertheless, for some commentators who note the
continuities between New Labour and their predecessor Conservative administration, there is little beyond the changing rhetoric to
suggest that New Labour reflects a radical break with the pro-
market policies of the New Conservatives.

The consequences of political ideologies for leisure policy

In this section, a set of leisure policies will be identified which are
consistent with each of the ideologies outlined, while in the following section the relationship between these ideologies and feminist
and race perspectives will be considered. The purpose here is to
provide a link between the discussion of what the major ideological
positions represent, and an explanation of the historical development of leisure policy from the 1980s to the end of the 1990s, which
will form the subject matter of the following chapters. There is no
suggestion here that ideology or even party political programmes
are always the sole, or even principal, determinants of policy
development. Rather the emphasis of the section is on demonstrating that there are consequences for leisure policy of holding to
particular ideological positions, and on illustrating how the notion
that leisure is somehow beyond the concerns of politics is in itself an
ideological position.

In the discussion of liberal ideology we made the distinction
between the anarchistic liberalism of Rothbard and the minimalism
of Nozick on the one hand, and on the other, the more mainstream
political philosophies represented in the economics of Friedman and
the 'conservative liberalism' of Hayek. Clearly, since the former
leaves little or no room for state intervention, the consequences for

public leisure policy of this brand of liberalism are severely limited. However, Friedman does not wish to adopt the radically minimalist position, and in *Capitalism and Freedom* (Friedman, 1962) he sets out a statement of the criteria which justify the limited state intervention which he advocates. There are three types of argument which can be used to justify state intervention. The first is that the state should perform the role of impartial arbiter, ensuring (e.g. through the maintenance of a police force, the prevention of market monopolies) that individuals are able to pursue their own interests through the operation of the free market. The second type of situation in which state intervention is justified is when the free market works imperfectly. For example it may be the case that some industries can only operate profitably where a monopoly exists. Where such 'natural' monopolies exist the state should regulate them to prevent abuse. A similar market imperfection occurs where it is impractical or impossible to charge those who benefit from a service in the case of public or merit goods or where externalities occur. Friedman illustrates this aspect of his argument with an example drawn from the field of leisure services:

> For the city park, it is extremely difficult to identify those people who benefit from it and charge them for the benefits they receive. If there is a park in the middle of the city the houses on all sides get the benefit of the green space and people who walk through it or by it also benefit. To maintain toll collections at the gate or to impose annual charges per window would be very difficult. (Friedman, 1962: 20)

The final criterion employed by Friedman to justify state involvement is that of paternalism. However he is reluctant to employ this argument beyond very limited circumstances. For example, while he accepts that in the case of the mentally ill (who cannot identify or pursue their own interests) the state has a legitimate role to play, in the case of provision of education for children he is prepared to consider this as a responsibility of the family rather than of the state.

Such a limited view of the role of the state would seem to require a marked reduction in government activity in the leisure field. Indeed the rhetoric of some Conservative politicians indicated their wish to see such a reduction. In a Commons debate held in the early days of the first Thatcher administration, for example, on a motion recommending the formation of a unifying Ministry of Leisure with wide-ranging responsibilities, John Page, the Conservative spokesperson, indicated the government's total opposition to state expansion of this kind.

> The idea of a new Cabinet Minister and a Department of Leisure is totally unacceptable ... I believe that the Prime Minister would have nothing to do with a motion such as this. She believes in letting in the icy, gusty, lusty, thrusty winds of reality and competition to blow away the sleep from people's eyes and the cobwebs from the machinery of our industrial life. (Official Report, Commons 24/1/80: col. 815)

Similarly Philip Holland MP, in a series of books and pamphlets published by the Conservative Party in the early 1980s attacking quangos (Holland, 1979, 1981, 1982), recommended the abolition of a range of such organisations with responsibilities for leisure, and also advocated that the activities of the Arts and Sports Councils be restricted.

In the field of arts provision the influence of the New Right was evidenced from its earliest days as a force within the Party in a number of statements advocating a policy shift away from heavy reliance on public subsidy (Amis, 1979; Brough, 1978; Selsdon Group, 1978). Of these, Kingsley Amis's paper to a fringe meeting of the 1979 Conservative Conference was, in many ways, the most radical. Amis's attack was directed evenly against proposals put forward in the late 1970s for Conservative Party policy (in *The Arts: The Way Forward*, Conservative Party, 1979) and those for the Labour Party (represented in *The Arts and the People: Labour's Policy Towards the Arts*, Labour Party, 1977):

> I've said nothing so far ₃₀ut the Conservative document about arts policy ... tʰ ₃₀st sentence goes 'any government, whatever its politi₃ ₃₀ue, should take some steps to encourage the arts'. ˙₃₀. The arts ... have their own momentum and must be allowed to pursue it unmolested by encouragement as much as by censorship. (Amis, 1979: 9)

This type of statement might be seen as consistent with traditional 'one-nation' conservative views, but Amis goes on to identify classic liberal objections to state subsidy. His objections are based on the claim that such subsidy encourages the wasteful use of resources, particularly on experimental, *avant garde* projects which are value-less (in aesthetic and market terms). Aesthetic value and monetary value are equated here insofar as Amis wishes to argue that, if a work has value, it is unnecessary for the state to step in with subsidy (though it should be said that he does allow of some exceptions). By encouraging art, particularly experimental art of little or no value, through public subsidy, the state, Amis argues, is damaging the cause of excellence in the arts. Liberalism can therefore be said to espouse a form of 'cultural democracy', allowing people to define and meet their own cultural wants and needs through the market-place, in opposition to 'democratisation of culture', a policy of educating the masses to appreciate superior art forms. This rela-tively minimalist liberal approach is one which increasingly char-acterised Conservative Party policy. Though wholesale dismantling of arts funding did not take place, throughout the 1980s and early 1990s, increasing emphasis was placed on reducing state funding and complementing, or in some cases replacing, it with other sources such as business sponsorship, and ultimately in the early 1990s under John Major, the National Lottery.

Minimalism in relation to sports policy also is reflected in New Right thinking. As discussed in more detail below (see Chapter 3), the reduction of local government spending which had hit hard by the 1990s, took its toll on public investment in leisure (CIPFA, 1995). By the early 1990s the then Minister for Sport, Robert Atkin, explicitly relegated sport for all as a concern from central to local government while denying the financial means to promote Sport for All at local level (Department of Education and Science, 1991). The advent of the Lottery in 1994, though it did involve intervention in the policy domain of leisure had an appeal both for the New Right since it allowed for the part replacement/part supplementing of public investment through 'private' funds, and for the One Nation approach, in that it allowed decisions in relation to support for the arts and sport to be taken by 'advisory groups' at arm's length from government.

The consequences for leisure policy of 'one nation conservatism' are perhaps more complex than those associated with liberalism. There are, however, clear implications in the field of arts policy where conservative values of authority, allegiance and tradition are consistent with the promotion and protection of the high arts, the cultural trappings of tradition and social structure. Thus 'democratisation of culture' might logically be expected to be the policy line promoted by the 'traditional conservative', advocating the protection of the nation's 'cultural heritage' and the education of the population to appreciate that heritage.

Scruton provides an interesting illustration of a conservative view on the role of leisure in social life. Leisure in general, and sport in particular, he argues, are 'autonomous institutions' with intrinsic goals which are to be valued for their own sake, 'the truly satisfying activities are often those with no purpose' (1980: 142). Thus if the state uses sport and leisure for extrinsic purposes such as the curbing of delinquent behaviour among the young, it is likely to corrupt the very nature of these phenomena. Ironically, sport, when entered into for its own sake, does have positive benefits for the community. Traditional team games in particular, Scruton argues, instil positive social values:

> The pursuit symbolises the social values which are inspired by it – loyalty, courage, competition, endurance. Here then is a simple and spontaneous institution, which in pursuing its internal purposes generates a consciousness of social ends ... Every activity which allows men to value an activity for its own sake will also provide them with a paradigm through which to understand the ends of life. (Scruton, 1980: 143, 155)

Such values promote social solidarity and resist the instability inherent in the pursuit of the utopian ideals of left and right.

Scruton's analysis draws on the same intellectual tradition as that of European conservative commentators on leisure, Huizinga (1938), Pieper (1946) and Caillois (1961). Like Scruton, these writers reject the materialist arguments of the Marxist tradition and identify the separateness of leisure and play from the serious elements of economic, political and social life as one of the primary defining features of these phenomena. Indeed, for Huizinga and Caillois, the treatment of sport as a serious pursuit, with its attendant professionalism and pressure to improve performance, for example by the use of drugs or other forms of cheating, is an indicator of degeneracy in our society. Leisure in such circumstances is no longer seen as autonomous, and becomes corrupted. The state therefore, apart from providing an infrastructure within which autonomous institutions such as leisure will flourish, should not actively involve itself in provision of leisure opportunities to further its own ends. Such an approach would be self-defeating, destroying the very phenomenon it wished to employ:

> The role of the state is guardian and foster parent. It cannot invade the institutions of leisure without perverting them to its own uses and losing sight in the process of what those uses are. (Scruton, 1980: 168)

The conservative prescription, therefore casts the state in an enabling role which avoids the directive approach associated with state socialism However, unlike the minimalist liberal prescription, it is consistent with the sort of indirect funding that is operated in the 'arm's-length' approach to support for the arts and sport through quasi-autonomous bodies, such as the Arts and Sports Councils, or through independent advisory groups for example in the disbursement of Lottery grants.

The construction of a unified ministry with responsibility for sport, the arts and tourism in 1992, in the form of the Department of National Heritage, was something which, though it might imply more programmatic intervention in leisure, had the appeal to One-Nation Conservatives of implying a unitary national heritage (rather than a plural or multicultural set of heritages). It was also related to the concern with national sporting performance which figured so strongly in the Conservative policy statement *Sport: Raising the Game* (Department of National Heritage, 1995a).

In contrast to both liberal and conservative implications for leisure policy, socialist interest in leisure is likely to reflect a central concern with achieving equality through collective action. However, the place of leisure in the policy priorities of the socialist will depend to a great extent on the type of socialism with which one is dealing. For the purposes of this analysis, we will employ the three branches of socialist political thought identified earlier in this chapter, each of which has implications for leisure policy – traditional (structural) Marxism, with its emphasis on the primacy of economic issues; the neo-Marxist inspired analysis of the New Urban Left, centred on the Gramscian concept of hegemony; and revisionist or utopian socialism, which rejects an analysis based on class and advocates piecemeal reform financed out of economic growth in a mixed economy.

Since traditional Marxist accounts have premised the achievement of equality in areas of social policy (including leisure) on fundamental economic reform, concern with leisure on the part of this branch of socialist thought is likely to be limited and perhaps to be seen as misdirected since primacy must be given to economic questions. The role of competitive sport is viewed critically by structuralist Marxists in that it encapsulates and reinforces the values of capitalism through its structure of apparently meritocratic, goal-oriented activity, involving division of labour, specialism of task, and most importantly winning and losing (Gruneau, 1975). Lefebvre (1971) argues that sport is a 'cultural illusion', serving no other purpose than to act as a compensatory stratagem in industrialised societies, while Brohm (1978a) also argues that, in its present form, sport simply performs an ideological function and predicts that,

> Sport is alienating. It will disappear in a universal communist society. (Brohm, 1978b: 52)

Indeed for a short period in the post-revolutionary USSR attempts were made to ban sporting activities because of their bourgeois nature (Riordan, 1978). Nevertheless, most state socialist countries were later keen to promote state involvement in sport for military, political and social reasons, a strategy equally condemned by Brohm (Brohm, 1978b: 79–87) whose critique of sport finds echoes in the work of other western Marxists such as Marcuse (1964) and Lefebvre (1971) who describe the emergence of the modern individual respectively as 'a happy robot' and as 'le cybernathrope', a robotic type with an affinity for sport and other non-utilitarian pleasures.

One would also expect the role of art in structuralist Marxist analysis to be analogous to that for sport. However, even Althusser himself wishes to accord some freedom from materialist forces for art, arguing that art has the potential to reflect and highlight the contradictions of capitalism. Such a move on his part, however, undermines the nature of his holistic, functionalist explanation. How artists are able to break through 'ideology' to uncover the real nature of social relations is as difficult to explain as the ability of intellectuals (i.e. Marxist theoreticians) to gain such insights. In

ideal-typical terms, therefore, the role of leisure forms for traditional, structuralist Marxist accounts should be seen as 'ideological'
(in the Althusserian sense), masking reality.

While the function of sport, the arts and leisure may be 'ideological' for the structuralist Marxist tradition, its function for the New
Urban Left is 'hegemonic'. The thinking which underlies this
position involves a rejection of both the base-superstructure distinction of 'vulgar Marxism', and cultural idealism which treats the
material and the cultural as entirely independent spheres. The
approach to cultural policy of the New Urban Left draws on the
notion of the 'relative independence' of the material and the
intellectual, a position reflected in the work of critical theorists of
the Frankfurt school. Art was regarded by Frankfurt School
theorists as a potentially powerful consciousness-raising tool,
though only if it was not deployed overtly for political ends. David
Held illustrates this point in reviewing the work of Adorno:

> Adorno always insisted that art loses its significance if it tries to
> create specific political or didactic effects; art should compel
> rather than demand a change in attitude ... The truth value of
> art resides in its capacity to create awareness of, and thematize,
> social contradictions and antinomies. (Held, 1980: 82–3, 84)

Of course art can also perform an ideological function by presenting
a vision of spurious harmony, but such art is viewed by critical
theorists as valueless.

One area of leisure policy which has interested some radicals is
that of community arts and its potential role in developing working-
class consciousness and thus its usefulness in stimulating political
action. The corollary of espousal of community arts, for some
theorists, is that high arts are rejected as irrelevant to the experiences and interests of working-class people (Braden, 1977; Clark,
1980). In opposition to the commentators of the Frankfurt
School who argue for the emancipatory potential of some works
of high art, the role of the high arts in the critique of Braden and
Clark is seen largely as a matter of status conferral, through, for
example, the acquisition of 'cultural competence' or 'cultural
capital' (Bourdieu, 1989).

However, such an approach to the high arts is not necessarily
associated with the New Left. The Greater London Council, which

presented perhaps the archetype of New Left cultural politics in the 1980s, promoted both access to traditional art forms and radical arts initiatives. Nevertheless, although access to the high arts was retained by the GLC as a policy goal, there was a concern on the part of Tony Banks (the then GLC Chair of the Arts and Recreation Committee), in particular, to move away from traditional definitions of culture as a site of individual excellence towards a definition focused on collective experience, popular culture (including sport) and the media. State control of art forms and arts production was also rejected since this fostered the paternalism of state professionals. Thus the GLC placed heavy emphasis on the promotion of leisure opportunities through finance to the voluntary sector.

The GLC's cultural policy involved three major policy strands (Bianchini, 1987; Bianchini, 1989); these are discussed more fully in an analysis of local government leisure policy in Chapter 4, and in the discussion of post-Fordism in Chapter 7. These policy strands were the use of leisure forms to promote a positive image of socialist authorities; the use of cultural events and services to promote other aspects of socialist policy (e.g. the Rock Against Racism concerts of the 1980s); and the development of strategies to allow cultural minorities to develop their own production and distribution systems in the open market. These three policy strategies were developed within what became a highly publicised cultural programme, bringing leisure into the mainstream of local political thinking.

The key difference between the cultural or leisure policy associated with the New Urban Left, and that of 'revisionist' or 'Fabian' socialism is that while the former is used for overt political purposes to challenge the hegemonic dominance of capital and its economic dominance of the cultural industries, the leisure policies of the latter are rather more concerned with reducing inequalities in leisure opportunities. Concomitant with that aim is an improvement in the responsiveness and accountability of organisations providing and controlling leisure to the wishes of the workforce, consumers and the electorate. Although leisure is not to be used as a political tool, the promotion of leisure opportunities is seen by 'utopian' socialists as a political issue, and provision of leisure opportunities should not, therefore, rest in the hands of professional groups of self-interested technocrats or be left to market forces.

Some 'socialist' arts policy documents of the 1970s and 1980s (Labour Party, 1977; Labour Party, 1986; Trades Union Congress,

1976) and the sports policy recommendations of Whannel (1983) and the TUC (1980) focused on the need to democratise the system of control of arts and sports provision. The general formula promoted for democratising the Arts and Sports Councils, for example, and other sporting organisations, was to be one of providing representation on such controlling bodies for worker interests (through unions and/or professional associations), for users of the service, and for elected representatives and professional administrators.

Despite a common ambivalence among socialists concerning the role of the state, there have been those who have advocated a greater state involvement in the leisure field arguing that this is a prerequisite for redressing existing inequalities. The late Dennis Howell, for example, regularly raised, throughout the 1980s, the issue of reinforcing and unifying government control, advocating the formation of a new Ministry of Leisure and Cultural Affairs. He had some support in Labour ranks. James Callaghan MP (not the former Prime Minister), for example, introduced a Private Member's Bill in 1980 advocating a similar move. However, the fact that this was a Private Member's Bill and not a party motion, and the level of attendance at the debate on the motion, might be taken as an indication of the low priority accorded by the Parliamentary Labour Party to leisure policy generally and to this issue specifically. Nevertheless the formation of a new ministry was subsequently adopted in the 1987 pre-election policy programme as a policy goal for a future Labour government (Kinnock, 1987), and after the Conservative innovation of the Department of National Heritage in 1992, the New Labour government of 1997 similarly united the concerns of sport and the arts in the Department of Culture, Media and Sport.

Gary Whannel articulated the fears of many socialists in respect of state intervention, in relation to sport:

> In the case of sport, proposals must avoid the danger of control by a faceless state. The idea should be to give power to those who work in and use the sports centres, recreation grounds and swimming baths, football clubs and so on. (Whannel, 1983: 102)

This fear of the corporate state is related to the former Liberal Party's traditional commitment to community politics, and was a primary bond in the merger with the Social Democrats as well as being a concern of free marketeers. What is different about the socialist concern from that of many Social and Liberal Democrats is, perhaps, the nature of the solutions proposed. Whannel promoted three further principles (in addition to that of democratic control of resources) which he argued should underpin a socialist sports policy. These are:

(a) an egalitarian intention; genuine sport for all, with positive discrimination to counter existing attitudes and structures;
(b) adequate funding and facilities to make sport for all feasible;
(c) social ownership of stadiums, sports centres, recreation land and subsidiary leisure industries.

The first two of these were broadly supported in the TUC (1980) pamphlet *Sport and Recreation*.

Labour Party and TUC policy documents on the arts, from the mid-1970s onwards, adopted a less radical approach than that associated with the New Urban Left. These documents supported the view that it is important for the public sector to sustain the high arts and that there is a need to educate popular taste to understand and appreciate such art forms. Nevertheless the documents also advocated a greater emphasis on popular art forms and community arts. In contrast to the unitary view of cultural need associated with traditional conservatism, what was being presented here was a form of cultural pluralism, arguing that the range of tastes to be supported should be as wide as possible, with an attendant emphasis on widening access. This form of cultural pluralism represented an attempt to meet the cultural wants of a range of interest groups which are not met by the market, but fell short of the use of cultural policy to mount a hegemonic challenge.

Fabian socialism does, however, have something to say not only about the kinds of art, but also about the kinds of leisure forms which it is appropriate to foster through subsidy. Whannel argues that the public sector should discriminate positively in favour of activities which have relatively higher rates of participation among disadvantaged groups (such as women and ethnic minorities), and in particular the state should subsidise those activities which are cheap and accessible with demonstrable appeal. These are, Whannel claims, important parameters which should guide policy thinking if such policies are to be successful in achieving egalitarian goals. In addition, Whannel also sees certain sports, and types of contest, as alien to socialist ideals. Specifically, he questions the morality of boxing, the martial arts, hunting and fishing. (In this sense his commentary has something in common with the New Urban Left concerns about the role of sport in promoting particular political values.) Following Brohm, he sees international competition (though not all forms of sporting competition) in a negative light:

> National sport has proved a highly successful element of bourgeois ideology. It creates a largely artificial sense of national belonging-ness, an imaginary coherence. It masks social divisions and antagonisms, offering a unity which we all too easily fall in with ... It helps to circulate unreal expectations of our own merit and derogatory stereotypes of everybody else. (Whannel, 1983: 105)

Despite some differences about strategy, provision through state patronage or devolution of power to community groups, Fabian socialism is concerned to promote equality of opportunity and rejects leisure activities which are inconsistent with the notion of collective responsibility for the welfare of the community. This implies a very different policy prescription from those derived from liberalism and conservatism, and yet leisure policy goals pursued by central governments of both major parties have, in the past, tended to be remarkably similar. This is even the case in the initial period of Conservative government up to the mid-1980s, and it will be one of the concerns of the next chapter to outline why, despite the erosion of political consensus in the 1970s, this should have been the case.

If the core values of New Labour are those of stake-holding, inclusiveness and community, the vehicle for operationalising this is the setting of a new balance between the state and the market, the framework for which is established in the government's modernisa-tion programme (UK Government, 1999). In the resetting of this balance in the fields of sport and the arts, the government is fortunate to be able to draw on income from the National Lottery to offset aspects of the continuing squeeze on public sector, and in particular local government, budgets. The use of a commercial lottery for funding good causes reflects the approach of the 'clever state and intelligent market' promoted by New Labour advocates.

Under a New Labour approach, sport and the arts are to be valued for the performance of four principle generic functions. The first is their value in establishing community and promoting social inclusion. The Social Exclusion Unit, established in the Cabinet Office in 1997 has sought to establish the rationales for, and examples of good practice in, sport and the arts for tackling social exclusion (Collins, Henry and Houlihan 1999). The second function is their use in promotional terms. Culture has been used by New Labour for political promotion in, for example, the much publicised post-1997 election gatherings at Downing Street receptions of media figures (including high-profile figures such as Ben Elton and members of Oasis). It has also been used in place promotion – the Lowry Gallery in Salford, and the Millennium Dome reflect this approach. The third function represents the use of sport and the arts for economic development purposes, as reflected in the promotion of England's bids to host the World Cup in Athletics, the Football World Cup, and the Olympics under the leadership of Tony Banks, who was moved 'sideways' in a ministerial reshuffle in 1999 to take responsibility for securing global sporting events for the UK. The final function of sport and the arts which might be said to flow from New Labour's approach is the use of sport and the arts to foster national pride in excellence (as outlined for example in the Labour policy document *A Sporting Future for All*, Department of Culture Media and Sport, 2000b). This is a counterbalance to New Labour's embracing of global markets which may threaten the stability of people's sense of identity and thus dilute their commitment to the national polity.

The shift of responsibility for sport and the arts from a Department of National Heritage under the Conservatives, to a Department for Culture, Media and Sport under New Labour is emblematic. The mixture of functions accorded to sport and the arts, of hedonistic celebration, economic development through attraction of global events, promotion of national excellence at a time of reducing national sovereignty, and the combating of the development of a two tier society produced by shifts in the global economy, fits well with the image of a politics for a postmodern world. Postmodern politics is described by advocates in positive terms as an advance on the old conflict-ridden class politics of industrial society, of left versus right and of market versus state (Heller and Fehér, 1991). It is said to reflect the multifaceted requirements of a globalised world in which multiple and hybrid identities (Hall, 1992) incorporate a set of demands which are too complex and fast changing to be met with an adequate response by the traditional state. The emphasis in terms of provision is thus to be on the third sector – all those organisations which are neither purely commercial nor part of government – families, universities, sports clubs, trades unions, social service voluntary organisations and self-help groups (Blair, 1996), as well as on an intelligent market. The enabler state is one which can foster, promote and challenge the market and the third sector to respond to human need, and which invests in the development of the human capital required to allow the market and the third sector to respond effectively. Rather more negatively, particularly for commentators of the traditional left, postmodern politics is said to be simply a triumph of style over substance, which, while dismissing the traditional class-based politics of modernity, ignores the growing polarisation of society in the name of celebrating difference.

Tables 2.1 and 2.2 summarise the nature of the argument concerning the relationship between political ideologies and leisure policy developed in this chapter. It should be noted that what have been described in this account are ideal types. The distinctions between, for example, Fabian socialism and social democracy may in some instances be difficult to sustain, and individual authors may be drawn upon in different ways to support the arguments underpinning different ideological positions. Individual cases invariably depart from ideal types in some way but the types themselves provide a benchmark against which to measure the direction and degree of that departure.

Gender, race, political ideologies, and leisure policy

Feminist ideologies have not been considered in detail here since, with the exception perhaps of radical feminism, feminist thought might be seen more readily as informing a wide range of political positions rather than necessarily constituting a separate set of ideologies themselves. It has become conventional to characterise the range of feminist positions by reference to the spectrum from liberal feminist, through Marxist and radical feminism, to socialist feminism: to these might be added non-feminist, anti-feminist and post-feminist positions.

Table 2.1 Political ideology and sports policy

Political label	Traditional Conservatism	Liberalism/New Right	Labourism/Utopian Socialism	New Urban Left	Structural Marxism/Scientific Socialism.	New Labour
Cultural Policy	Democratisation of culture	← Cultural Democracy →		Provision to facilitate class expression	Provision promotes false consciousness	Provision to promote inclusion, and celebrate identity
Key concepts	Tradition and social solidarity	Individual freedom	Equality	Hegemony	Ideology	Stakeholding, inclusion, community
Cultural Values	Elitism	Free Market Pluralism	Mixed Market Pluralism	Socialism through a Modified Market	Economic Determinism	Supply-side 'socialism'
Arguments Supporting Sports Policy Analysis	1. Sports promotes positive social values, e.g. courage endurance, cooperation competitiveness 2. Sport is corrupted if used	1. Individual free to choose leisure forms through market. State only acts where market imperfections occur e.g. neighbourhood effects externalities	1. No sports/leisure forms can be said to be superior 2. Reduction of inequalities of access a major goal	1. Sport can be employed as a tool for promoting a positive image of socialism, or for other political purposes e.g. sanctions against racist regimes	1. Sport forms reflect and reinforce dominant values 2. Play and spontaneous fun lost in institutionalised sport forms	1. Sport is a vehicle for social inclusion, generally and specifically of socialising the young 2. Sport is a celebration of

	for political purposes by the state or for other purposes by the individual (e.g. body building linked to narcissism) 3. Sport and leisure are separate from material elements of life	2. Leisure forms/ sports experiences which are 'valuable' are those people will pay for	3. Some sports uneconomic but contribute to individual/group well-being, and therefore should be supported	2. Sport can be used for promoting positive self-image for disadvantaged groups and challenging dominant views of such groups 3. Non-socialist sport forms (e.g. boxing, hunting) to be challenged	3. Sport will whither in a socialist society	identity – national, regional, local 3. Sport is a means of generating income
Sports Policy	Promote sport but at arm's length via independent sports bodies	Market forces dictate sports provision. State involvement limited to instrumental uses of sport e.g. in inner city	State supports uneconomic leisure forms where affordable, to maximise range of opportunities for all by subsidy	Sports selected for state support are those which heighten social awareness (of self or other disadvantaged individuals/or groups) or promote positive image of political organisation	None	Provision devolved to third sector and commercial sector or retained in public sector if it gives best value
Proponents or Theorists drawn upon	Scruton, Huizinga, Pieper	Friedman, Phillip Holland, Ken Roberts	Whannel	Clarke and Critcher	Brohm, Lefebvre, Adorno	Durkheim, Etzioni, Giddens

Table 2.2 *Political ideology and cultural policy*

Political Label	Traditional Conservatism	Liberalism/New Right	Labourism/Utopian Socialism	New Urban Left	Structural Marxism/Scientific Ssocialism	New Labour
Cultural Policy	Democratisation of Culture →	← Cultural Democracy →		Provision to Facilitate Class Expression	Provision promotes False Consciousness	Provision to promote inclusion, and celebrate identity
Key Concepts	Tradition and Social Solidarity	Individual Freedom	Equality	Hegemony	Ideology	Stakeholding, inclusion, community
Cultural Values	Elitism/Cultural Idealism	Free Market Pluralism	Mixed Market Pluralism	Socialism through a Modified Market	Economic Determinism	Supply-side 'socialism'
Arguments Supporting Arts Policy Analysis	1. National unity preserved by conserving our national heritage 2. Our cultural heritage consists of high arts evolved via tradition	1. Freedom of individual to choose cultural artifacts through market 2. State intervention distorts supply and demand, economic wastage	1. No single cultural form inherently superior to any other 2. Inequalities deny individuals and groups cultural	1. Arts policy can be highly visible means of demonstrating socialist ethos as caring and progressive 2. Art can be a medium for	1. Function of cultural forms is ideological, legitimating position/values of dominant group 2. Art cannot raise working-class consciousness,	1. Arts are a vehicle for social inclusion, generally and specifically of socialising the young 2. Arts serve to celebrate identity – national, regional, local

61

	3. Aesthetically superior art forms can be identified 4. Art as an autonomous institution is perverted if used for other purposes	3. Avoid state paternalism dilution of individual freedom and artistic expression 4. State subsidy fosters poor taste: aesthetic judgement no different from market judgements	opportunities and resources 3. Role of the state to support uneconomic forms and protect minority tastes: education of people re cultural possibilities	challenging hegemony 3. Cultural industries source of exploitation of labour. State can unify small scale cultural producers to give them power in market to combat stranglehold of multinationals on distribution	because it is shaped by dominant group 3. Real cultural needs of working-class people only if economy changes form	3. Arts are a means of generating income
Arts Policy Goals	Promote traditional high arts: educate people to appreciate them	Allow market rather than state to judge people's cultural wants	Promote those art forms unable to survive in market: educate people to appreciate high arts: promote access	Promote arts with potential for raising consciousness. Control the market rather than circumvent it, allowing consumers wider choice by combatting oligopolies	None – cultural policy secondary to economic policy	Provision devolved to third sector and commercial sector or retained in public sector if it gives best value
Proponents or Theorists Drawn Upon	Scruton, Leavis	Amis, Brough, Selsdon Group, Friedman	Raymond Williams, William Morris	Sue Braden, Gramsci, Adorno, Nicholas Garnham	Althusser, Bourdieu	Giddens, Etzioni, Durkheim

Anti-feminist views of the social world account for gender inequalities by appeal to biological differences between the sexes that describe women as 'physically weaker', 'emotionally less stable', and in intellectual terms 'less rational' than their male counterparts. These views, though discredited, are seen as widely held. The gendered nature of sports performance is such that female failure to equal male performance is deemed to support such views. Thus male 'superiority' is to be regarded as 'natural' and 'inevitable' (viz. Willis, 1982). This notion of the sexual division of labour as natural is related to traditional conservatism's argument that hierarchies within society are inevitable and that such social institutions represent the lessons of history

Non-feminist ideology indicates a failure to register the existence or the significance of gender inequalities. This failure to acknowledge gender as an issue on social explanation or policy programmes clearly reinforces the status quo of gender disadvantage and under-representation. Non-feminist approaches share with the liberal individualism of the New Right the denial of the importance of social structures in accounts of social phenomena. To assert, as Mrs Thatcher did, that there is no such thing as society, only individuals, is to assert that collective interests, whether of class, race or gender, do not exist.

Liberal feminism incorporates a potentially confusing use of the term 'liberal' in that we have employed the term in this chapter so far to refer to *economic* liberalism, rather than to liberalism in the sense of support for mild social reform, which is the connotation of liberal feminism. Thus liberal feminism is associated with the concern to reduce inequalities evident in Fabian or utopian socialism. Equal opportunities legislation is the hallmark of this approach, but despite more than a decade of such legislation inequalities persist, and have even widened in the period since 1979 (European Commission, 2000; Pond, 1989). The application of liberal feminist thinking to leisure policy implies promotion of equal representation in leisure policy decision-making and in leisure management, coupled with equal access to leisure opportunities. Progress in these respects has been unimpressive (White, 1988).

Marxist feminism seeks to explain the function of patriarchy as that of a subsystem of capitalism. In the same way as leisure is portrayed by traditional Marxism as simply a means of reproducing the values of capitalism, so for Marxist feminists, sport forms, by their gendered character and by their representation in media reporting, reproduce images of women as weaker and less able than men, representing them as objects of sexual interest (in the media focus on physical appearance and the sexuality of female athletes). Art forms also, whether the popular arts (e.g. 'pulp' romance novels) or the high arts (e.g. representation of female sexuality in classical painting and sculpture), represent women in ways which reinforce heterosexuality and thereby the conventional dominance of the male, and dependence of the female, in sexual partnerships. The sexual division of labour, which is crucial to the interests of capital, is thus reproduced in part through the ideological influence of sport and the arts.

For radical feminists the significance of the sexual division of labour is that it reflects the interests of all men and not simply capitalists. Working-class males and their employers benefit from the unwaged female work within the household that both repro-duces the labour force and reproduces patriarchal relations. Thus, for radical feminists, the principal ideological impact of leisure forms is the reproduction of patriarchy. Capitalism is seen as subordinate to the needs of male domination in a patriarchal system. Liberal feminism promotes the goal of sexual equality, while Marxist feminism promotes the replacement of capitalist relations of exploitation (of which patriarchal relations are only a subsystem). As such, they represent variants, rather than independent, political ideologies. However, radical feminism promotes a different set of goals the replacement of the system of patriarchy as an end in itself, and as such it constitutes a separate ideological programme. Never-theless, radical feminism suffers from some of the fundamental criticisms levelled at structuralist Marxism in that it assumes that all cultural forms simply reproduce patriarchal values and relations with little scope for cultural resistance (see the discussion of theories of the state in Chapter 3 for a fuller discussion of these issues). The implication of this approach to explanation of the significance of leisure and culture is that women will require their own cultural forms independent of 'malestream' society to ensure that feminist, anti-patriarchal values are promoted. The function of all other cultural forms is therefore consigned to that of mere cultural reproduction of patriarchal relations.

The radical feminist position is premised in part on the rejection of other ways of viewing the world as ideologically flawed. These flawed visions are the product of a gendered consciousness, reinforced by the values, perceptions and implicit social explanations evident in drama, literature, sport, education and all other cultural forms. All other inequalities are simply a function of the need to sustain patriarchal dominance. Socialist feminists reject this view, with two principal arguments. The first is that although patriarchal relations are the source of important inequalities, they are not the only source. The class position, race, age, disability and knowledge of individuals and groups can be additional sources of inequality and oppression. Thus the unemployed black, male, Briton living in the inner city may be said to be less powerful, more oppressed, than many white, female, middle-class suburbanites. The second argument is that leisure and cultural forms are not merely reflections of the dominance of gender or class, but can challenge the hegemony of gender, race or class. In an important sense, therefore, the socialist feminist position is strongly related to that of the New Urban Left, and although for the former group the focus of attention may be on patriarchy as underemphasised by socialist thinkers, both share a hegemonic strategy.

For the range of feminist views covered above, the position of the female is a matter of social structure – either one 'describes' the position of women (and men) in relation to this position in the social structure (e.g. liberal feminism), or 'explains' that position as produced by social structures (e.g. radical or Marxist feminist), or a mixture of the two (e.g. socialist feminist). In contrast, post-feminist analysis has tended to focus rather more on discourse and identity, and in particular on deconstructing the way that certain forms of discourse 'define' or 'shape' the identities (or normalise the typically heterosexual identities) of women. One of the main tenets for most post-feminists is the rejection of the notion that identities are essentially biologically founded; and thus post-feminists have sought to challenge the ways in which normative roles of women have been reproduced.

Much of the advance of post-feminist approaches has been linked to developments in postmodern analysis. The postmodern rejection of grand political narratives and logocentrism (the centrality of scientific reasoning to understanding of truth) has fostered the ways in which some post-feminists give expression to their ideas. Hélène Cixous argues that feminists who strive for a place in the mainstream/'malestream' system for respect for their ideas, and for legitimation of their position, are simply 'playing the patriarchal game' (Cixous and Clément, 1987). Post-feminist discourse must look for a place in its writing and performance which goes beyond the binary logic of Western philosophical discourse (i.e. does not fall into the trap of binary discourse: true–false; male–female; white–black – where the meaning of one term is defined by its subordinate relationship to another). Instead she promotes a mode of writing, *écriture feminine*, which does not conform to norms but disrupts traditional frameworks and permits contradictions. Other art forms such as dance (at least when liberated from strictures of classical dance such as ballet) are valued because they allow the expression of the 'unsayable' and have the potential to permit women to communicate outside of the frame of reference of the patriarchal world (Wolff, 1993).

For post-feminists the celebration of identity, whether through art, or sexual or other forms of everyday behaviour, has the potential to either reproduce or resist dominant cultural significations (Butler, 1990), with the role and presentation of the body as critical in such processes (Hughes and Witz, 1997). Leisure and cultural forms therefore have a key place in the hegemonic challenge to dominant ideals of the feminine, and cultural forms in particular are important in that they may allow such challenges to be located to some extent outside the male-dominated epistemology of mainstream political and 'scientific' debate.

Thus key concepts in feminist ideologies range from the biological determinism of anti-feminists, through the individualism of non-feminists, to the focus on inequality of liberal feminists, the focus on ideology/false consciousness of Marxist and radical feminists to the celebration of difference and identity of post-feminists, and the notion of hegemonic challenge inherent in socialist feminist strategies. The arguments which stem from these key concepts are summarised in Table 2.3.

Parallel arguments can be made for ideologies which follow from race theories. Arguments which stem from the 'biological determinism' of race groupings have been discredited, but continue to resurface not simply in explicitly racist literature but also in 'scientific' explanations of for example sports performance. 'Individualist' accounts which de-emphasise the significance of social structures in mediating life chances, devalue the importance of race in social and economic processes (Coakley, 1990; Jarvie, 1991). (One reading of the 'parading' of successful black British entrepreneurs at Conservative Party conferences of the 1980s was the implicit assertion that individual effort, rather than the social structure of race, is the key factor in explaining economic success.) The race relations industry has pinned its hopes on reducing inequalities through legislation, while Marxist accounts of race identify the role of black Britons as one of providing a reserve army of labour which may be laid off in times of recession. Meanwhile radical race theories, promoted in particular by black separatist movements (such as Louis Farakhan's Nation of Islam in the United States), see racism as so deeply ingrained as to be impossible to challenge within the existing social system. Postcolonial theory shares post-feminist concerns with deconstructing discourse (in the case of postcolonial theory, of the dominant West). Finally, socialist accounts emphasise the interplay of race with class, gender and other social structures in reproducing inequality and oppression. Thus, as with feminist accounts, all but radical separatist strategies draw on the same range of assumptions about the nature of disadvantage as other political ideologies but with a specific focus on the issue of racism. Both feminist and race-based arguments have provided powerful critiques of the welfare state and the 'post-welfare era' which it would become increasingly impossible to ignore in the 1980s and 1990s.

The erosion of the social democratic consensus

The key features of post-war government in Britain until the mid-1970s had been management of the economy based on Keynesian principles; the initiation and expansion of welfare provision funded from the increasing revenues derived from economic growth; and the incorporation of labour and capital with government in 'rational' social and economic planning. The nature of this 'social democratic' compromise between competing ideologies is well-documented in the literature, and dominated policy thinking in both parties (Drucker, 1983; Hall and Jacques, 1983; Loney, Boswell, and Clarke, 1983). Consensus, compromise politics it seemed was both possible and desirable since the interests of the constituencies of both the major parties could be satisfied, with for business a profitable private sector, economic growth and a strong currency, and for the working class an expanding network of welfare rights and services.

Leisure policy was seen by both parties as enhancing the quality of life for participants. Thus, when policy initiatives were introduced by the post-war Labour governments, not only did the Heath administration (1970–74) not attempt to rescind such arrangements, it continued to fund increasing levels of finance for the leisure quangos. These were just part of a redesigned network of corporatist organisations which were intended to reshape and invigorate British politics in the late 1960s and early 1970s. Traditional political structures were remodelled, with the appearance of new quangos, the recasting of social services, the health service and local government, which incorporated leisure as a unified policy area in most localities for the first time. Leisure policy and leisure departments were a logical extension of state welfare and economic planning.

Consensual politics and social democratic values, however, were subject to challenge in the deteriorating economic situation of the 1970s. The turbulent circumstances of that period, with the flotation of major currencies in 1971, British membership of the EEC and the explosive growth of oil prices in 1974, together with Britain's outdated industrial structure, combined to generate 'stagflation', a combination of factors, unemployment and inflation, which Keynesian theory had regarded as mutually incompatible. The Keynesian economic approach, therefore, with its emphasis on state spending to stimulate demand, and the social welfare institutions which such state spending supported, were soon under pressure, exposing the nature of the contradictory ideological positions which had been subsumed within the pragmatic approach to social and economic policy which social democracy represents.

The rise of the New Right in the Conservative Party in the 1970s, and the capturing of the Tory leadership by Margaret Thatcher, fuelled the liberal critique of social democratic practices and institutions. Centralised planning, through the unwieldy mechanics of the corporate state, was seen as a major factor in Britain's failure to respond effectively to the volatile economic environment of the 1970s. If the economy was to be regenerated taxation burdens and government intervention generally would have to be reduced in order to allow the flexibility of the free market to facilitate adaptation and change to meet new market opportunities. The

Table 2.3 The relationship between feminist thought, political ideologies and leisure policy

Type of Feminism	Anti-feminist	Non-feminist	'Liberal' Feminist	Socialist Feminist	Marxist Feminist	Radical Feminist	Post-feminist
Key Concepts	Biological determinism	Individualism	Inequality	Hegemony	Ideology	Ideology	Difference
Explanation of gender disadvantage	Inequalities are 'natural'; they result from the biological differences between men and women	Gender and other structural variables are unimportant in explaining people's success or failure in social and economic interaction. No such thing as collective (gender) interests	Failure to promote the membership of women on key decision making groups	Patriarchy is one of a number of social structures which must be attacked if inequalities are to be seriously tackled – others include race, class	Patriarchal relations are an essential requirement of the success of capitalism	Oppression of women is a feature of most forms of social organisation, not simply capitalist forms. Patriarchy operates independently of capitalism	Post-feminism rejects the political correctness of feminism which casts women as victims. Looks for female empowerment without telling women how to experience their sexuality – celebrate and explore difference
Typical Arguments supporting analysis of leisure policy	'Male' sport is more valuable than 'female' sport because it incorporates	Market should allow individuals to meet their own needs	Policy should promote equal access to sport and culture and equality of	Cultural forms can be used to challenge hegemonic masculinity e.g.	Sport and culture are merely sites of exploitation and cultural	Sport and culture are merely sites of exploitation and cultural	Hedonistic and playful use of art, sport and all cultural forms to explore

		higher standards of performance	representation on policy making bodies	feminist publishers, female sports participation on equal footing with males	reproduction of capitalism and patriarchy. Marxist feminist theory required to 'see through' ideological functions of leisure	reproduction of capitalism and patriarchy. Radical feminist theory required to 'see through' functions of leisure	difference and empower women and celebrate identities
Political Ideology to which the form of feminist thought is most closely related	Traditional Conservatism	Liberalism/ New Right	Utopian Socialism/ Labourism	New Urban Left	Structural Marxism/ Scientific Marxism	None	None

social democratic model of state policy was to be replaced by the minimalism of a Thatcherite administration which regarded social democratic policies of universal welfare services and redistributive taxation as a form of 'back door socialism'.

The polarisation which was evident in the Conservative Party was evident also in the Labour Party. Marxist critiques of the failure of post-war Labour administrations to achieve real socialist gains, to redistribute wealth and welfare, explained this failure as a function of the compromise with capital which the corporate arrangements of social democracy entailed. Such arrangements had failed to gain real concessions from capital and had even failed to avoid industrial conflict. Socialist economic strategies were sought by the left to combat deindustrialisation, which meant control of the export of capital and the import of goods (and therefore leaving the European Economic Community: Callaghan, 1990; Holland, 1971). However, it was not simply a dissatisfaction with economic strategy which marked the disenchantment of the left in the Labour Party. The institutions of the welfare state such as the health service, the education service and other local government services were seen to have been ineffective in meeting the needs of those members of the community who were most disadvantaged. Large-scale bureaucracies, staffed by white-collar professionals, generated alienated clients receiving poor levels of service and having little opportunity to influence the decisions which affected them. Socialists looked to the development of alternative means of providing social services and advocated the abandonment of large-scale social welfare organisations in favour of smaller, client-centred units. Meanwhile, Labour also began to lose some of its traditional class-based support, as sectoral cleavages, especially in the housing market, began to appear (Dunleavy, 1980). Home owners employed in the private sector, it seemed, were more likely to be influenced by the critique of the New Right with its vision of the welfare state as undermining the principles of self-help, the family and hard work.

Attacks on the achievements of social democracy were not limited to Marxist or free-market liberal thinkers. The SDP/Liberal Alliance in the early 1980s certainly maintained support for a mixed economy, 'not as a reluctant compromise, or as a temporary expedient but as the best way of reconciling human needs and capabilities' (Williams, 1981b: 4), but nevertheless recognised limitations in the centralised planning that social democratic practice had adopted. Sharing many of the arguments of the liberal right, the Alliance with its stress on community politics and popular partici- pation developed a critique of the large-scale governmental units and quangos which were insulated from public influence (Owen, 1981). Decentralisation and devolution of powers to regions and communities, therefore, were key features of the Alliance pro- gramme aimed at alleviating unresponsiveness of state bureaucra- cies, alienation on the part of individuals and communities, and at promoting the concept of 'active citizenship' (Plant, 1983).

The social democratic welfare state was also under attack by feminists who regarded the notion of 'welfarism' as grounded in the separation of public and private spheres. The framework of welfare services was built on differential treatment and role expectations of men and women, and therefore served to reinforce the inequalities of the sexual division of labour. Moreover, when welfare services were withdrawn to be replaced by 'community care', the conse- quence was seen to be that women were left with the burden of substituting for state provision.

With the breadth and vigour of the critique of welfare provision, it was hardly surprising that the policy system should be revised. However, perhaps what was surprising was that in the early part of the 1980s leisure provision, as the 'luxury' end of the welfare services framework, was not immediately reduced or even dismantled. It was only in the second half of the decade that major restructuring of service provision began to have a clear impact on leisure. It is therefore to leisure policy in the ensuing period that we now turn our attention.

3 Leisure, the State and Policy: New Labour in the New Millennium

Introduction

This chapter has two major aims. The first part resumes the account of the politics of leisure policy developed in preceding chapters, and focuses on an explanation of policy change in the period following the breakdown of the post-war social democratic consensus. The second half of the chapter locates the account of the development of leisure policy within a discussion of theories of the state, evaluating the adequacy of those theoretical accounts of the state by virtue of their ability to accommodate explanations of the development of leisure and policy.

'New economic realism' and the restructuring of the Welfare State: some leisure policy continuities across Labour and Conservative governments, 1976–84

In the previous chapter an account was given of the resurgence of ideology in British politics in the late 1970s, which resulted in apparently differing approaches to social policy being advocated by the major political parties. This polarisation of party politics did result in major difficulties at the local state level and in terms of central–local relations. However, in terms of central government policy *per se*, leisure was, ironically, one policy area in which strong continuities were to emerge across the Labour administration's approach under James Callaghan, and the incoming Conservative government of Margaret Thatcher. Under this new, restricted consensus the notion of leisure as a right of citizenship was to be replaced by the advocacy of leisure as a social and economic tool, and it was only gradually across the 1980s that evidence of this giving way to a more clearly New Right approach to leisure policy was to emerge.

With the welfare policies of the post-war period under attack from all sides by the late 1970s, one might have expected leisure, as the newest addition to the portfolio of welfare services, to be the service area most immediately under threat because of the economic difficulties of the 1970s and 1980s, and the general loss of faith in welfare practices. However, leisure provides an interesting example of the changing face of the welfare system in the 1980s. Leisure policy was not deleted from the political agenda of the public sector. As Gough (1979) had argued, what was to occur was not the *dismantling* of the welfare state, but rather its *restructuring* in particular ways. This shift has been characterised as the supplanting of the hegemony of social democracy, with its emphasis on rights of citizenship and increasing provision to combat social inequalities, by that of 'authoritarian populism' (Hall and Jacques, 1983; Hargreaves, 1985) which emphasised the use of a reduced state welfare expenditure to promote social order, and to foster self-reliance on the part of the individual, the family and community groups.

The 1975 White Paper *Sport and Recreation* reflected the beginnings of this restructuring of state expenditure on leisure because, although it rehearsed both the social democratic rationale for leisure provision (i.e. that such services reflect 'one of the community's everyday needs'), it also developed the pragmatic promotion of leisure services on the basis of the externalities which accrue from leisure provision:

> By reducing boredom and urban frustration, participation in active recreation contributes to the reduction of hooliganism and delinquency among young people ... The need to provide for people to make the best use of their leisure must be seen in this context. (Department of Environment, 1975: 2)

This tension between leisure as an end and leisure as a means (i.e. of social control) is reflected also in the White Paper *Policy for the Inner Cities* (DoE, 1977) which promotes the provision of leisure services in areas of deprivation as a means of offsetting expenditure on policing and vandalism. The introduction of such pragmatic forms of justification coincides with the introduction by the Labour administration of public spending limits, which marked the end of the expansion of welfare services.

The Commons debates on leisure held under Labour and Conservative administrations in 1977 and 1980, provide evidence of the similarity of thinking in both major parties, with Labour and Conservative spokespersons alluding to the savings to be made in respect of inner-city costs through investment in sport and recreation. Firm evidence to support the contention that such externalities do accrue was lacking (Bramham, Haywood, and Henry, 1982), yet government (e.g. in the 1975 and 1977 White Papers, *Sport and Recreation*, and *Policy for the Inner Cities*), government departments (Department of Environment, 1977) and politicians (Scarman, 1981) continued to make such assertions. As a result, governments of both political persuasions tended from the mid-1970s to the mid-1980s to fund recreation in similar ways. Both sought to reduce local government leisure spending (though with little immediate success) while increasing public sector leisure investment in the inner city.

The 1976 White Paper *The Government's Expenditure Plans* outlined Labour's proposals to reduce central government's contribution to local government revenue expenditure on 'other environmental services' (which included recreation) from £971.9 million in 1975–76 to £845 million in 1978–79. The second of the Thatcher government's expenditure White Papers (Treasury, 1981) outlined similar reductions (see Table 3.1). This is one of the few expenditure White Papers to give a detailed breakdown of recreation expenditure and demonstrates both the success of the Labour government in containing central government's contribution to recreation spending by local government (though not the leisure spending of local government *per se*), and the Conservative government's intentions of sustaining that trend. However, it also demonstrates the exponential growth of the Urban Programme under both governments (from £12 million in 1975–76 to £203 million in 1981–82). In designated programme areas the Urban Programme had become an important source of public sector investment in leisure services. The total investment in leisure through the Urban Programme is difficult to quantify though some indication is provided in the expenditure White Papers of the mid-1980s. In 1985–86 approximately 20 per cent of expenditure on Partnership Authorities (£13 million) and 18 per cent of expenditure on Programme Authorities (£10.9 million) was spent on recreation projects (Treasury, 1987), while in 1984–85, £84 million was spent on 'social projects' including 495 community centres and buildings with 204 000 visits by users per week, 4380 sport and recreation projects

Table 3.1 *Public sector leisure expenditure 1972/3–1990/1 (selected years) and 1991/2–1999/2000*

Year	Local govt. revenue estimates for leisure[1]	Sports Council[2]	English Sports Council	UK Sports Council	Arts Council[2]	Arts Council of England	Countryside Commission[2]
1972/3	453	3.6			13.7		
1977/8	882	11.5			41.7		11.1
1982/3	1189	28.0			90.8		22.6
1987/8	1725	37.1			138.4		29.7[5]
1991/2	1781	46.0			205.0		42.6
1992/3	1762	47.6			221.2		45.6
1993/4	1786	50.6			225.8		45.0
1994/5	1839	49.8			NA[4]	186.0	42.1
1995/6	1935	49.8			NA	191.1	25.4[5,6]
1996/7	1937	47.4			NA	186.1	
1997/8	2010	NA[3]	36.9	11.8	NA	185.9	
1998/9	2066	NA	36.5	11.6	NA	189.4	
1999/2000		NA	37.9	12.6	NA	218.8	NA

1 *Source:* C.I.P.F.A. Annual Leisure Revenue Estimates.
2 *Source:* Government Expenditure Plans White Papers; Sports Council, Arts Council of GB and Countryside Commission Annual Reports.
3 The Sports Council ceased to exist (replaced by the UK Sports Council and the English Sports Council) in 1997.
4 The Arts Council was replaced in England by the Arts Council of England in 1994 with separate Arts Councils established for Scotland and Wales.
5 The Countryside Commission merged with the Rural Development Commission in 1999 to form the Countryside Agency.
6 The Countryside Commission budgets are inflated in 1991 and deflated in 1997 by the initial addition and the subsequent withdrawal of responsibility for the Countryside Stewardship grant-aiding scheme.

with 364 000 visits by users per week, and 460 health projects with 86 000 visits by users per week (Treasury, 1986). Although the increase in Urban Programme leisure spending did not compensate in financial terms for the anticipated reduction in local government expenditure on leisure services, nevertheless it did represent a significant investment. Despite subtle differences in the way the Urban Programme was administered under the Conservative regime, with greater emphasis on capital rather than revenue projects, and on economic and environmental rather than social projects, it seems clear that public sector investment in sport and recreation was not subject to cuts in all types of service from the early 1980s. Particular kinds of leisure service, those which are appropriate for particular groups within the inner city were continuing to attract government funding. The anticipation of, and shock waves from, urban riots in the early 1980s were, of course, instrumental in shaping Conservative views on inner-city leisure spending.

There was a further striking resemblance in approach between the Labour and Conservative governments of the 1970s and early 1980s, and that is in their willingness to provide additional funds for the Sports Council, and to 'earmark' those funds (despite the Sports Council's quasi-autonomous status) for schemes to combat urban deprivation. In 1978, the Labour government, in addition to an increase in grant aid to the Council, made a further £1.8 million available in mid-financial year for the schemes aimed largely at urban deprived populations (Sports Council, 1979). Subsequent Conservative White Papers on expenditure announcing the level of grant aid for the Sports Council, frequently stressed how funds should be used. The 1986 White Paper for example points out that:

> Provision for 1986/7 has been increased from Cmnd. 9428 by £6 million to be devoted principally to support provision of facilities in the inner-city areas. (Treasury, 1986: 167)

The White Paper for the following year highlighted a willingness on the part of government to make use of resources from other programmes to foster its recreation policy aims:

> In responding to Government priorities, the [Sports] Council is increasing its expenditure in the inner cities and other stress areas from 20% of grant-in-aid to 30% (some £11 million) in 1986/7. It

is seeking with success to attract private sponsorship for its campaigns (e.g. to boost mass participation) and for sports generally ... Schemes to encourage an increase in participation have been further developed including the broadening of the Action Sport Programme (linked with the MSC's Community Programme) – this will provide for 1100 sports leaders to work with disadvantaged groups particularly in the inner city.

(Treasury, 1987: 175)

The usefulness of employing sport and recreation as a means of reinforcing the values of community and family are also rehearsed in the expenditure White Papers:

The (Sports) Council's grant has been substantially increased in recent years, reflecting the Government's recognition of the importance of sport and recreation in family and community life. (Treasury, 1984: 55)

Thus in terms of policy objectives, or at least the means of achieving policy objectives, the redirection of sport and recreation funding towards the inner city represents a continuity in policy rather than a policy break for the Callaghan and Thatcher governments.

The process which was begun by the Labour administration of the mid-1970s with reluctant cuts, thus culminated, not in the wholesale dismantling of the welfare state, but in its restructuring. The nature of that restructuring is perhaps best captured by O'Connor's (1973) typology of state expenditures. O'Connor argues that all state expenditures fall into one of three primary categories:

- social investment: expenditure to raise productivity, e.g. investment in a transport network;
- social consumption: expenditure to lower the costs of reproducing labour power, e.g. housing, education, leisure;
- social expenses: expenditure to maintain social integration, e.g. policing.

These categories are not of course discrete. Education, for example, is both an area of social consumption expenditure and of social investment, since an educated workforce will be more productive. However, the categories are intended to illustrate the dominant functions which public expenditures fulfil. The shift in government spending towards community recreation and community arts in the inner city represents a shift in the function of leisure spending away from 'social consumption' and towards 'social expenses', with leisure being seen as having the potential to be employed as a form of 'soft' policing, particularly in the wake of Britain's inner-city disorders of the first half of the 1980s. The rationale for growth in community recreation schemes was increasingly being couched in terms of externalities, rather than simply in terms of alleviating recreational disadvantage, or fostering community development.

The consequence of this form of justification was therefore that the emphasis in provision was placed on groups which are perceived as volatile and troublesome, typically young, male, unemployed, often black, inner-city residents, while other equally disadvantaged groups are relatively neglected (e.g. elderly people, 'housebound' mothers, single parents, the handicapped) because provision for such groups cannot be justified by reference to similar financial benefits.

The role of state spending on the arts could not be as readily defended as a social priority as was the case for sport and recreation. However, just as community recreation initiatives in the inner city benefited from increased urban programme funding, so community arts projects (particularly for the more volatile elements in the inner city) were more likely to receive funding from such sources under Labour. However, community arts are regarded somewhat suspiciously by Conservatives since they have a traditional association with radical community development programmes.

The impact of the tensions in leisure policy thinking during this period of 'new economic realism' and the subsequent 'state privatisation and disinvestment' are illustrated in Figure 3.1, which traces the growth of grant-in-aid to the leisure quangos in real terms from 1974 to 1997.

State flexibilisation and disinvestment: Part 1 – the emergence of a New Right leisure policy agenda in the later Thatcher governments 1985–90

Although we have stressed important continuities between the policy approaches of Labour and Conservative governments, nevertheless significantly New Right-oriented policies began to emerge

Figure 3.1   *Grant in aid to leisure quangos at constant 1985 prices*

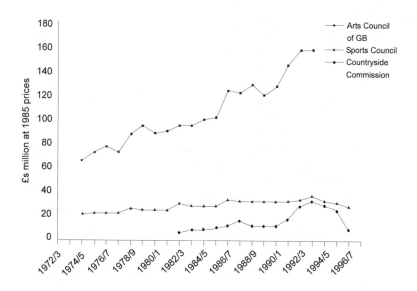

with the advent of the first Thatcher government and grew in strength and volume particularly in the later 1980s.

Even before the 1979 election the arts lobby suspected that the New Right might wish to target Arts Council funding as part of its strategy for reducing reliance on state expenditure. Shortly before the Conservatives gained power in 1979, the Chairman of the Arts Council wrote to Mrs Thatcher asking for some reassurance that the arts would not be subject to reductions in government subsidy and specifically that the Arts Council should not have its grant reduced. Mrs Thatcher replied in a letter to the Chairman that, when elected, the new Conservative administration would not be looking to achieve 'candle end' economies by cutting spending on the arts which was relatively insignificant in terms of the overall public sector bill. However, the incoming government did reduce the Arts Council grant by £1.114 million with virtually immediate effect (viz . Baldry, 1981: 32), intending that the deficit be met by increases in private sponsorship.

As Table 3.1 illustrates, Arts Council grant-in-aid was reduced in real terms across the 1980s when measured against the general rate of inflation, and even this is an underestimate in the sense that arts inflation is generally higher than the retail price index, since the arts are inevitably labour-intensive. During the decade there were periodic crises of funding when the Council was unable to continue to provide funds to meet the revenue costs of some clients (Beck, 1989; Ridley, 1987). Arts Council clients, it appeared, had become 'grant dependent', a cardinal sin in New Right terms. Two reports, one initiated by the Council itself, *The Glory in the Garden* (Arts Council, 1984) and one by the Minister for the Arts (Wilding, 1989) advocated devolution of responsibility for prioritising grant aid recipients to the Regional Arts Associations and their successor bodies, and indeed this was to occur in 1994 with the disbanding of the Arts Council of Great Britain and its replacement with Arts Councils for England, Wales and Scotland, and the devolving of much funding to the regions. This had the merit of allowing decisions to be made by local bodies, while also (more cynically) reducing the risk of emotive national campaigns relating to the termination of grant aid to clients. The government also encouraged the Council to establish grants which should be regarded as incentive funding, that is, an incentive be provided for organisations to obtain support from non-governmental sources, rather than that grants be regarded as part of a programme of ongoing revenue funding (Treasury, 1988).

Other features of arts policy also indicated New Right influence. The government introduced in the mid-1980s two schemes, the Business Sponsorship Incentive Scheme providing tax incentives for such sponsorship, and Arts Marketing providing grants to arts organisations seeking to improve their marketing, although the Arts Marketing Grants amounted to a relatively small sum (£150 000 for 70 awards in 1988/9). However, as Table 3.2 indicates, the Business Sponsorship Incentive Scheme represented a considerable invest-ment. Both these schemes circumvented the Arts Council, being operated directly by government, rather than operating through the quango, reflecting perhaps a traditional New Right distrust of service professionals.

Throughout the 1980s there was controversy over appointments to key positions in the Council. Luke Rittner, until 1990 Secretary General of the Arts Council, was an appointee who was not the original choice of the Council, having relatively little top-flight experience as an arts administrator. His appointment was heavily

Table 3.2   *Business sponsorship incentive funding for the arts, 1985/6–1990/1*

	1985/6	*1986/7*	*1987/8*	*1988/9*	*1989/90*	*1990/1*
Business Sponsorship Incentive Scheme Grants	1.3	1.8	1.9	3.0	3.25	3.5
Business Sponsorship Generated by Grants	2.7	3.6	2.9	6.1	–	–

Source: Treasury (1988).

promoted by the Minister, his claim to preference being apparently related to his success in attracting business sponsorship for arts events. Ironically he resigned over plans to decentralise funding, weakening the influence of the Arts Council itself. The appointment to the Chair of the Council of Peter Palumbo also raised objections from the arts establishment since he was regarded as not having the requisite background in the arts to warrant such a high-profile appointment. His reputation had been established in business as a property developer, and as such his sympathy for New Right ideology was seen as an important factor in his preferment.

A review of the arguments raised in Arts Council Annual Reports in defence of public subsidy of the arts in the 1980s indicates a move from a rationale based on criteria relating to aesthetic standards and promotion of access, to one which emphasised the economic importance of the arts (Myerscough, 1988). This rationale was of course likely to be more favourably received in the prevailing economic and political climate and the public expenditure White Paper of 1988 reflects this. However, though sport, the arts and tourism may contribute to the regeneration of urban economies, the determination of central government to control expenditure, even on tourism, from the public purse was clearly evident by the end of the 1980s (Treasury, 1989).

Countryside recreation policy also experienced the effects of New Right policy throughout the 1980s. The Countryside Commission was granted quango status in 1982 having previously operated under the aegis of the Department of the Environment. The set of circumstances in which the Arts Council and Sports Council had been quasi-autonomous, while the Countryside Commission had in effect been directly accountable to a government minister, is explained by Coalter *et al.* (1987) as resulting from the fact that while the Arts and Sports Councils were traditionally seen as almost exclusively concerned with consumption issues, the work of the Countryside Commission impinged directly on production interests in the form of agriculture and the extractive industries. In pursuing its conservation and recreation goals the Countryside Commission was likely to clash with other government ministries, and the potential for conflict was therefore considerable. Blunden and Curry (1985) cite various instances in which the objectives of the Country-side Commission's grant-aiding schemes conflicted with those of other ministries. For example, a landowner could obtain a grant from the Countryside Commission for preserving a wetland habitat, or one from the Ministry for Agriculture, Fisheries and Food for reclaiming boggy land for agricultural production, and on occasions government departments appeared to be attempting to outbid one another offering grant aid to achieve conflicting goals.

These tensions within government came to a head when the Department of Transport planned the route of the M25 through a designated Area of Outstanding Natural Beauty (Coalter *et al.*, 1987). The Countryside Commission objected formally within the context of a public enquiry set up to investigate the planned route, and counsel for the Department of Transport attempted unsuccessfully to argue that the Countryside Commission did not have the right to raise formal objections to planning outwith the National Parks. Central government was faced with the embarrassment of funding legal costs for both sides, proposers of, and objectors to, the route, and the friction generated was an important factor in the subsequent granting of quango status to the Countryside Commission.

In other circumstances quango status might have strengthened the hand of the Countryside Commission. However, in the light of the predominance given to economic issues over social, aesthetic or conservation measures by the New Right, it was always likely that quango status would marginalise the Commission's position. The passage of the Countryside and Wildlife Act 1981 illustrates the way in which this marginalisation process took effect. The Labour Government had introduced legislation in the 1970s aimed at controlling the loss of valued habitats, following the findings of the Porchester Enquiry. The Enquiry had been inspired by the discovery of the extent to which landscape, of amenity value or conservation interest, was being lost to agriculture. However, the

Countryside Bill of 1978 was 'talked out' by the Conservative opposition, after effective lobbying by the National Farmers' Union and the Country Landowners' Association. Shortly after the Conservatives came to power in 1979, representatives of the National Farmers Union and the Country Landowners Association met with government ministers to discuss alternative legislation, and on 20 June 1979 the Countryside and Wildlife Bill was announced. Blunden and Curry (1985) give a detailed account of the preparation of consultative papers, of which six were drafted in consultation with the National Farmers Union and Country Landowners Association. The Countryside Commission was not even consulted by government until after the consultation of the general public, while the National Farmers Union and Country Landowners Association were instrumental in the development of the Bill. This episode illustrates the extent to which recreation and conservation interests were marginalised in government decision-making.

As with membership of the Arts Council, the membership of National Park Boards and Committees increasingly reflected the primacy given to economic concerns, with landowning and industrial interests growing disproportionately on such bodies (MacEwan and MacEwan, 1982) and on the Countryside Commission and Nature Conservancy Council. The balance of government concerns in the 1980s seems, therefore, to have shifted away from access to the countryside for recreation, and from conservation of natural assets, towards the accommodation of business interests in the rural environment. The Countryside Commission's difficulties were compounded by the fact that where grant aid was intended to promote activity by local government, the financial situation in which local authorities found themselves was such that stimulation of local authority spending had become increasingly difficult.

In respect of sport and recreation and inner-city policy itself, there was evidence by the end of the 1980s of a sea change. Whereas in the early 1980s expenditure White Papers had indicated a commitment to growth in this kind of funding, by the 1990 White Paper there had been a reduction of investment by Programme Area Authorities in Sport and Recreation from £20.7 million in 1987/8 to £12.23 million in 1989/90 (see Table 3.3), and the Labour spokesperson on sport, Tom Pendry, claimed that there had been a general reduction in the general Urban Programme expenditure on sport of £60 million between 1986/7 and 1991/2 (Pendry, 1991). The relative distance, and the lack of any lasting effects, from the major urban riots of 1981 and 1984, or the conviction that social regeneration was largely dependent on economic regeneration, may well be the explanations of this change in funding emphasis. However, the rationale for Sports Council funding was in effect being modified by central government with greater emphasis on its economic, rather than social, role in the inner city.

Table 3.3   *Inner area programme expenditure 1987–90 (£ millions)*

	1987/8	*1988/9*	*1989/90*
Sport and recreation	20.7	19.3	12.2
Community centres	18.3	13.1	10.2
Health	12.2	11.6	11.9
Education	9.2	6.4	4.7
All social objectives	83.3	66.7	56.6
Housing objectives	24.4	24.6	24.6
Environmental objectives	49.1	46.1	44.3
Economic objectives	100.5	115.6	120.5

Source: Treasury (1990).

The increasing evidence of New Right thinking over the 1980s was not simply limited to central government arts, countryside or inner-city policy. It became clear during the later 1980s that sports policy itself was also likely to be subject to major review. The first evidence of this lay perhaps with increasingly evident New Right credentials of the succeeding Ministers for Sport over the period. The succession from Monro, through Macfarlane, Tracey and Moynihan to Robert Atkins tended to lead from the wet to the dry side of the Party (Grundy, 1990). Furthermore, the streamlining of the membership of the Council in 1988 and the appointment of Sports Council members with an acknowledged sympathy with the economic ideology of the New Right, such as the then Chairman and one of the two Vice-Chairmen (John Smith and Sebastian Coe respectively) further eroded the myth of the autonomy of the Council from government (see Coghlan, with Webb, 1990, for a detailed account of government intervention in the policies and membership of the Sports Council).

The nature of government funding policy for sport was subject to redirection. Traditionally a large proportion of the Council's grant-in-aid was awarded to meet the revenue costs of the governing bodies of sport. However, the government declared its intention that this system of ongoing annual revenue grants should be at least partially replaced by a system of incentive funding, similar to that intended for the Arts Council:

> The [Sports] Council has again assisted in securing private sector sponsorship for Olympic preparation and to encourage participation by women and young people. The Council will continue to look for ways to attract private sector investment into sport including, inter alia, incentive funding schemes. (Treasury, 1990: 37)

In addition competitive tendering for the management of the National Sports Centres was announced to take effect from the early 1990s.

These policy developments followed the publication in November 1987 of an open letter from Colin Moynihan, the then Minister for Sport, to the Chairman of the Sports Council. In this letter Moynihan proposes a reorienting of the Sports Council's mission, suggesting that Council might reduce in size, that it might disengage from provision of support for élite competitors, and that it might assist governing bodies in looking towards private sector funding rather than government support (Moynihan, 1987).

Competitive tendering and the restructuring of Council membership had already been introduced by the late 1980s. With the announcement of the government's plans to reduce the Sports Council's budget in real terms in the early 1990s (Treasury, 1990) and the restructuring of Sports Council spending with emphasis on incentive funding, the changes in policy seemed set to follow the rest of the agenda set out in the Moynihan letter. Indeed his successor wrote to the Chairman of the Sports Council shortly after his appointment to signal his intention that the review of Sports Council policy and management should be actively pursued (Atkins, 1990). However, the recasting of the Sports Council's work and structure was to take an even more significantly neo-liberal orientation with the government abandonment of the policy of Sport for All as a policy philosophy in the early 1990s (Rodda, 1994).

The rationale for central government support for leisure in the late 1980s was, thus, not simply a less ambitious form of that which obtained during more expansionist times, but was qualitatively different. The social democratic strands in the leisure policy of central government such as the concern to tackle recreation disadvantage, to 'plug the gaps' in provision in the commercial and voluntary sectors in order to foster cultural democracy or 'recreation for all' (the slogan advocated by the House of Lords Select Committee, 1973) gave way in the late 1970s and early 1980s to the pragmatic cost–benefit analysis of policies based largely on financial savings in other areas.

Flexibilisation and disinvestment: Part 2 – leisure policy and the Major administrations, 1990–7

When Mrs Thatcher fell from grace in the Conservative leadership campaign of 1990 it was assumed that her perceived weaknesses, the poll tax debacle, her relative antipathy to Europe, and her autocratic and aggressive leadership style, would have to be addressed by her successor if the Party were to be united, and indeed John Major set about tackling these very issues. Most notably he brought a new, less confrontational leadership style, seeking to build coalitions in the Party and in wider society with his averred aim of producing a 'classless society'. Legislation was introduced repealing the poll tax, and Major was a signatory to the Treaty on European Union at Maastricht, though he did negotiate a special position for Britain, most notably in the 'opt out' for the social chapter.

However, in significant respects, John Major's administrations did not seek to undermine, or even deviate from, the neo-liberal direction of his predecessor's governments. Privatisations continued with British Coal and British Rail being added to the list of utilities privatised by Mrs Thatcher, and the introduction of market principles into aspects of the civil service's work was continued through the employment of the agency principle with, by 1994, three-quarters of civil servants working in agencies. Market principles were introduced or reinforced in the health service reforms introduced by the previous government, with fundholding general practices and NHS Trusts fostering market mechanisms, and in schools, where local budget holding and opting out were enthusiastically implemented. There were also differences in emphasis. Major sought some options other than privatisation to provide consumers with choices, and this was reflected in his introduction of the *Citizen's Charter* in early 1991, which set out to define consumers' rights more clearly and to provide information on levels of service, performance and redress. However, despite the rhetoric, the Charter approach reinforced the notion of a direct relationship between provider and consumer but gave much less emphasis on the role and accountability of governments to citizens (Theakston, 1999).

In sports policy, ironically, the Major government was, if anything, more radical than that of Margaret Thatcher (Allison, 1994: 21). Thatcher had been uninterested in sport *per se*, and therefore merely reactive, whereas Major and a number of members of his government were very interested in the field of sport. However, the New Right agenda of reducing bureaucratisation and the social policy budget were reflected in proposals for the reorganisation of the Sports Council. Robert Atkins had announced in 1991 the intention of government to reorganise the Sports Council of Great Britain into two bodies, a UK Sports Council (which would deal with international matters) and an English Sports Council (which would deal with teams competing for England, rather than Great Britain or the UK, and would take responsibility for English domestic sports policy). However, in July 1994, his successor Ian Sproat announced that the proposed UK Sports Council and English Sports Council would be significantly smaller than their predecessor, that more influence and policy input would come from the British Olympic Association, that the £34 million savings thus made would go to élite sports people, and that 'Sports for All campaigns would be scrapped along with those for leisure pursuits and health promotion' (*Guardian* Editorial, 1994: 21). Responsibility for these latter campaigns was to pass to local government but a local government squeezed of resources with which to accommodate additional responsibilities.

In addition, Major's concern with uniting the Party, and for that matter the nation, implied considerable intervention in cultural affairs. In a widely reported speech on St George's day (the patron saint of *England*) in 1993, the Prime Minister of Great Britain

sought to evoke a traditionalist vision of an England with
reference to,

> the long shadows falling across the county ground, the warm
> beer, the invincible green suburbs, dog lovers and pools fillers ...
> old maids bicycling to Holy Communion through the morning
> mist ... (Quoted in Holt and Tomlinson, 1994)

This vision is of course both redolent of the one-nation Conservative monoculturalism of an (imagined) shared cultural heritage, and
reflective of the danger of exclusion of others from such a vision.
The Scottish rejection of the Conservative Party in the 1997 election
brought home some of the dangers of such a strategy. Cultural
policy was to take this approach further, as reflected most strongly
in the establishment of the new super ministry of culture and leisure,
significantly named the Department of National Heritage, the
establishing of a unified, core education curriculum for schools,
and the publication in 1995 of the policy paper *Sport: Raising the
Game* (Department of National Heritage, 1995a) which carried a
personal endorsement and foreword by the Prime Minister. These
moves were particularly significant since national identity had
become an increasingly significant political issue with the sharpen-
ing of debates around national sovereignty during and following the
debates around the adoption of the Maastricht Treaty.

The establishment of the Department of National Heritage after
the 1992 election, with responsibilities for the arts, sport, broadcasting and the press, tourism and heritage, and with a minister of
Cabinet rank, was an unexpected stroke. Its first minister, David
Mellor, had been a close supporter of Major in the Party leadership
contest, and combined a keen interest in sport and the arts which, it
was argued, would serve him well given his ministerial portfolio.
Robert Hewison argues that Major's concern for the arts was
evident even before he assumed the role of Prime Minister:

> it was under his brief Chancellorship that the first of a series of
> substantial increases in arts and heritage spending was announced:
> in 1989 a 12.9 per cent increase to £540 million for 1990–91. In
> 1990 under Major's first Chancellor Norman Lamont, this rose
> again, by 14 per cent to £560 million for 1991–92; and in 1991 by
> 8.9 per cent to £610 million for 1992–93. (Hewison, 1994: 420)

The Arts Council's grant rose by 20 per cent across this three-year period, while in 1992, £6 million was dedicated to a celebration of British and European culture to commemorate Britain's presidency of the European Union, and £10.8 million was granted to English National Opera towards the purchase cost of the freehold of the Coliseum in London. This was seen to reflect, in part, the influence of David Mellor.

Mellor's time at the DNH was, however, to be short-lived. When two minor scandals in quick succession effectively ended his ministerial career. Mellor's successor, Peter Brooke, was a less flamboyant character who presided over a decline in the DNH's budget, with severe financial implications for the Arts Council in particular. The system of three-year grant allocation plans (indicative funding plans were introduced in 1989) was abandoned, and what had been predicted as a 3.5 per cent increase turned into a 1.8 per cent increase, a cut in real terms in 1993–94.

The Wilding Report of 1989 had recommended that the relationship between Regional Arts Associations and the Arts Council be completely overhauled, that Regional Arts Boards (fewer in number and more strategically planned in terms of their constituencies) should take over all non-national level funding. Tim Renton, who was Minister for the Arts in Major's first administration, suggested in 1992, while still in office, that Britain's national companies should be handled directly by government, with the rest funded by the Regional Arts Boards, and in the following year called for the abolition of the Arts Council itself.

From 1994 the Arts Council of Britain ceased to exist, with the Arts Councils for Scotland and Wales (previously sub-committees for the Arts Council of Great Britain) to be funded directly by the Scottish and Welsh Offices. The Arts Council of England, smaller and less significant than its predecessor, came into being in April 1994 following a year of planning by its predecessor, the Arts Council of Great Britain, which involved it in preparing for its first ever cash cut of £3.2 million, a year in which proposals to cut off the grants to 10 regional theatres and two of the three London orchestras were withdrawn. Hewison's concluding comments on this period of turmoil reflect the desperation of the arts establishment at being faced with the inevitable impact of the reassertion of neo-liberal principles to public arts subsidy:

It is fair to say that the Arts Council of Great Britain's last year of existence was also its worst, and that it lost all of its credibility with the arts constituency. The brief period when arts funding had risen decisively came to an end, with many companies technically insolvent because of their deficits. If this was a kindlier face to the arts, it did not feel like it to those about to go out of business. (Hewison, 1994: 429)

But if the arts demonstrated the twin pressures inherent in the defence of cultural unity and the promotion of neo-liberal economics, what of sport? The publication of *Sport: Raising the Game*, with a foreword by the Prime Minister in July 1995, was the first fundamental governmental policy statement for sport since the publication of the 1975 White Paper *Sport and Recreation* (Department of Environment, 1975). Its principal policy goals – aid to élite sport and in particular the establishment of a British Academy of Sport, promotion of sponsorship through schemes such as Sportsmatch (pound for pound matching of business sponsorship), promotion of core team games and competitive sport in school, and the funding of sports scholarships at Britain's universities, represented a mixture of near market approaches, and an appeal to nationalistic sporting aspirations with schemes to be funded through the National Lottery. The emphasis on sponsorship, on the market value to schools and universities of sport (in attracting students and therefore funds) reflects a judicious mixture of neo-liberal economics and the one-nation philosophy of traditional Conservatism in the paper.

John Major's own introduction to the statement is indicative of the ideological implications of these policy initiatives. He lays great emphasis on the unifying qualities attributed to sport:

Sport is a binding force between generations and across borders. But, by a miraculous paradox, it is at the same time one of the defining characteristics of nationhood and of local pride. We should cherish it for both of these reasons. (Major, 1995: 2)

The point is made more directly in relation to British identity:

Sport is a central part of Britain's National Heritage [sic] We invented the majority of the world's great sports. And most of those we did not invent we codified and helped popularise throughout the world. It could be argued that nineteenth century Britain was the cradle of a leisure revolution every bit as significant as the agricultural and industrial revolutions we launched in the century before. (Major, 1995: 2)

Sport, and culture more broadly, are policy areas which lend themselves to such assertions. It is perhaps not coincidental that at the beginning of the run-up to the 1997 general election, and at a point when the Conservative Party was riven by internal battles between 'Euro-enthusiasts', and 'Euro-sceptics', the Prime Minister could promote a high-profile policy statement, arguing for £100 million pounds of investment in a British Academy of Sport, to foster British sporting success. Such a move would have wide populist support, would emphasise the Conservative commitment to British cultural sovereignty (though legal and political sovereignty would prove to be an ongoing source of strife, viz. Laffan, O'Donnell, and Smith, 2000) but would be funded outside the tax system by the Lottery. The Prime Minister's interest in the sports field is well-documented, and this explains to some degree his enthusiastic and high-profile support for the policy statement, but the timing of the statement, its tone and message chime so well with the needs of the Party and Government. Nationalism was an essential element both in one-nation Conservative thinking and in Mrs Thatcher's own philosophy, which tempered free market neo-liberalism with commitment to the idea of the British nation (Hayes, 1994: 92).

The claims made about the value of sport, and therefore the rationale for promoting certain types of sport in schools, are also redolent of Roger Scruton's position referred to in the last chapter, and outlined in his book *The Meaning of Conservatism* (Scruton, 1980):

Competitive sport teaches valuable lessons which last for life. Every game delivers both a winner and a loser. Sports men [sic] must learn to be both. (Major, 1995: 2)

As with the establishment of a core curriculum in physical education, the emphasis placed on school sport was on competitive sport, and on what Major referred to as 'our great traditional sports – cricket, hockey, swimming, athletics, football, netball, rugby, tennis and the like [which are to be] put firmly at the centre of the stage.'

(Major, 1995: 3). The emphasis on tradition, on heritage, and on national pride, borrowed from the one-nation Conservative line, while the funding of the initiatives through the National Lottery avoided the breaching of neo-liberal spending concerns.

The lasting contribution of the Major administration would not, however, be the new UK Academy of Sport, proposed in *Raising the Game*, and which would take on an altogether different form under New Labour, but was to be the National Lottery. The introduction of the Lottery in November 1994 was a master stroke in terms of leisure policy, since it allowed the Conservative government to both decrease tax-driven subsidy and to increase financial support for sport, the arts and heritage, three of four good causes (the other being the Millennium Fund) which were to benefit from this new source of funding. Despite attracting some initial criticism that it constituted a tax on the less affluent who bought most tickets, it proved to be highly popular and a huge commercial success. It vastly increased the amounts of money in the public sector sports and arts economy. In England alone, by April 1999, the government had committed £1.01 billion to the arts and by April 2000 £1.12 billion to sport since the first draw. This greatly exceeded Exchequer support, which even for 2000/1 stood at £237 million for the Arts Council of England, £38 million for the English Sports Council and £12.6 million for the UK Sports Council (Department of Culture Media and Sport, 1999c).

The Lottery did not, however, constitute a replacement for welfare spending, since funding depended on successful bidding rather than on straightforward assessment of need. The bidding process, particularly initially, was complex, demanded professional resources, and, in the case of the sports fund, required a financial contribution of 35 per cent of the total project costs to be made by the applicant (this was only 5 per cent in the case of the arts fund). Disadvantaged communities, which arguably were most in need of financial support, were thus least able to bid successfully, since they were least likely to have access to planning, accounting and other professional skills to present a strong case, and were least likely to be able to generate the 35 per cent contribution required.

The Sports Council responded to this situation and by January 1996 had launched a Priority Areas Initiative, identifying 70 geographical areas of greatest need, for which up to 90 per cent project funding would be made available. However, criticism that the selection of priority areas was inconsistent and left out large numbers of disadvantaged groups, was evident from the first announcement (Duncan, 1995), and the strategy failed to generate a sufficiently significant increase in successful applications from disadvantaged groups (English Sports Council, 1998), a problem to be addressed by New Labour in its revamping of the Lottery in the 1998 Lottery Act.

While arts lottery finding was used for both new schemes and the shoring up of arts organisations in financial crisis under the 'stabilisation' and 'recovery' elements of the arts funding programme, sports grants were limited initially to new capital grants. Thus initially it was possible to bid for new sports schemes but not to off-set the revenue costs of existing provision, revenue costs which local authorities were finding it increasingly difficult to meet given a continuing squeeze on local authority budgets.

The introduction of the Lottery replaced a welfare culture (where services are planned and targeted given a particular policy rationale, but where grant dependency may set in) with a bidding culture (where funds go to those able to bid most effectively). Challenge funding and bidding may have been accompanied by a growth in the funds available to sport and the arts, but a major concern was that the eventual beneficiaries would not be those most in need of support. Such a system was, if unmodified, likely to increase the distance between affluent communities and those in need.

It is clear that, although the Major administration represented a departure from the overtly confrontational and aggressive style of Thatcherite government, it broadly continued the reduced emphasis on public sector spending and greater reliance on market funding in leisure as in other fields of policy. It is ironic, therefore, that while the divided nature of the British social structure was becoming more apparent (Levitas, 1998), and while a bidding culture in sport and the arts, if anything, expanded such divisions, the Conservative appeal to a 'common culture' was also an evident theme in leisure policy pronouncements.

New Labour and the search for a responsible market

When Tony Blair came to the leadership of the Labour Party in 1994, he set himself the task of 'modernising' the Party, a process which had been inaugurated by his predecessors but which he was to accelerate and shape. New Labour was to be new in at least one significant respect, which is reflected in the amendment of Clause IV, and that is the absence of left-wing rhetoric or influence:

> The key difference between the Labour Party of today and the party led by Ramsay MacDonald and his successors, up to and including Neil Kinnock, is the absence now of the socialist left which collapsed suddenly in the 1990s. (Rubinstein, 1997: 339)

Indeed the term 'socialism' was to be used less and less frequently in public pronouncements by senior party members, and the traditional commitment of socialism to redistribution and public ownership had given way to themes of equal opportunity and encouragement of the free market, though tempered by social responsibility, so that all could have a stake in society (Kavanagh, 1997). Thus, in terms of macroeconomic policy in particular, in the run up to the 1997 general election, there was precious little difference between the proposals of the two major parties, with Labour combating its traditional 'tax and spend' image through a commitment to follow the Conservative spending plans for the first two years of a new government. Labour acknowledged that privatisation of utilities implemented by the Conservatives should not be reversed, though it declared an intention to levy a one-off 'windfall tax' on those who had profited from the selling-off of public utilities at what were described as below-market rates.

In relation to leisure policy, the early days of the Labour government showed few surprises in terms of policy initiatives. The renaming of the Department of National Heritage as Culture, Media and Sport (with Chris Smith as Secretary of State, the first openly gay MP to be elected to Parliament) and the appointment of Tony Banks as Minister for Sport (with his background of radical work in local government leisure policy with the Greater London Council in the early 1980s, Bianchini, 1987) might seem to indicate a drift away from a concern with tradition and national heritage. However, the Labour government agreed to implement the Conservative policy proposal to establish a national Academy of Sport (to be named the British Institute of Sport) though with a series of regional centres rather than a single greenfield site as envisaged by Major. The government also signalled the end of compulsory competitive tendering (CCT) in local government services (including leisure). However CCT had not proved as revolutionary as the Conservatives had intended, and it was to be replaced anyway by a requirement that each local authority should demonstrate that it is obtaining 'best value' from the arrangements for service delivery which it adopts, implying a far from straightforward return to traditional public sector management (for a discussion of this policy initiative see Chapter 4). Market approaches were seen as wholly acceptable, assuming the market could be persuaded or regulated to act in a 'responsible' manner.

Thus, although the period of the latter half of the Thatcher era and the Major years is described in our typology as a period of 'flexibilisation and disinvestment' on the part of government, the early days of the Labour government appeared to many not to have offered a radical alternative. The active pursuit of privatisation was not evident but the concern to control local government expenditure was a common theme, as was the concern to disempower the major leisure quangos (the Arts Council of England had its staff halved in 1998). Some commentators of the left have referred disparagingly to 'Blaijorism' (Hay, 1994) as a form of muted neo-liberal consensus of the 1990s, paralleling the muted socialism in Butskelism, the social democratic post-war consensus. The globalisation of the economy, and the interconnectedness of polities, means, for some commentators, that there is little room for government manoeuvre (as, for example, the failed Keynesian experiments of the Socialist government in France in the early 1980s demonstrated).

> The discourse of globalisation ... is the all too familiar 'logic of no alternative'. The liberalisation of financial regulations and the heightened mobility of both industrial and financial capital on a global stage that this has facilitated, it is argued, simply leave no space for macro-economic measures that are not fiscally austere, budgets that are not balanced, or welfare states that are not in the process of retrenchment. (Hay, 1994: 377)

Thus, as we pointed out in the opening paragraphs of this book, just as in the early 1960s Daniel Bell felt able to pronounce *The End of Ideology* (Bell, 1960), arguing that 'we are all social democrats now', so, in the early 1990s, Fukuyama could ask whether, in real terms, the 'end of history' had occurred with the dominance of the neo-liberal political paradigm (Fukuyama, 1993).

However, just as Bell's claims proved to be mistaken, so Fukuyama's overstate the case for ideological hegemony in the other direction. There is room for 'local' difference within nation-states in terms of political response, and though there are some obvious policy continuities between the Major and New Labour administrations, there are also some significant policy differences which have emerged. Perhaps the most significant difference between the Blair government and its predecessor is New Labour's avowed commitment to tackling social exclusion in and through sport and the arts. The Social Exclusion Unit set up by the Cabinet Office in 1997 incorporated programme action teams, focusing on different aspects of exclusion, and its Programme Action Team 10 reported in 1999 (Department of Culture Media and Sport, 2000a) on policy options to be adopted.

This policy advice underpinned, for example, the establishment by Sport England (the new name for the English Sports Council from 1999) of Sport Action Zones in 2000, which were priority areas for promotion of sports development:

> The Government's Social Exclusion Unit's Policy Action Team on sport and arts (PAT10) puts forward clear recommendations and key principles for how sport should be used to help combat social exclusion. The implementation of Sport England's Lottery Fund Strategy 1999–2009 sets out initial proposals for how Sport Action Zones will be implemented as part of our concerted effort to help reduce economic and social deprivation through sport. (Sport England, 2000)

The SAZs, like their predecessors 'Areas of Special Need' defined by the Sports Council in the previous Labour administration of the 1970s, were selected on the basis of indicators of deprivation from the Department of Environment, Transport and the Regions' 'Index of Local Conditions'. They thus shared with their predecessors all the limitations of an area-based, social-indicator-constructed, focus for policy (Henry, 1984d). However, they did reflect New Labour's concern to mediate the impact of the reduction of welfare policies. While the Conservatives announced in the early 1990s the abandonment of Sport for All as a policy goal (or at least a piece of policy rhetoric) in 1994 (Rodda, 1994), Labour reasserted its commitment to Sport for All both in its pre-election document (Labour Party,

1997) and in the Government's sports policy statement *A Sporting Future for All* (Department of Culture Media and Sport, 2000b). In addition, it recognised the inequities inherent in a bidding culture for funding via the National Lottery and introduced legislation in the 1998 National Lottery Act to allow distributors to be proactive in seeking grants from underrepresented communities. The planned distribution of grants for 2000 by the Arts and Sports Councils of England, is illustrated in Figure 3.2 and Table 3.4 and highlights how, in sport in particular, but also in the arts, there has been a real attempt to ensure that resources reach disadvantaged communities.

Table 3.4   *Arts Council Published Spending Plans for Lottery Income*

	1999/2000 (£m)	2000/2001 (£m)	2001/2002 (£m)
Capital	86.1	65.0	40.0
National Foundation for Youth Music	10.0	10.0	10.0
Dance and drama grants	4.2	–	–
Stabilisation and recovery programmes	17.2	23.4	18.1
Film production	33.8	27.0	27.0
Publications, recordings and distribution	–	3.0	3.0
National Touring Programme	–	10.0	10.0
Regionally managed programmes			
Small-scale capital	6.5	6.5	6.5
Regional Arts Lottery Programme (revenue)	13.0	13.0	15.5
Small grants, including Awards for All	4.7	5.0	5.0
Year of the Artist	3.5	–	–

Source: Arts Council of England (1999).

Ancillary to the concern with social exclusion was a concern to promote access in sport, the arts and in countryside recreation. In the cultural sphere an additional sum of £290 million for the Department of Culture, Media and Sport was announced in July 1998 in part to foster free access to museums and art galleries. Even where exclusive art forms had been funded as with the £78.5 million lottery grant to the Royal Opera House to refurbish Covent Garden, on top of the annual grant to that body from the Arts Council (£16 million in 1999), government insisted that ticket

Figure 3.2 *Sport England's planned distribution of lottery funds from 2002*

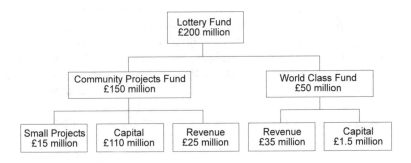

prices be reduced by the Opera House to allow wider access to productions.

In relation to countryside recreation the government announced its intention to introduce legislation to allow 'freedom to roam' in 1999 (McCloy, 1999) though the potential efficacy of the proposals was challenged by some (Shoard, 1999). Announcement by the government in 1999 of the forthcoming designation of two new national parks, the first since the 1949 National Parks Act, in the South Downs and the New Forest, also indicates a willingness to regulate commercial activity for the purposes of conservation and recreation which was unlikely to have found favour with their Conservative predecessors.

While both the Labour government's policy paper *A Sporting Future for All* and the Conservatives' *Sport: Raising the Game* placed great emphasis on sport in schools, the emphasis on the part of Labour is with the use of schools as community focal points, particularly in disadvantaged communities where the school may represent one of the few physical and policy resources available to foster improvements. Labour announced its intention to expand the number of Specialist Sports Colleges to 110, and to use them as a vehicle not simply for developing young talent, but also to develop sports provision in other associated schools in the catchment. Six hundred school sports coordinators were to be employed to promote wider participation, the sale of playing fields was to be halted, and 'after-school clubs' funded by the Lottery from the New Opportunities Fund would promote sporting opportunities and would be an additional source of physical education teaching in a less-formal setting. All this stands in contrast to the emphasis on positive socialisation and national identity through traditional team sports which represents the emphasis for education in *Raising the Game.*

Although their Conservative predecessors had fostered devolution of funding decision-making in the arts to Regional Arts Boards, they had done the opposite in relation to sport. The Regional Councils for Sport and Recreation were finally disbanded in the early 1990s. Devolution for New Labour was, however, a key issue, not only at the national level with a Scottish Parliament and National Assemblies for Wales and Northern Ireland, but also at the regional level with the establishment of Regional Development Agencies and the possibility of regional assemblies for those regions which might choose such an option. The government also promoted the development of strategies at regional level, requiring each region to complete a cultural strategy by 2002 and fostering the development of leisure and tourism strategies for local authorities (Department of Culture Media and Sport, 1999a).

In the arts field, New Labour declared:

> three overarching goals for arts policy. First, that access to the arts should be open to the many, not just the few … access and excellence go hand in hand. Second that we must nurture the creative industries on which much of our country's economic future will depend. These cultural industries will be there where many of the jobs and much of the wealth of a new century will come from. And third, that education – not just at school but throughout life – must foster the creative spark and skill of individual citizens. (Smith, 1998a: 4)

However, New Labour was seen, at least in the early period of office, as less enthusiastic about high art than about more popular forms of culture. The Arts Council budget in the first year of the government was, for example, cut by £1.4 million (which followed five years of cuts or frozen budgets, *Guardian* Leader, 1997). Hugo Young in an article sub-titled 'They Prefer to be seen with Noel Gallagher' suggested that Chris Smith, the Minister for Culture, saw 'no difference between high and low culture' and that he and his colleagues 'embrace culture that has a populist economic base, and place in peril the high arts that cannot be relied on to qualify for that status' (Young, 1998: 20). While it is the case that in the period pre- and post-election New Labour sought to enhance its image of youth, the popular touch, and of 'Cool Britannia' by association with media figures (Tony Blair being seen heading footballs with Kevin Keegan; Noel Gallagher, Harry Enfield and others being invited to receptions at 10 Downing Street), nevertheless the government in 1998 increased the Arts Council of England's grant allocation from £190.7 million for 1998/9 to £227.3 million for 1999/ 2000 with a further rise to £252.3 by 2001/2. This incorporated a significant increase in grant aid to the Royal Opera House, the arts institution with perhaps the worst reputation for élitism.

A further distinctive feature of New Labour's approach was its willingness to regulate the free market by (selective rather than widespread) intervention. The dangers of the interpenetration of ownership between media interests and those of professional sport, particularly in the British case professional football, is one high-profile area where market regulation has been evident. The government's blocking in 1999 of the BSkyB bid to buy a controlling interest in Manchester United was the most publicised such intervention. However, the establishing of the Football Task Force and its subsequent final report (Football Task Force, 1999), seeks to find ways of protecting the interests of consumers by modifying the ticketing and merchandising practices of clubs, and promoting supporter influence in the running of clubs, which had been greatly affected by the increasing tendency for clubs to be floated on the stock exchange.

The nature of the state, or what is seen as the state's legitimate role in leisure, had shifted in the last two decades of the twentieth century. While the strident ideology of Thatcherism was no longer evident, the balance between the market, the state and the rest of civil society had been reset; and with an increasingly globalised economy (and globalised polity, with the deepening of the European Union) there seemed, to some commentators, to be less opportunity for intervention at the level of the nation-state to 'make a difference'. In the preceding section on New Labour, we have suggested that such claims are overstated and that there has been evidence of an approach to leisure policy on the part of New Labour which distinguishes it, to some degree, from its Conservative predecessors. Of course this difference may only have been sustainable in areas of policy which are peripheral to central concerns such as economic policy and national sovereignty. Such arguments imply a debate about different ways of theorising the state's role and it is therefore on such issues that we now focus.

Leisure, the state and social theory

The analysis of the politics of leisure undertaken in this and preceding chapters has focused on material relating to leisure politics and policy with reference to the central rather than the local state. Yet, since most leisure provision is made by local government under permissive legislation, it is at the level of the local state that the major public sector investments have been traditionally decided and implemented. However, before embarking on a detailed analysis of the politics of leisure policy at the local level, it will be important to contextualise that analysis by reviewing and evaluating theoretical accounts of the nature of the local state and its relationship with the central state. Theories of the state may, on the one hand, be prescriptive or normative, in effect specifying how the state ought to operate; or they may be analytic, or heuristic, seeking to illustrate and explain how the state does in fact operate. An understanding of both normative goals and heuristic frameworks is a prerequisite to the generating of adequate accounts of the articulation between central state and local politics and policy.

The following discussion deals with the major theoretical accounts of the central and local state broadly in line with the chronology of their development. The material conditions under which such accounts were, or are, generated reflect the changing nature of central–local relations, and the problematics which they have sought to identify or explain. Pluralist theories of the state, for example, enjoyed their strongest support (at least in their heuristic form) in the period of post-war growth when lobbying for the extension of welfare rights could be effective. The development of radical Weberian accounts of urban managerialism was influenced by the emergence of research evidence in the late 1960s and early 1970s which underlined the failure of welfare policy to meet the needs of the most disadvantaged, for whom they were primarily intended. The resurgence of Marxist accounts and the articulation of Marxist theories of the state in the 1970s reflects the recognition of the political and policy impacts of the deepening economic recession. The dual-state thesis illustrates the separate and sometimes conflicting roles of the central and local state as clashes between first Labour, and subsequently Conservative, central governments, and local government grew in severity and frequency at the end of the 1970s and the beginning of the 1980s. The importance of New Right prescriptive theories of the state which guided government policy in the 1980s and into the 1990s is a function of the hegemonic leadership established by the New Right during the 1980s and its treatment of local government. Feminist accounts of the state have also grown as the contradictory position of women in the public economy and in the household economy has become more apparent with the growing proportion of women in work. Finally, at the beginning of the twenty-first century it has become increasingly difficult to deny the impact of globalisation on the role of the state and the way this has been conceptualised.

Until relatively recently the received wisdom concerning local government was that it represented a neutral vehicle for local administration (Lloyd, 1985). This was underpinned by the assumptions of democratic pluralism, which included the notion of free competition between interest groups across a range of issues, with local political parties representing shifting alliances of such interest groups in the political process. The classic statement of local pluralism was Dahl's (1961) analysis of politics in New Haven which examined a range of issues or decisions, and describes how no single interest group was able to dominate all such decisions. Although not all groups have equal access to resources, the nature of the local political process means that where an issue is sufficiently important to a group, greater efforts may be made, for example, to lobby decision-makers and mobilise public opinion so that the desired outcome may be achieved by pressure politics. The principal role of the local state in such an explanation is one of ensuring that interest groups have a forum for expressing their preferences. State intervention in the form of social provision is restricted to those instances where a consensus exists supporting such intervention. These instances are likely to be rare and the democratic pluralist argument therefore implies a minor role for state intervention in general and in leisure provision specifically.

This analysis is consistent with Roberts' (1978) account of leisure participation as reflecting a fragmented pattern of 'taste publics'.

The state should, he argued, avoid positive involvement in leisure provision, limiting itself to generating the conditions under which individuals and groups may meet their own needs. However, where a consensus supporting state involvement does exist (perhaps for example in promotion of national fitness or conservation of art forms) or where the market operates inefficiently, the state may step in. Nevertheless, such state involvement is insulated from the competition of interest groups by employing 'neutral', 'technical' experts often in quangos, such as the Arts and Sports Councils, to make decisions about the precise nature of resource allocation.

A number of difficulties with the premises of the pluralist argument seriously undermine this explanation. First, the notion of local polities being responsive to voter pressure has not always stood up to scrutiny (Dunleavy, 1980; Newton, 1976). Second, the pluralist explanation of local policy ignores the pivotal role played by 'urban managers' (Pahl, 1977) or local state bureaucrats in the setting of the policy agenda. As Bachrach and Baratz (1970) have demonstrated, local bureaucrats may be able to influence significantly the local political agenda, filtering out undesired policy options and identifying those interest groups among the local community which can be defined as 'responsible'. As such, these professionals are crucial gate-keepers, controlling access to public services. Pahl's analysis largely draws on examples from the field of housing and has been employed in the analysis of urban planning, but the establishment of the new, large, leisure services departments in the post-1974 period, and the professionalisation of leisure services, gave leisure professionals greater access to resources, and the opportunity to influence corporate planning, and helped to develop a degree of autonomy in defining leisure needs. Such a situation invites analysis of leisure professionals' influence on resource allocation decisions.

Marxist critiques of the pluralist and urban managerialist explanations of the local state point to their failure to locate the activities of interest groups and urban managers in the context of the structural demands of capitalism. Perhaps the most influential Marxist account of this type was developed by Castells (1976), who sought to explain the 'crisis of the local state' as a consequence of its contradictory functions, meeting the long-term needs of capital while responding to working-class demands for increased social expenditure (expressed through urban movements). In seeking to sustain an increasing rate of profit, capital traditionally socialised the costs of reproduction of labour power, with education, health, housing and even leisure provision becoming responsibilities of the state. However, as the rate of profit falls, capital seeks to reduce costs by pressing for lower taxation, while working-class demands for social expenditure increase. Thus the costs of 'collective consumption' exceed revenues, and, Castells argued, this basic contradiction of capitalism was likely to manifest itself in the form of struggles around consumption issues, many of which directly involve local government. The 'Poll Tax riots' of the late 1980s might, for example, be subject to explanations of this nature.

This type of explanation of the welfare state (and of the role of the local state) has significant implications for leisure policy. As has already been suggested, if collective consumption was to be cut back in periods of economic stringency, one might have expected leisure to be one of the first service areas to suffer, since resistance to cuts seemed likely to be keenest in more 'basic' service areas such as health, housing and education. However, as social expenditure was reduced, social expenses accrued because of the need to secure public order in the face of resistance to cuts. Such social expenses may take the form of policing, vandalism repair, or even 'preventive recreation'. Opposition to the cuts may foster new alliances, for instance between local state professionals and client groups (Whitsun, 1984) generating new urban social movements.

There are, however, a number of problems with the structuralist analysis of Castells and other functionalist Marxist accounts of the local state (e.g. Cockburn, 1977). Perhaps the three most important of these are the circularity implied in such functionalist explanations, the 'problem of specificity', and the failure to address the gendered nature of power relations within the state and between the state and civil society. We will return to the issue of the state, gender and power below, but let us deal here with the first two objections cited. Any forms of state intervention which might appear to benefit working-class interests, such as the development of welfare services, are explained in the Marxist account as representing the interests of capital, in the final analysis, by buying off working-class opposition to capital accumulation. However, such an argument will not allow of any realistic counter-example of the state acting against the interests of capital (Saunders, 1981). Thus if the state reduces expenditure on public services it is said by Marxists to be acting in the interests of capital by saving on taxes. If, however, the state increases the level of public sector investment in services and therefore of taxes, it is also said to be acting in the interests of capital by assuaging working-class opposition to contemporary social arrangements. The conclusions of such Marxist analysis are therefore built into the premises which underpin any empirical work in this field. The tautological nature of the argument and the impossibility of describing a state of affairs in which the state acts against the interests of capital, serve, therefore, to devalue the Marxist account. However, even if the circularity of this argument is ignored, this kind of Marxist account is functionalist and explains state activity only by reference to general principles, such as the need to reproduce labour power, and fails to explain how and why particular policies arise at particular points in time. Yet such explanation of detail must be a criterion of the adequacy of social theory, and in this sense also the Marxist explanation is inadequate.

The shortcomings of traditional Marxist analysis of the local state as an undifferentiated element in a functional whole, led Saunders and Cawson (Saunders, 1984) to develop the 'dual-state thesis'. The local tier of government was regarded in this thesis as performing different and often conflicting functions to those of central government. According to this account the allocation of responsibilities for various functions to different tiers of government represents the way in which the state manages to accommodate such conflicts.

There are problems for this explanation of the operation of the local state. It should be noted for example, that some production issues (e.g. highways), are the responsibility of local government, while control of some consumption services is spread across more than one tier (e.g. the National Health Service). However, the separation of production and consumption functions between different tiers of government might perhaps be regarded as an organising tendency which will admit of some exceptions. A potentially more serious objection, however, was produced by Dunleavy (1980) who argued that, if the operation of local government is indeed best characterised as pluralist, one would expect to find a great variation in the level, quality and variety of consumption policies across local authorities. However, what is striking about such consumption policies is their uniformity in apparently disparate settings. Thus, for Dunleavy, the major difficulty with the dual-state thesis is its failure to acknowledge the pivotal role of the public sector professional in influencing policy. The advent of Best Value in local government and its attendant technocratic monitoring and planning, if anything, seems even more likely to promote the role of public sector professionals (at least those working in the 'core' of local government policy) over that of local politicians.

A major feature of the appeal of the dual-state thesis was that it eschewed description of the state as a monolith, seeking to capture the differential operation of the state machinery at different levels of government without collapsing into atheoretical, anecdotal accounts. It should be said in defence of Saunders' argument that he was promoting a thesis, rather than a theory. The significance of this distinction is that the status of 'thesis' invites disconfirmation or support from empirical investigation rather than simply 'explaining' the phenomenon in question. Dunleavy's major objection to the thesis, the characterisation of local policy-making as professionally dominated, is a potentially serious problem, but it is also open to evaluation in the light of empirical studies. Thus the dual-state thesis offers what, in some respects, is an interesting organising framework for considering the analysis of local government leisure policy.

However, it is debatable whether the dual-state thesis ever accurately reflected political and organisational practice. As an 'ideal type' it may have served to illustrate ways in which the state departed from, rather than conformed with, the thesis. The thesis was to be regarded simply as an heuristic device which attempted to explain how contradictory consumption and production functions are accommodated within government. Critics of both left and right might suggest that, whether or not the dual-state thesis accurately characterises the nature of the state, the thesis, as a basis for a prescriptive theory of how the state ought to operate, is doomed to fail. The development of central–local relations across the 1980s illustrates this point clearly, since the vigour with which the central state has sought to control local state spending has severely constrained the nature of the local state's ability to make decisions about local consumption. In a sense the central state also attempted to induce competitive politics at local level by the introduction of the community charge, and subsequently in a more subtle fashion by its replacement, the council tax. Instead of individuals voting at local elections according to support for the national parties, it is intended that by presenting the local electorate with costs more directly tied to the individual's tax bill for local spending, there would be a starker choice between spending on local services and reducing individuals' levels of taxation. However, central government has also *undermined* local political competition of this sort by threatening to 'cap' council tax levels for those local authorities which wished to spend beyond the limits advised by central government.

The New Right model of the state, at least as a prescription for how the state should operate, dominated the political arena in the 1980s and early 1990s. There are perhaps two major strands to New Right theories of the state, namely public choice theory and the Austrian school of economic (and moral) theory (Dunleavy and O'Leary, 1987). In the same way as classical economics highlights the nature of market imperfections, public choice theorists focus on the nature of imperfections in the political marketplace, that is tendencies for the political and administrative system to produce negative outcomes. The economic crisis of the early 1970s, or at least the reasons why that recession hit Britain's economy harder than that of other developed nations, is explained by the New Right reference to these 'state imperfections' (Bacon and Eltis, 1978; Olson, 1982). This has lead the New Right to adopt an approach to state organisation which is anti-planning and anti-interventionist, using instead the market as a vehicle for learning about consumer preferences and how to meet them (Hayek, 1976).

Public choice theorists point to a range of imperfections in the operation of the political system. Voting procedures, for example, are seen as crude measures of aggregated individual, or collective, interests. In Britain, with the exception of very rare public referenda, voters go to the polls, placing a single vote, to decide both on personnel (who their political representative should be) and policies (usually grouped together in the form of a party manifesto). In order, therefore, for candidates or parties to attract votes, they have to bundle together policies with an appeal to a wide range of voters, thus invariably generating commitments which may win elections, but which, as a total package, are unaffordable. Furthermore, policy trade-offs, where support is given by one group to another's policy goals in exchange for support for their own, and the attempts by individual politicians to ensure that their own constituencies of interest receive benefits, generate further commitments.

Government organisations and policy programmes, once started, are difficult to terminate. Unlike the marketplace, where firms meet market needs or die, government departments, quangos and funding programmes continue unless questioned, in part because of the traditional incrementalist budgetary practices of government whereby budgets for one year are employed as bases from which to plan the following year's budget (Danziger, 1978), building into the policy system an inherent conservatism. Thus governmental organisations exhibit entropic tendencies, they become ossified. This is partly a function of size (the impossibility of undertaking comprehensive reviews of all governmental programmes annually) and is partly a function of entrenched interests ('empire building' politicians and 'budget maximising' officials). This generates the problem of 'government overload' in the sense of placing an intolerable burden on government in terms both of monitoring its own programmes and departments, and of the economic resources required to run this ever-growing volume of state business.

The operation of liberal democratic conventions has, according to the New Right, led to an increasingly interventionist state which acts against the individual and collective interests of society. The consequences of this for New Right thinkers in terms of prescriptive theories of the state are either that one should modify the particular forms of political inputs in liberal democracy which generate this form of state imperfection (Hayek, 1976, goes so far as to advocate restricting the franchise), or that one should more strictly delimit the legitimate areas of political outputs or policies, restricting areas for state intervention.

The Thatcher administration sought to adopt aspects of the New Right's prescription for restricting political outputs in order to avoid political market imperfections. Corporatism, as a form of political oligopoly, was rejected. Organisational entropy was attacked, with, for example, a fundamental review of the number and powers of quangos, the abolition of a tier of local government, and exposure to market forces of various areas of local government activity through the introduction of compulsory competitive tendering. Furthermore, the introduction of the community charge also sought to erode the opportunity for the 'buying' of votes with policy promises, because it transferred some of the real costs of meeting those policy promises onto the wider electorate.

The New Right theory of the state is both descriptive/analytic in its explanation of how policies were developed in the past (e.g. in its explanation of government overload), and is *prescriptive* in its advocacy of a minimalist form of provision. However, as a theoretical account of the state it is inadequate in a number of ways. Perhaps its most significant weakness is its failure to theorise the nature of the relationship between the state, social structure and the market. An account of public demands leading to government provision of services (and ultimately 'overload') may explain how the state comes to provide services, but it fails to explain why such services disproportionately benefit particular groups (e.g. gender, race, class). It also fails to explain the impact on social structure of such provision.

In addition, the New Right's account of the state is premised on the denial that one can talk meaningfully about the 'collective interests' of social groups (hence Mrs Thatcher's much publicised claim that there is no such thing as society, only individuals). This is in part derived from the New Right's wish to dismiss Marxist accounts of social needs (and subsequent Marxist prescriptions of how the state should meet such needs) which are premised on the concept of 'false consciousness'. Structuralist Marxists wished to deny that individuals in capitalist societies could identify their real interests. However, as Giddens (1979: 189) points out, one can deny Marxist accounts of false consciousness without dismissing the possibility that individuals may be unconscious of their own interests. Individuals have conscious wants. Giddens identifies individuals as working in their own interests if they are adopting the means to achieve their conscious wants. The point for Giddens, then, is that we can be conscious of our wants but unconscious of our interests, in the sense of being unconscious of the means to achieve those wants. Furthermore, we may be said to have 'collective interests' if, as a group, by virtue of our structural or spatial location in society, we share the means required to achieve our wants as individuals. This 'philosophical' point is of significance in the sense that state politicians and professionals can be said to be acting in the interests of social groups (whether or not those groups are conscious of their interests), a possibility which the New Right wishes to deny.

Some of the most powerful critiques of the operation of the state in liberal democracies to emerge in recent years are derived from the work of feminist writers. These critiques have varied in their focus and adequacy, depending on the particular form of feminist analysis adopted. Such contributions have not generally sought to develop a theory of the state as such, but rather to develop critical analysis of the gendered nature of political representation, government institutions and policy outcomes. Nevertheless they have generated important insights. Sylvia Walby (1990), for example, reviews the major theoretical traditions in feminist thinking and their implications for analysis of the state, while Sheila Scraton (1988) develops similar discussion of feminist perspectives and their implications for the sociology of sport, with particular implications for understanding the role of the state in sports policy.

The central concern of liberal feminists has been with the absence of women from decision-making positions. This is certainly the case in respect of the absence of women in key roles among state professionals in leisure (White, 1988). The exclusion of women is explained by reference to factors such as enculturation, role expectations and male conspiracy within state institutions. The implication of liberal feminist analysis is that strategies should be sought to locate women in powerful positions within the state. This, however, is naïve in that it offers no guarantee of redressing gender imbalances. The relatively recent example of a woman holding the highest political office in Britain illustrates that simply putting women in positions of power will not of itself result in the redressing of gender inequalities.

Marxist feminists explain the oppression of women by the state as a function of the needs of capital. The state, for example, fosters the family as the major unit of labour reproduction, through fiscal and other incentives, and the promotion of familial ideologies. Capital benefits from cheap reproduction of labour power through the family, which is serviced largely by the unpaid domestic labour of women. Such an account fails, however, to acknowledge that men in general (not just capitalists) benefit materially from the oppression of women, and radical feminists have therefore focused on patriarchy rather than capitalism as the major source of oppression, arguing that the state always acts in the interests of patriarchy (rather than those of capital). Crucially, however, both Marxist and radical feminists fail to account for the contradictory nature of the state which can occasionally act in the interests of women. The outcomes of state activity are not structurally determined by the needs of capitalism or of patriarchy, but rather such outcomes are contingent. Women have won some important reforms, yet such contradictory outcomes are as difficult to explain for radical and Marxist feminists, as the political and policy advances of the working class have been for traditional Marxists.

Dual-systems theory advocated by Walby, and socialist feminism, by Scraton, suggest that giving primacy to either gender or class is misplaced. The state will act in different interests at different times, and the outcome of struggles relating to the state will therefore be contingent. In addition, structures other than class and gender may be important in mediating life chances (in particular race but also potentially, for example, age, 'knowledge', disability). Such an approach while not constituting a theory of the state *per se*, does point to the requirement that an adequate account should be able to explain the differential relationship of the state to different gender, class, race and other groups. A way forward in this respect is offered in the 'strategic relational' approach of theorists such as Jessop (1990c), who suggest that the state should be seen as the outcome of past struggles between social groups, which also forms the context of, and resources for, contemporary struggles. The outcomes of these past struggles will invariably reflect the interests of the most powerful groups in society.

Such an approach has six fundamental benefits, since it illustrates or emphasises:

(a) the relationship between the state and civil society, the social structure and relations of power other than those of the formal political system;

(b) the contradictory nature of the state – e.g. sometimes groups, disadvantaged in terms of gender, class, race, age etc. do win their struggles;

(c) the state is fragmented – e.g. women's interests may be more strongly represented in say the local state, or in some local states, because of the history of local struggle;

(d) the outcomes of state activity are contingent, they are not determined;

(e) nevertheless, these outcomes are likely to reflect the interests of the most powerful;

(f) and finally a strategic relations approach fosters the analysis of the relationship between not only the state and civil society within national boundaries, but invites analysis of wider relations in the transnational sphere.

Thus the strategic relations conceptualisation of the state invites empirical analysis to evaluate whose interests have been reflected in the activity of the state, in what ways, and how the primacy of these interests has been effected. Much of this analysis in respect of leisure will require detailed discussion in respect of local government and it is therefore to leisure policy and politics at the local level that three of the following chapters will be principally addressed.

Recent work on the phenomenon of globalisation has significant implications for the way in which the role of the state may be understood. Much of the initial work reflected on the growing economic interdependence between national economies (Rhodes and van Apeldoorn, 1998). Political interdependence has also been subject to considerable debate (Casanova, 1996; Rosenau, 1989), and in particular the impact of globalising tendencies on the role of the nation-state (Hirst and Thompson, 1995; Morris, 1997; Shaw, 1997; Smith, 1998b). This is allied to the apparent growth in importance of the region and the city as the locus of significant political activity (Andrew and Goldsmith, 1998; Jones, 1998; Keil, 1998). In addition, considerable research effort has gone into identifying ways in which cultural or leisure forms have been either, or both, a reflection of such tendencies or a reaction to globalising phenomena (Featherstone, 1990, 1995; Maguire, 1999; Robertson, 1992)

Two of the most influential explanations of the nature of globalisation are provided by Anthony Giddens and David Harvey. Giddens (1990) characterises globalisation in terms of time-space distanciation, that is the phenomenon of people's lives being increasingly less tied to local circumstances, while Harvey (1989) focuses on 'time-space compression', the speeding up of processes given technological and economic change, in particular across the period since the end of the 1960s. Both acknowledge the increasingly transparent interdependence between markets, polities and everyday life in formerly spatially, culturally, politically and economically distinct constituencies. The hierarchy of causes of such globalising phenomena are subject to considerable debate, with some authors giving primacy to economic factors (Sklair, 1991; Wallerstein, 1983) others to advances in technology (Rosenau, 1989) or culture (Perlmutter, 1991), while Giddens (1990) and Robertson (1992) both argue that globalisation represents the results of multiple dimensions of change.

The concept of governance is intrinsically bound up with that of globalisation. As Rhodes comments, the term governance is well-used in the literature but is imprecise. He identifies six connotations of the term, namely: the minimal state; corporate governance; the new public management; 'good governance'; socio-cybernetic systems; and self-organising networks; and goes on to provide his own stipulative definition of governance as consisting in 'self-organising, inter-organisational networks' (Rhodes, 1996: 652). The use of the term 'governance', in place of 'government', reflects a recognition that in contemporary developed economies governing decisions can no longer be taken by governments alone (whether national or local). Rather, effective decision-making will need to incorporate other stakeholders from the commercial and/or voluntary sectors. This in turn is a reflection of the interconnectedness of change. As economic competition has increasingly globalised, so pressures have been induced for nation-states to adopt a *neo-liberal*, free-market philosophy, reducing state expenditures in order to lower taxation and maintain a competitive position in relation to industrial costs. Thus the notions of the *minimal state*, or the *hollowing out of the state* are associated with globalisation of the economy, and have key significance in terms of issues of governance.

The hollowing out of the state or the minimisation of its activities does not simply imply an overall reduction in state activities, but rather a reduction in particular kinds of activities. Thus as Gamble (1988) illustrates in relation to 1980s Britain, a reduction in state activity in certain areas, may require a strengthening of the state's powers in others. The pressure for the reduction of state activity is predominantly to be felt in the welfare domain (Taylor Gooby, 1991; Wilding, 1992) and thus a *restructuring* if not *withering of welfare states* has ensued in many national contexts (Pierson, 1991). Indeed Jessop has characterised the restructuring of welfare policy in the developed economies as a shift from the welfare state to the *Schumpeterian workfare state* (Jessop, 1995b). The state is Schumpeterian in the sense of conforming to the neo-liberal precepts of Joseph Schumpeter, and workfare in the sense of allying social policy to economic development and work-related goals.

While the transnational organising of capital has proceeded apace, outflanking to a considerable degree the national organisation of labour, a need has been increasingly evident to organise economic policy on a transnational basis. The European Union, the development of the single market, and moves towards political integration reflect such an approach. The increasing significance of transnational governmental activity conflicts with the tendency to reduce governmental activity, and it is at the transnational level that some social legislation is possible if the costs of social policy advances are not simply to be visited on the economies of 'progressive' states. Thus the EU has, for example, been the site of discussion and legislation for workers' rights, marginal though the gains may have been in most instances. The activities of the EU are of course coordinated by the governments of nation-states, though power is shared between the institutions of the European Parliament, the European Commission and the Council of Ministers (which is drawn from national governments). However, direct accountability is perceived as a problem, and results in what is described as 'democratic deficit' (Bellamy and Warleigh, 1998; MacCormick, 1997).

The weakening of the role of nation-states in economic terms has meant not just an increase in economic significance of governance at the transnational level, but also a growing role for sub-national economies. Cities in particular have come to see themselves involved in an inter-urban competition which is no longer bounded by the nation-state (Barlow, 1995; Kantor, Savitch, and Haddock, 1997), and city governments have increasingly become involved in economic development activities, focusing more on 'selling' their cities to prospective investors, and less on the delivery and management of traditional public sector services.

Thus theorising the position of the nation-state requires a situating of explanation within an understanding of the impacts of globalisation processes and their relationship to the structural context of British society and to systems of local, national and transnational governance. The final two chapters of this book take up this issue. Chapter 6 locates a discussion of leisure policy within the context of a general frame of regulation theory, evaluating ideal-typical accounts of Fordist and post-Fordist social regulation against the detailed analysis of the development of leisure policy in a major British city, while the final chapter considers aspects of strategic relations, in particular at the transnational level, by focusing on the intervention of the European Union in aspects of leisure policy.

4 Local Government and Leisure Policy: From the Thatcher Era to the Modernisation Agenda

Introduction

Despite the ideological significance and traditionally high public profile of the leisure quangos, local government is by far the most significant vehicle for the delivery of leisure services. Local government current expenditure estimates for 1999/2000 exceeded £2066 million (CIPFA, 1999b), compared to which the budgets for the same year of the UK and English Sports Councils combined of £50.7 million, and the Arts Council of England of £218.8 million (Department of Culture Media and Sport, 1999c) were relatively small, even when combined with the £400 million to be allocated from the Lottery to sport and the arts. The breakdown of local government leisure expenditure in Figure 4.1 illustrates the fact that the vast majority of local government spending in this area is on sport and recreation. Nevertheless, the local government budget in general and the budget for leisure in particular was subjected to sustained pressure over the period from the mid-1970s, and the Blair government continued to apply this budgetary pressure when it came to power in 1997.

As already noted in Chapter 2, a squeeze on local government spending was initially invoked by the Wilson/Callaghan Labour administration in response to conditions imposed by the International Monetary Fund, when granting a request for a loan in 1976, to ease Britain's balance of payments problems. The subsequent imposition of spending restrictions by Labour resulted in a considerable reduction in capital spending, though revenue expenditure remained at relatively high levels (Newton and Karan, 1985). Nevertheless, notwithstanding the reduction in capital spending in

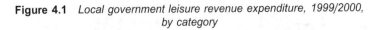

Figure 4.1 *Local government leisure revenue expenditure, 1999/2000, by category*

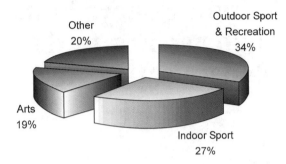

Source: CIPFA (1999).

the late 1970s, the growth in the number of local authority facilities across the 1970s was remarkable (Sports Council, 1983, 1988). However, in the 1980s several factors combined to move the emphasis of local government leisure policy away from a simple provision of additional physical facilities. The first of these was the expenditure squeeze. This was accompanied by a second factor, a questioning of the assumption that subsidised facilities served the interests of those unable to meet their own needs in the free market. Research findings indicated that public sector cultural and sporting facilities (as with welfare services generally) were failing to attract the most disadvantaged (Audit Commission, 1989). The third factor relates to the fact that concern with attracting the disadvantaged was heightened by the major urban disorders of the early 1980s, it being recognised that non-traditional forms and styles of provision would be required to attract non-standard users. Some non-standard forms of provision were employed as expressions of resistance by Labour local authorities (in particular the Greater London Council) to the political and ideological pressures from central government. Finally, in the 1990s new pressures were to emerge with the implications of the introduction of CCT in leisure services, and subsequently Best Value (introduced in the 1999 Local Government Act and due for implementation from April 2000) both of which fostered local government interest in means of service delivery other than direct provision.

Local government leisure services in the 1970s: an arm of the Welfare State

When local government had been reorganised in 1974 (for most parts of England and Wales) the rationale which informed this process could be described as built on political consensus and corporate management. The system was intended to be pluralist in operation, with increased opportunities for citizen involvement, and to enhance the effectiveness and importance of local government. The reorganisation was politically consensualist in that both major parties accepted the need for reform to replace the fragmented system of reactive local government units (though there were disagreements relating to the placing of boundaries and the political advantage thus obtained). The new system was to involve setting up large-scale authorities since size was seen as promoting several benefits. Bigger governmental units could provide large-scale solutions to the large-scale social, economic and environmental problems faced by local authorities. Large-scale local government would attract able and ambitious politicians and bureaucrats, because with increased size would come greater political and professional kudos and larger salaries. The new system promoted corporate management both by amalgamating service areas into larger service departments (the new personal social services and leisure services departments were obvious examples of this), and by promoting the establishment of policy and resources committees and chief officers' management teams to ensure the establishment and monitoring of corporate objectives across the whole of the authority. An integral feature of the new framework was the structure planning system which incorporated mechanisms for participation based on pluralist assumptions, with the recommendations of the Skeffington Report (Skeffington, 1969) on citizen participation in planning inscribed within the system.

However, once in place, reorganised local government attracted severe criticism. The size of the new authorities militated against local participation and created alienation in communities which felt organisationally, socially and often geographically remote from the locus of decision-making. The pluralist inspired structure planning system proved unwieldy and unresponsive to local interests and changing political priorities (Brindley, Rydin, and Stoker, 1989).

The corporate management philosophy imported from the commercial sector in times of stable growth had been seriously questioned by commercial management analysts in the volatile markets of the 1970s, and proved unworkable in the turbulent political and social environment of local government of the 1970s (Haynes, 1980).

Local government and new economic realism, 1976–85

While the Labour governments of Wilson and Callaghan had sought to control local government expenditure through 'fiscal persuasion', the Conservative government of Margaret Thatcher set about this task with an altogether more determined approach. Friction within local authorities grew as the more overtly ideological, neo-liberal themes of the Conservative Party nationally percolated through to the local level. By the beginning of the 1980s the consensualist nature of local politics had been eroded, particularly in Metropolitan districts which had to deal with the worst aspects of the restructuring of the economy and its social consequences. These authorities were predominantly controlled by Labour councils, a number of which became locked in conflict with Conservative central government. Table 4.1 summarises data on sport and recreation expenditure by districts, for Labour, Conservative and all authorities. These figures have to be treated with considerable caution. Political control was established by data from the *Municipal Year Book* and can be presumed to be accurate, but expenditure data for this table are from the CIPFA annual estimates (CIPFA, 1982, 1984, 1988, 1995, 1999a) and although accounting procedures were to become much more uniform between authorities from the early 1980s (Stabler, 1984), the response rate to CIPFA's annual questionnaire by local authorities over the 1980s had decreased alarmingly. A fear of rate-capping, or community charge-capping, seems to have militated against the openness of the system of financial reporting. Thus comparison, particularly across years, must be conducted with caution.

In respect of London boroughs the gap in spending on sport and recreation between Labour and Conservative-controlled authorities would appear at first sight to have closed in the later 1980s. However, among the 10 authorities which did not respond in

1988/9 were a number of high-spending Labour authorities from earlier years. The figures for non-metropolitan districts reveal a larger rate of increase for Labour authorities across the time period and a wider discrepancy between Labour and Conservative authorities. Indeed the per capita expenditure level for non-metropolitan Labour-controlled authorities exceeds that for their metropolitan counterparts, in three of the five years reported.

When the Conservative government came to power in 1979 its policy agenda was dominated by New Right concerns to impose monetarist prescriptions on public spending and to introduce market discipline in areas of work traditionally seen as public sector dominated. In the first half of the 1980s, government concerns were almost wholly taken up in attempts through legislation to contain and reduce local government spending by increasing the powers of central government to intervene in the process of local authority raising of finance, and expenditure. The first of these measures, enacted after the Conservative government came to power in 1979, was the Local Government Planning and Land Act 1980. This replaced the system of central government funding of local authorities, introducing a Block Grant based on central government's assessment of what local expenditure needs were. The new system incorporated a 'grant taper' for overspending authorities in which those going beyond the expenditure limits anticipated by central government would receive progressively reduced funding. This system was subsequently made more rigorous with the introduction of 'grant penalties' for those authorities spending 10 per cent or more above prescribed limits.

The 1980 Act also enhanced central government's control over local capital spending, introducing cash limits for such expenditure. The targets and limits were seen by some commentators as politically manipulated (Newton and Karan, 1985) with in 1983–84 Conservative authorities receiving penalties amounting to £24 million compared with £217 million imposed on Labour-controlled authorities. Furthermore, the system of sliding grant scales, imposition of penalties and rule changes taking place within a given financial year had a significantly deleterious effect on local authority financial management and planning according to the government's own watchdog, the Audit Commission, which was established in 1982 (Audit Commission, 1984).

Table 4.1 *Per capita revenue expenditure estimates for sport, recreation and leisure services for English authorities for selected years*

	1982/3				
	Mean	Std. devn	Min.	Max.	N
All London boroughs (LBs)	16.0	8.6	5.6	44.5	32
Labour-controlled LBs	19.9	9.0	9.5	44.5	15
Conservative-controlled LBs	11.1	3.8	5.6	19.2	16
All metropolitan districts (MDs)	11.6	3.2	6.1	19.3	26
Labour-controlled MDs	12.0	3.2	7.6	19.3	26
Conservative-controlled MDs	9.7	1.9	6.1	11.6	6
All non-metropolitan districts	7.1	4.7	0.0	37.2	291
Labour-controlled non-MDs	11.6	4.8	3.8	27.2	55
Conservative-controlled non-MDs	6.5	4.2	0.1	37.2	148

	1995/6				
	Mean	Std. devn	Min.	Max.	N
All London boroughs (LBs)	31.0	11.1	15.7	60.1	19
Labour-controlled LBs	33.0	12.6	21.6	60.1	8
Conservative-controlled LBs	31.6	7.1	23.5	36.3	3
All metropolitan districts (MDs)	30.0	8.9	11.7	55.9	25
Labour-controlled MDs	31.6	10.0	18.7	55.9	13
Conservative-controlled MDs	24.5	–	24.5	24.5	1
All non-metropolitan districts	21.5	10.7	3.3	70.1	211
Labour-controlled non-MDs	32.3	12.2	5.82	70.1	47
Conservative-controlled non-MDs	15.7	6.5	3.3	32.4	52
All unitary authorities (UAs)					
Labour-controlled UAs					
Conservative-controlled UAs					

1. Caution should be exercised in comparisons across years since this is subject to changing accounting conventions, and in comparison between Labour and Conservative-controlled authorities in specific categories since increased non-reporting of financial data is apparent.

	1984/5					1998/9			
Mean	Std. devn	Min.	Max.	N	Mean	Std. devn	Min.	Max.	N
17.0	8.6	8.3	40.1	25	22.6	7.5	13.8	45.8	22
26.5	7.9	16.0	40.1	7	24.7	5.5	17.5	33.2	6
12.0	3.3	8.3	18.1	15	21.2	5.8	13.8	32.4	10
15.0	4.8	8.0	24.7	21	19.9	7.3	9.9	44.4	32
15.0	4.8	8.0	24.7	21	20.9	7.9	9.9	44.4	24
11.2	2.5	7.0	13.1	5	10.56	–	–	–	1
8.9	5.5	–0.2	33.8	285	12.8	7.6	0.3	42.4	263
15.4	6.8	2.3	33.8	52	22.0	8.1	6.8	42.4	42
7.6	3.6	–0.2	18.8	137	10.9	5.7	0.3	28.3	131

	1999/2000			
Mean	Std. devn	Min.	Max.	N
29.8	14.7	9.3	68.0	27
35.2	16.5	13.2	68.0	14
30.3	7.1	23.0	37.2	3
29.8	9.9	15.1	64.9	26
31.1	10.4	19.5	65.0	21
–	–	–	–	–
22.5	10.1	4.4	74.7	165
27.4	12.3	7.9	74.7	54
17.7	6.0	10.0	25.5	7
38.6	13.6	12.4	67.8	27
45.0	11.3	26.6	67.8	17
12.6	–	12.6	12.6	1

Source: CIPFA Leisure and Recreation Estimates, for the years cited above.

The ability of local authorities to resist central government pressures resulted in further legislation in the form of the Local Government Finance Act 1982. This legalised retrospectively the system of targets and penalties introduced to supplement the 1980 Act, and prevented local authorities from raising a supplementary rate or precept within a financial year. It was followed by the Rates Act 1984 which empowered the Secretary of State to limit the rates of local authorities. Eighteen authorities were rate-capped in 1985/6 of which only one was not Labour-controlled (Brent, which was controlled by a Labour–Liberal alliance). Of the rate--capped authorities in the following two years only Liberal-controlled Tower Hamlets and Conservative-controlled Portsmouth were not Labour authorities. However, even this failed to suppress some local authorities' expenditure plans as imaginative efforts to raise funds by sale of mortgage debt, lease-back arrangements, and creative accounting were employed to find alternative sources of funds.

A campaign to combat what were seen as attacks on local autonomy was launched by rate-capped authorities together with some authorities threatened with rate-capping. Despite some success with popular opinion, this campaign was effectively quashed when Liverpool and Lambeth councillors were surcharged and disqualified from office for refusing to set a legal rate in 1987 (Lansley, Goss, and Wolmar, 1989). The Local Government Act 1985 also swept away one tier of local government, the Metropolitan Counties and Greater London Council, which had been particularly visible in organising opposition to central government.

The remaining legislation in the mid-1980s attempted to turn the spending screw even tighter, reducing opportunities for local government to circumvent central government expenditure limits. The Local Government Acts of 1986 and 1987 restricted local authority sale of mortgage debt, and removed from local government any right of appeal or of judicial review of past or present ministerial decisions about allocation of grants or of accounting practices. The impact of these measures began to be felt in the inability of local government to fund the growth of leisure services, and budgets remained relatively stationary in real terms until the reflationary budgets of Chancellor of the Exchequer, Nigel Lawson, at the end of the decade.

Flexibilisation and disinvestment in local government leisure services: the Conservative governments of 1985–97

The squeeze on local authority spending exerted by the Major administrations, if anything, had a greater impact on local authority leisure budgets in the first half of the 1990s as Figure 4.2 illustrates. In 1992/3 there was even a fall in cash terms, while in real terms budgets have remained static or fallen across the decade, having risen in the briefly reflationary period at the end of the 1980s. While attempts to control local government expenditure were key to Conservative local government policy, this by no means marked the end of Conservative ambitions. It was not simply that Conservatives wished to reduce the costs associated with operating the machinery of local government, they wished to change the nature of the machinery itself, to reduce it in size, and to make what remained more flexible and responsive to market conditions. A range of initiatives were thus introduced from the middle of the 1980s, across the later Thatcher and the Major administrations. These are discussed below under five headings: compulsory competitive tendering (CCT); new urban policy initiatives (including the 'delocalising' of local government, rationalising urban grants and instilling

Figure 4.2 *Local government leisure revenue estimates at current and at 1985 prices*

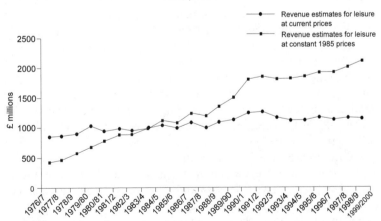

Source: CIPFA *Leisure and Recreation Estimates (various years).*

competition in the urban grant-allocation process); the restructuring of local taxation; the restructuring of local government; and subsequently some local leisure policy responses by the New Urban Left.

Compulsory competitive tendering

Compulsory competitive tendering was originally introduced in the Local Government Planning and Land Act 1980 for some services, and the logic and approach underpinning this was simply extended in the Local Government Act 1988 to include other service areas including street cleaning, refuse collection, ground and vehicle maintenance. Management of a variety of sport and leisure facilities and services was subsequently added in a Parliamentary Order (Competition in Sports and Leisure Facilities, November 1989). The list of facilities affected included sports centres, leisure centres, swimming pools, golf courses, bowling greens, putting greens, tennis courts, athletics tracks, pitches for team and other games, cycle tracks, water sports facilities, artificial ski slopes, skating rinks, indoor bowls areas and beaches. 'Management' in the context of sport and leisure was described as including the following; taking bookings; collection of fees and charges; cleaning and maintenance of grounds, buildings, plant and so on; supervising activities (e.g. lifeguards at swimming pools); instruction in sport and recreation activities; provision and hire of equipment; paying for heating and lighting of premises; and security of premises. Thus a considerable tranche of what constituted the work of leisure service departments was included in these proposals with a considerable potential impact on the nature of provision and management of such services. All such facilities in local authority ownership were to be subject to the tendering process in England by January 1993 and in Wales by 1994. The only exceptions to this requirement were for facilities for which the primary use was not sport and recreation, or those premises used primarily by educational institutions.

The way in which the initiative was implemented meant that local authority leisure service departments, in effect, became the clients of contractors who managed their services. The leisure services department could of course also bid to win its own contracts and therefore continue to manage its own facilities, but the nature of the relationship between facility or service management and the authority was nevertheless radically altered, since the authority had a responsibility for ensuring that the terms of the contract were adhered to, whether by its own direct labour organisation, or by a commercial contract winner.

The local authority letting a particular contract had responsibility for specifying the terms of the contract, as well as for monitoring implementation. Contracts could dictate (though this was optional) the pricing policy to be pursued at a given facility, and the programming requirements for particular groups (e.g. sports centre sessions for the unemployed, for women only, for young people, or for the disabled, or the balance between club and causal usage could be specified by the authority). Contracts could not, however, specify the type and quality of instructors, of staff training, of customer care programmes, and other such requirements (except those relating to health and safety) since the Parliamentary Order specifically precluded the inclusion of 'reference to non-commercial matters' in such contracts.

Where local authorities won the contracts they themselves had let, the authority had to generate an organisational structure to allow for the different functions (client monitoring of management performance, and contract management of the service) to be separately and adequately accomplished. This required the establishment at officer level, *either* of separate sections within a department (one to undertake the client role the other to manage the facility or service), *or* of separate departments or of 'management boards' (of officers and members) which could act in a way analogous to the board of a private company employed to carry out the terms of a management contract. Local authority committee structures were also generally altered in ways which would allow the oversight of the development of contract specifications, and the monitoring of contract performance on the one hand, and the management of contract compliance on the other, to be accomplished separately.

The operation by a local authority of its own facilities generally took one of three forms of management, the first being the most common, management by a Direct Service Organisation (DSO), the council's own workforce; the second a 'management buyout', where the existing local authority workforce set itself up as a private company to submit a tender to run the facilities; and the third management by an outside contractor. The forms of contract let under compulsory competitive tendering were as follows (Audit Commission, 1990):

- 'deficit guarantee', or 'franchise' contracts where the operator ran the facility at a preset level of subsidy, or for a fixed fee to be paid to the authority, with the operator taking all income or costs;
- profit-sharing' where net income was shared;
- 'income-sharing' where the gross income was shared;
- or the simple 'management fee' where an authority simply paid the contractor to operate a given facility or service.

Each of these arrangements had implications in terms of how the risks were allocated between client and contractor. However, it seemed likely from the outset that where commercial-sector operators gained from the generation of income in a facility, the social objectives of leisure provision were likely to be squeezed. Unless, therefore, social priorities were clearly specified in contracts, and performance monitored accordingly, user profiles for publicly owned/privately managed facilities were likely to reflect the more lucrative segments of the market, rather than reflecting those most in need.

Not surprisingly, in the early days of CCT in leisure there were problems for commercial operators. The vast majority of the companies involved in competitive bidding were established for the purpose of competing in this market, many formed by ex-local authority managers who may have been inexperienced in commercial management practice. The Public Services Privatisation Unit (1992) reported in the findings of a survey of 141 of the sport and leisure contracts let by local government by 1991, that 42 per cent (59) had been won by 18 private contractors, but of these 22 contracts had been terminated largely because of private contractors going into liquidation. In 1990, Clifford Barnet was liquidated with seven contracts, followed by Crossland Leisure in 1991 with 11 contracts and four other single contract companies. This left only 12 companies of which Serco with six contracts was the biggest. Ironically, Serco took over three Crossland contracts and gained the other three in taking over Community Leisure Management. At that stage, it was the company with the largest number of contracts, without ever having won a competitive tender.

Table 4.2   *Leading management contractors in the public sector leisure
centre and swimming pools market, 1997*

Contractor	No. of sites
Relaxion Group	44
DC Leisure	31
Circa Leisure plc	30
Civic Leisure (Vardon plc)	27
Serco Resource Management (Serco Facilities plc)	23
City Centre Leisure (Apollo Leisure plc)	22
Glendale Leisure Ltd	13
Sports and Leisure Management Ltd	13
Quadron Services Ltd	9
Holmes Place plc	4

Source: Mintel (1998).

Nevertheless as experience was gained, the commercial presence
developed in size and strength. Table 4.2 summarises the sites held
by leading management contractors in the public sector leisure
centre and swimming pools market in 1997.

It is not that the local government leisure sector was swamped by
commercial contractors who had won contracts to manage public
facilities. Mintel (1998), citing research by the Local Government
Management Board, notes that by 1997 private contractors had won
26 per cent of the sport and leisure management contracts put out to
tender, but this amounted to only 15.7 per cent of the total value of
such contracts, with the average value of private contractors' contracts being £287 000 compared with that of £558 000 for contracts
won by direct service organisations (DSOs). Local authorities were
able to undermine competition by 'bundling', that is placing very
attractive facilities with much less attractive entities in the same
contract. Very large contracts implying higher risks and greater
diversity of management requirements also proved less attractive to
commercial companies. Nevertheless, across the 1990s the leading
companies were operating in a profitable manner. Figure 4.3 illustrates the generally very healthy pre-tax profits earned by the leading
companies across the period. Even the decline in year-on-year
operating profit in 1996 for Circa Leisure and in 1994 for Civic
Leisure is explained by the companies as attributable to investment
costs for refurbishment and redevelopment of facilities.

Figure 4.3   *Operating profit of leading commercial operators of local government facilities, 1992–96*

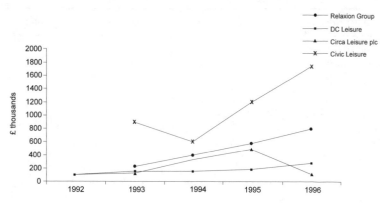

Source: Mintel (1998).

The level of commercial competition for contracts was certainly variable, with Conservative authorities attracting far more commercial-sector bids for contracts than their Labour counterparts. Indeed in the first tranche of contracts investigated by the Centre for Leisure and Tourism, Conservative authorities were almost three times more likely to attract a commercial bidder while in the second set of contracts the ratio had risen to 4:1 (Centre for Leisure and Tourism Studies, 1992). There were also regional differences, with considerably more commercial contractor success in the South. The LGMB indicates that in London and the South East more than 40 per cent of all contracts were won by commercial contractors, while in Wales, the Northern region, West Midlands and Yorkshire and Humberside, the figure stood at below 10 per cent (Mintel, 1998). Labour authorities were more likely to stipulate opening hours and prices in their contracts, but they were very much more likely than Conservative authorities to stipulate programming requirements for target groups. Just over 30 per cent of all Conservative authorities included programming requirements in contracts compared to over 60 per cent of Labour authorities (Centre for Leisure and Tourism Studies, 1992). Thus CCT seems to have exacerbated political differences (Nicholls and Taylor, 1995).

    The LGMB research also indicated that in the bidding for almost half of all contracts (49.6 per cent) there was no competition

(Mintel, 1998). However, even though the level of competition was low, the process of competition certainly affected wages and conditions in many authorities:

> In many cases in-house contracts were won at a price with job losses and the deterioration of pay and conditions being imposed despite the fact that there was no competition. (Public Service Privatisation Unit, 1992: 27)

In the PSPU study, 19 local authorities had reduced pay and/or conditions. Pay reductions had been largely achieved by reductions in bonus, overtime and shift pay allowances, but five local authorities had actually reduced pay levels, two had moved to performance-related pay and two had cut annual leave allowances. Some job losses were also reported, these being largely in managerial posts, though managerial salaries were reported as less subject to cuts than those of the non-managerial workforce. The PSPU also report that although there was a dearth of information on pay and conditions offered by commercial contractors 'the available information indicates that their terms and conditions are worse than those of the public sector' (p. 27). Although the European Court of Justice had decided that the arrangements for CCT fell within the provisions of the EC directive covering the transfer of public enterprises to commercial companies (TUPE), the precise nature of the application of the TUPE regulations in the case of CCT gave rise to considerable confusion and it is evident that conditions of service were routinely altered after contracts had been won. The TUPE regulations should have been able to protect the jobs and conditions of service of employees in any transfer from public to private sector, but it seems clear that they did not (Tichlear, 1998).

Notwithstanding the important implications of the introduction of CCT for those working in publicly owned facilities, potentially the most significant impact was on the nature of the service provided and the markets served by the contracted management. One of the major benefits of the review of public sector services undertaken in introducing CCT had been the recognition of the need to specify policy goals for public sector leisure provision. In the past these had often remained unexpressed and unclear. The Audit Commission promoted the notion that contracts should be drawn up in the context of sport and recreation strategies for each authority, stressing that it is impossible to establish whether value for money is being obtained unless one can identify what the investment in sport and recreation is designed to achieve. Nevertheless, the specification of social goals is not straightforward and, as studies of CCT indicate, programming goals are often left unstated (Centre for Leisure and Tourism Studies, 1992; Lawrence, Standeven, and Tomlinson, 1994). However, for those who failed to specify policy in contractual terms, the power to dictate policy directions would fall to contractors by default. Clearly, therefore, there was potential for considerable policy change through the introduction of competitive tendering since for leisure services, unlike other service areas such as refuse collection, policy outputs or performance measures may not be easily stipulated and monitored. The aims of public sector policy in the field of sport and recreation were therefore more at risk than those in other areas subjected to competition. Although Best Value shares many of the aims evident in the introduction of CCT, some effort has already been expended in defining social goals more clearly in preparation for the introduction of Best Value in 2000 (English Sports Council, 2000).

Compulsory competitive tendering undoubtedly had a significant impact on local government leisure services, not simply in terms of the economies gained, but also in terms of local government structures and culture. In addition to the requirement for separating out responsibility for the client and contractor function at both officer and member levels, the new regime fostered a focus on economy and efficiency, while neglecting in some instances social effectiveness since social goals were subordinated to financial objectives. Such a tendency is evident in other aspects of new managerialism, a matter considered in more detail in the following chapter (Clarke and Newman, 1997) (Lane, 1995; Leach, Stewart, and Walsh, 1994).

It is clear that one consequence of CCT was a reduction of costs in real terms for sport and leisure facilities. The consequences of such reductions in a single year (1995/6) were identified by local authority respondents to a survey conducted by the Centre for Leisure and Tourism Research (Centre for Leisure and Tourism Studies, 1996) as falling into nine categories:

- Service-level reductions;
- Price increases beyond inflation;
- Staff cuts or reductions;

- Facility closures;
- Maintenance savings or deferrals;
- Efficiency savings;
- Increased income generation;
- Organisational restructuring.

The impact of such phenomena on social polarisation in the use of public subsidy is likely to be significant. Indeed, as Figure 4.4 illustrates, social class differences in usage of facilities remain stubbornly high particularly in respect of regular usage.

New urban policy initiatives: 'delocalising' local government; rationalising urban grants and instilling competition in the urban grant allocation process

A second vehicle for the implementation of central government policy, employed by the Thatcher and Major administrations, was that of setting aside normal local authority controls by the establish-

Figure 4.4   *Visitors to leisure centres: social class by frequency, 1997*

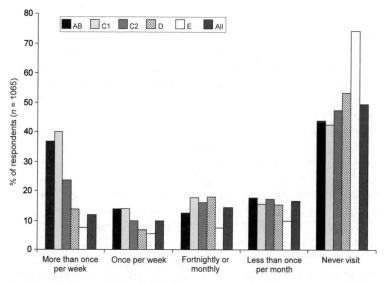

Source: Adapted from Mintel (1998).

ing of quango-like bodies with special powers, the memberships of which are determined by central government. These bodies included Enterprise Zones, Urban Development Corporations, Inner City Task Forces, and Freeports. The purpose of such bodies was to foster economic development in areas of urban decline. Enterprise Zones and Urban Development Corporations represented the most significant of these new organisational forms, providing benefits such as tax and business rate reductions as incentives to economic and industrial investment, together with a reduction in the control of local authorities over development decisions. Although introduced in the early part of the 1980s, they took off principally in the latter half of the decade.

In the first two rounds of designation by central government in 1982–84, 24 Enterprise Zones were designated by the Secretary of State, while in addition to the establishment of London Docklands and Merseyside Development Corporations, further Urban Development Corporations were added in 1987. All 10 Urban Development Corporations were in Labour-controlled local authorities. The Urban Development Corporation/Enterprise Zone initiatives provide a classic example of the disjunction between concern for rational economic planning, and for local accountability through democratic processes. In such areas, central government having effectively relieved local government of most of its planning powers put in its place a tier of quasi-government, the Urban Development Corporation, which was unaccountable to the local electorate and whose membership and *modus operandi* were designed to aid business interests, which may not be local. Local interests (including those of local capital) were to be subservient to those of development capital. The impact of this change on consumption politics is illustrated by Klausner (1986) in his discussion of housing on the Becton Park development in Newham. The London Borough of Newham prepared land, including Becton Park, for housing development in the late 1970s to alleviate the local housing shortage and reduce the council-house waiting list. When the land was vested in the London Docklands Development Corporation in 1980, it was subsequently developed and sold for private housing units at prices well beyond the reach of most local residents, thus having little or no effect on local housing pressures or the length of the council-house waiting list. Such cases of disregard for local interests were not unexpected given that Urban Development Corporations were charged with commercial development. Carr and Weir (1986) illustrate quite clearly that leading appointees to Urban Development Corporation's had regarded consultation with local communities (at least in the early stages) as being of low priority and a potential source of problems, rather than a necessary element of the Urban Development Corporations operation and one in which useful ideas might be initiated or developed.

Even in economic terms, the success of these initiatives which centralised local decision-making (by placing powers in the hands of central government appointees) has been subject to question. Duncan and Goodwin (1988) point out that the effects of these schemes were minor and largely redistributive, with existing business investment moving to take advantage of increased subsidy, rather than new businesses starting up. They argue that savings through non-payment of rates were offset by higher rents and property prices inside designated zones, that much new industry is non-labour-intensive and therefore had little impact on unemployment, and that financial success was often dependent on investment from central government (Erikson and Syms, 1986; Shutt, 1984).

Since the major thrust of development initiatives such as the Urban Development Corporations and Enterprise Zones was aimed at circumventing local controls and taxes in order to foster economic development, it is hardly surprising that leisure investment proposed for these designated areas tended to focus on issues other than social welfare. Leisure investment in the Urban Development Corporations fell predominantly into three categories:

- commercial investment in directly profit-generating schemes, e.g. marina developments in Liverpool and Docklands, and Salford's multi-screen cinema;
- investment to attract or support other commercial activities e.g. greening of open space and private housing;
- city tourism and city marketing e.g. Liverpool's Albert Dock, with its Maritime Museum.

None of these forms of investment were aimed predominantly at enhancing leisure opportunities for the local community as such, with priority being accorded to the interests of development capital, although such provision may provide attractions for local people (Department of Environment, 1990).

There was a subtle shift to be added in the Major administration's approach to urban funding which was reflected in two measures. The first of these was the introduction of *City Challenge* by Michael Heseltine in 1991. Its philosophy was a subtle reflection of Conservative thinking in that it awarded grant aid, not on the basis of social or economic need, but on the quality of the bid for that funding in a competitive bidding process. In other words local authorities were to receive money to tackle urban problems not on the criterion of how much greater their need was than others, but on how much more imaginative, efficient and responsible was their bid compared to those of their competitors. By 1993 more than a quarter of all urban aid (£800 million per annum) provided by government was to be funded in this competitive bidding process, and in 1994 the government announced that it would be introducing the 'prize money' grant concept to incorporate £200 million of European Regional funding (Bevins, 1994). The second measure was the introduction of the Single Regeneration Budget which drew together a range of urban funding schemes under a single heading thus simplifying the system of funding considerably. The move, in line with New Right concerns about organisational and informational overload in government, also incorporated the competitive bidding approach (McHardy, 1994). The government also continued to reduce the amount of money in real terms available for such urban projects, and where those local authorities in need failed to obtain funding there was a politically useful implication that the 'blame' lay at local level, since the local authority had failed to 'compete' effectively.

Inducing local accountability: the restructuring of local taxation and the development of the Citizen's Charter

Ironically, while initiatives such as Urban Development Corporations and Enterprise Zones diminished local accountability, the Conservatives also sought to enhance political accountability to the local taxpayer via changes in the local taxation system, and accountability to the broader population via the development of the Citizen's Charter.

While central government had sought to circumvent or constrain local government powers, the introduction of the community charge in Scotland in April 1989, and in the rest of the UK in 1990, represented an attempt to place electoral pressure on higher spending local authorities to reduce expenditure. The existing system of property taxation, local rates, was seen by the Conservatives as unjust, in that local electors who in effect paid partial, or no rates, could vote for high spending authorities with little risk of cost to themselves but with a clear economic impact on their co-electors. The 'poll tax' meant that virtually all electors were to make a personal financial contribution in direct proportion to the size of their local authority's spending bill. Thus, it was argued they would be more likely to place pressure on local authorities to spend less, and to be more effective with what they did spend.

This particular strategy proved to be highly problematic, generating poll tax 'riots', very high rates of tax evasion, and representing a key factor in by-election reversals and in the fall from office of Margaret Thatcher. It was subsequently to be dropped by the John Major government. However, the abandonment of the community charge and its replacement by the council tax maintained high levels of local electoral accountability since the new arrangements meant a gearing of 7:1, that is a rise of 70 per cent in the council tax was required to generate 10 per cent of additional local funding (Young, 1994). If this ensured the local authority financial 'belts' remained tightened, there were in addition 'braces' available to central government since ministers retained capping powers. Financial accountability of local decision-makers to local taxpayers and to central government ministers, was thus ensured.

In July 1992, John Major launched the *Citizen's Charter*, a document which sought to ensure that public (and privatised bodies) were accountable to their customers. The Audit Commission was required to develop Citizen's Charter indicators to form the basis particularly of local authority reporting of performance to their own communities. By 1996, 42 national charters had been published (such as the Patient's Charter, and the Job Seeker's Charter), along with an estimated 10 000 local charters (Theakston, 1999). The approach was not regarded as a great success:

Rhetorically, the Citizen's Charter represented a populist assault on bureaucratic paternalism in the name of greater responsiveness to service users, yet the Major government's concept of 'citizenship' was susceptible to criticism that it was too narrow and limited, focusing as it did on the individual consumer of services ... The Charter(s) had not given citizens any new legal rights and ... the impact in practice was uneven.

The public and service users played little or no part in setting performance targets, some of which were 'soft' or unambitious ...critics could retort that the Government was seeking to distance itself from service-failure and the under-funding of public services. (Theakston, 1999: 31–2)

However, though the Charter approach was subject to criticism, it prefigured the approach to be adopted by the incoming Blair government in respect of Best Value in the 1999 Local Government Act. Indeed, the Labour opposition could claim that the whole notion of a Citizen's Charter had been developed by Labour local authorities in the mid-1980s.

The restructuring of local government

In the mid-1980s with the increasing role of Labour-controlled local governments as opposition to the ideological programme of central government, spearheaded by the largest of the local authorities, the Greater London Council, the government took the decision on the grounds of efficiency savings to abolish one tier of government, that of the Metropolitan Counties and the Greater London Council. The dynamics of the struggle between local and central government in which abolition was a strategic blow against a group of authorities that were all Labour-controlled is discussed more fully below, and in ensuing chapters. However, it should be noted here that abolition was only one element in an unfolding attempt to restructure local government. In March 1991, Michael Heseltine revealed the government's intention to reduce local government to a single tier of local authorities where practicable, a move which seemed likely to be accompanied by a reduction in the range of services (particularly education services) for which local government was to be responsible. Although when the Banham Commission reported in 1995 the subsequent implementation of the 'unitary authority' approach was limited to 46 authorities, and a simplification of functions took effect in those authorities, the remainder were largely unaffected.

The New Urban Left: Labour's local response to central government pressures in the 1980s and 1990s

Resistance to attempts to control local government from the centre, and frustration with the ineffectual nature of Labour's parliamentary opposition to government, were manifest in the emergence and activities of groups of relatively young, local authority Labour members, particularly in large cities, who were accorded the label, the New Urban Left. Gyford (1985) describes this relatively heterogeneous group as the ideological heirs to the community activism of the 1960s and early 1970s, incorporating such interests as black organisations, the women's movement, and ecological issues. If this group had a defining feature it was perhaps the rejection of a Labour militancy based solely on traditional class politics in favour of a politics which gives primacy to all forms of disadvantage, including racism, sexism and disability as well as economic disadvantage. Another important feature was their willingness to employ non-economic tools in any struggle to redress imbalances, and in this context cultural politics became for the left a significant tool in political battles. The key to this rejection of the narrower traditional politics of Labour was the adoption of a Gramscian concept of hegemony which denies the primacy of economic domination and implies that moral and political leadership can be challenged along a number of non-economic dimensions. Economic domination, the New Urban Left argued, is legitimated by a wide range of cultural, educational, political, familial and gendered practices and arguments, and could therefore be challenged by addressing these arguments and practices. Hence the Gramscian prescription for a wider politics adopted by the New Urban Left provides a more central and important role for the politics of culture and leisure.

Despite the differing nature of local socialism in different locations (Gyford, 1985), a number of themes have been identified in the strategies of local authorities controlled or influenced by the thinking of the New Urban Left. Stoker (1988) characterises their strategies as falling into two major categories, both of which were of significance in respect of leisure policy. The first relates to direct intervention by local authorities in local economies and in service provision. Traditional forms of leisure provision had certainly been enhanced for disadvantaged groups, with for example the introduction of 'passport to leisure' schemes, and improvement of access for disadvantaged groups. However, in addition, new forms of provision in community and minority arts had been developed by some authorities. Perhaps the best documented example of this is the Greater London Council's conscious efforts to promote cultural diversity and cultural confidence among its population through festivals, small and large-scale cultural events, and support for community groups (Mulgan and Worpole, 1986). In addition, as Bianchini's (1987, 1989) work has illustrated, the Greater London Council adopted a strategy of employing cultural events such as the London Marathon to provide publicity for policies such as the 'Fares Fair' subsidy of public transport, and the 'London for Jobs' and anti-racism campaigns. Cultural provision for the Left in the Greater London Council became not simply an end in itself but a feature of a wider hegemonic struggle which is paralleled elsewhere in for example the 'Rock Against Racism' concerts and political pop of Red Wedge, and artists such as Billy Bragg.

The development of a cultural industries strategy by the Greater London Council (Garnham, 1987) also marks a policy innovation which was adopted as a blue print elsewhere. This strategy recognised that cultural production and distribution networks (film companies, publishers, recording companies, retail outlets etc.) were largely controlled by oligopolies predominantly consisting of multi-nationals, and that small-scale local cultural producers were unable to break in to the cultural production and distribution industries. The Greater London Council, by lending its political and economic weight to new cultural producers (e.g. community video groups, feminist publishers, black musicians) was attempting to foster a more culturally diverse and representative industry. This was to be achieved both by grant aiding new companies, and by providing incentives to distributors to accept the cultural products of such groups.

The second type of strategy adopted by the New Urban Left represented a concern not simply with the services of local government, but also with the process by which local government went about its work. Thus democratising local government and opening it up to public participation was a major concern for some Labour-controlled authorities. Policies of decentralisation and of area management were associated with a number of socialist authorities including, Norwich, Hackney, Sheffield and Walsall. This strategy was intended to break down the diseconomies of scale of large local government bureaucracies, in order to make service provision more responsive and to counteract departmentalism, and thus to achieve greater efficiency. The establishment of area recreation officers in middle management posts with responsibility for areas within the local authority boundaries, and a remit covering a wide range of cultural needs of local communities, a mini and localised version of 'joined-up government, was one product of this concern.

However, in addition to decentralisation of provision there was also evidence of a concern to establish more open government among authorities influenced by New Urban Left thinking. This took the form of reducing the amount of information which was withheld as confidential from the general public and reducing the number of meetings held in camera, increasing levels of consultation with community groups, or coopting more community representatives onto decision-making bodies. Hackney Leisure Services, for example, established in 1985 committees representing black people, gay and lesbian people, and the disabled, to advise on policy making and provision in the borough. The problem which the New Urban Left faced was that by opening up decision-making to wider groups it was open to pressures from the anti-socialist predilections of some communities or interest groups, which could, for example, be racist or sexist. This represented a serious dilemma for socialist groups committed to opening up political processes.

Despite such policy resistance the space available for policy innovation at the local level was inexorably reduced as central government squeezed additional savings or revenue from local government across the later 1980s and 1990s.

In search of the responsible market: local government and New Labour's modernising agenda

When New Labour came to power in 1997 there was criticism, particularly in what remained of the party's left wing, that New Labour was 'Thatcherism in sheep's clothing'. Certainly for local government there seemed little respite from the experience of financial stringency of the 1980s and early 1990s, with the new government retaining the overall spending limits which its Conservative predecessors had declared for the period up to 2000. In other aspects of policy there were also apparent continuities. The replacement of Clause IV of the Labour Party Constitution indicated an acceptance of the market and of competition as an appropriate distributive vehicle, and in urban policy, challenge funding was maintained, albeit in modified form. Even John Major's 'big policy idea', the Citizen's Charter was adopted/adapted in New Labour's *Service First* initiative (Cabinet Office, 1998).

However, New Labour's approach to policy development was given its most explicit articulation in its White Paper *Modernising Government*, published in March 1999 (UK Government, 1999), which sought to define ways for improving policy performance based on three overarching principles:

- policy-making should be 'joined-up' and strategic;
- the primary focus of public services should be consumer rather than producer interests; and
- efficiency and high levels of quality in the provision of public services should be demonstrable.

The approach outlined in the White Paper does reflect some clear differences from the Conservative approach (Falconer, 1999). First, the document emphasises the need to involve and consult users of public services in making decisions about service provision. Second, the Conservative approach to policy had generally been to separate out the functions of, and responsibilities for, *making* policy on the one hand, and *delivering* it on the other (for example in splitting client and contractor roles in local government under CCT). In emphasising 'joined-up government', New Labour sought to avoid the inherent tensions in separating out functions which could reinforce competing interests in different arms of government. Third, partnership is emphasised – across levels of government as well as between commercial, voluntary and public sectors with special emphasis on vertical integration with devolved administrations.

In terms of their impact on leisure, these principles are well-illustrated in the integrated approach to planning developed and proposed by New Labour (see Figure 4.5). Having adopted devolution as a key theme in government, vertical integration in planning is clearly evident. New Labour has also placed a requirement on regional consortia and local authorities, as well as national agencies to develop strategic plans in the sport, leisure and cultural field (Department of

Figure 4.5 *Links between types of leisure/cultural strategies*

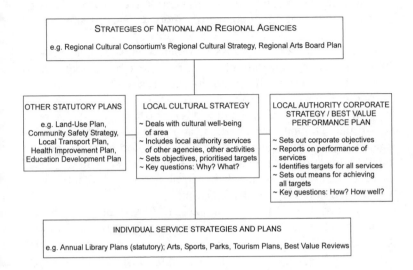

Source: Department of Culture Media and Sport (1999b).

Culture Media and Sport, 1999a, b). Horizontal integration between agencies in the cultural field and between different forms of planning is also built into the system. Thus integrated planning (to which the New Right has been antipathetic) is writ large in the system of leisure policy unfolding under New Labour.

However, in local government New Labour's policy cornerstone was to be Best Value, which is designed to fit with the generic concerns of *Modernising Government*. The Local Government Act 1999 rescinded the requirement for CCT in local government services and replaced it with a responsibility to demonstrate that the approach to service provision adopted by a local authority was one which produced 'best value'. The Best Value system was to be introduced in local government by April 2000. The principal elements through which a local authority was to establish what constitutes best value were to be:

- *Fundamental service reviews* (which required local authorities to challenge, compare, consult and compete); and

- *Best Value Performance Plans*, incorporating standards (both national and local) and performance targets based on wide community consultation (English Sports Council, 2000).

The fundamental service reviews are designed in particular to ensure horizontal policy integration, as leisure services are required to demonstrate their contribution to the cross-cutting, generic or corporate goals of the local authority. These goals are unlikely to be directly related to leisure, but will reflect concerns of the order of social and economic regeneration, anti-poverty, healthy lifestyles, community safety, community development, job creation, and so on. The Best Value approach requires that, as with other service areas, leisure services should demonstrate that they are contributing to the local authority's wider social priorities.

A number of consequences are likely to flow from this approach as it unfolds, but two are worth mentioning here. The first is that, unlike CCT where, at its best, social goals were inscribed only within the programming and pricing requirements of contracts, Best Value provides for a much more comprehensive review, allowing the expression and operationalisation of political priorities to have a more fundamental impact on service planning and delivery.

The second implication to highlight here is that, just as CCT had consequences for local government structures (in particular the separating out of client and contractor roles), so also Best Value will result in the addressing of organisational and political structures within local authorities, with the separation of policy and facility management being difficult to sustain. A range of solutions seems likely. Among Best Value pilot authorities established in 1998 some examples illustrate different approaches (English Sports Council, 1999). Leeds City and Lewisham Borough Councils have for example , adopted a 'Cabinet–style' system, reducing committee structures to facilitate a speeding up of decision-making. Thematic departments defined by local priorities are another structural solution that some authorities seem likely to adopt and many local authorities are restructuring and redefining services around key themes such as economic regeneration, social exclusion, lifelong learning, healthy living or community safety. To cite some examples from the Best Value pilot authorities:

Norwich City Council, North West Leicestershire Council and the London Borough of Lewisham are all examples of local authorities that are well on the way to reorganisation along thematic lines ... In Norwich, for example, sports development looks likely to align most strongly with those officer/member groups responsible for social inclusion and lifelong learning. In Lewisham, the same service looks likely to sit within and 'active lifestyles/ health' structural group, while leisure centres are likely to fall within a regeneration department. (English Sports Council, 1999: 23)

Thus in response to the injunction to identify and respond to 'challenge', the combination of policy conception and execution, together with the concern to reflect cross-cutting policy themes seem likely to lead to some innovatory structures in the local government context.

The Best Value approach is founded on the requirements of the four Cs (challenge, consult, compare and compete) which replace the Conservative emphasis on the three Es (economy, efficiency and effectiveness). Demonstrating that leisure can contribute to the *challenge* of generic policy goals will thus be a significant task for public sector leisure professionals. The requirement to 'consult' may also result in a number of initiatives. *Consultation* with the local population, users and non-users of services may be related to specific projects or to the general service, and may be conducted via area committees, stakeholder juries, citizen's panels, user or household surveys, and so forth. *Comparison* will be undertaken via performance indicators established nationally (via the Audit Commission), with target achievements for those indicators largely adapted and set locally by local authorities. The performance indicators selected and the associated targets adopted are required to be published by no later than 31 March each year by each local authority. The Best Value performance indicators set nationally and reviewed by government annually, are based on research undertaken by the Audit Commission which at the time of writing had just published performance indicators for 2000/1 (Audit Commission, 1999).

Table 4.3 illustrates the type of indicators being developed for cultural services in the Best Value framework, while the English Sports Council's publication on performance measurement in pools

Table 4.3   *Cultural and related services: sample of best value performance indicators*

Example of strategic objective indicator
Best Value performance indicator 114
Does the local authority have a cultural strategy? Yes/No
Definition
In accordance with the DCMS draft guidance on Local Cultural Strategies such strategies will cover a wide range of cultural activities including arts, media, sports, parks, museums, libraries, the built heritage, the countryside, playgrounds and tourism

Example of cost / efficiency indicator
Best Value performance indicator 116
Spend per head on cultural and recreational facilities and services
Definition
Spend on cultural and recreational facilities and activities ... divided by total population

Example of fair access indicator
Best Value performance indicator 119
Percentage of residents by targeted group satisfied with the local authority's cultural and recreational facilities and activities.
Definition
Percentage of women respondents fairly satisfied or very satisfied with cultural and recreational facilities and activities.
Percentage of minority ethnic community respondents fairly satisfied or very satisfied with cultural and recreational facilities and activities

---

Source: Audit Commission (1999).

and sports halls, following research by the Leisure Industries Research Centre (English Sports Council, 2000) gives an indication of the adaptation of performance measure to specific types of facilities in particular kinds of contexts.

Both consultation and comparison functions reflect the greater concern for local involvement on the part of the community than was evident under the CCT system. Local involvement on the part of the community in terms of consultation, and on the local polity in terms of setting targets which reflect local political priorities, are reinforced under the Best Value system.

The final requirement, to *compete*, is that which is most clearly redolent of the CCT system. The local authority is required to demonstrate that the option it adopts in terms of provision and management of facilities is the most cost-effective. There are in

effect three options open to a local authority which retains ownership of a facility; direct service management, voluntary sector
partnership, or commercial-sector partnership. A number of local
authorities as a result of the CCT process, or of the associated lack
of funds, handed over management of facilities to voluntary sector
bodies, charities, trusts or independent provident societies. In
addition, approximately one-quarter of all CCT leisure contracts
were managed by private contractors by 1998 (Mintel, 1998).
However, the majority of contracts remain with local authority
direct service organisations. Whatever the management arrangements, it is not open to local authorities under Best Value as it had
been under CCT, simply to exercise the option of requiring some
social goals to be taken into account by specifying pricing and
programming requirements, while awarding contracts to the lowest
bidder. Best Value requires that evaluation of service management
be undertaken by reference to defined social criteria, and this,
potentially at least, heralds a significant difference in policy practice.

Conclusion

CCT certainly dominated local government leisure policy in the
1990s. The twin pressures under the CCT system of the requirement
to compete and the squeeze on public sector budgets meant that
economic considerations were prioritised, and though efficiency
savings were achieved, service quality and access for specific groups
did suffer (Centre for Leisure and Tourism Studies, 1996). The
Conservative government sought to isolate service delivery from
policy-making in order to ensure that economies were achieved,
with an apparent dislocation between 'client' and 'contractor'
elements of the organisation. The Best Value regime, in line with
New Labour's modernising agenda, seeks to reintegrate service
delivery and policy decision-making, and to integrate policy across
generic themes. It seeks to identify performance measures, and
targets for those measures, as well as to require local authorities
to demonstrate value for money. The Best Value regime, therefore,
certainly has implications for the way that leisure professionals
address their core tasks, and this is the focus of the following
chapter. It remains to be seen, however, whether the requirement
to achieve social as well as economic challenges and to consult local

communities on their 'needs' can mediate the economic pressures of the continuing squeeze on local government expenditure and the requirement to 'compete'. The search is on for a set of policy solutions which is subject to market testing (whether voluntary, commercial or public sector management of services is adopted) but in which the market is tasked with delivering qualitatively and quantitatively evaluated social and economic goals.

5 The Leisure Professionals

Introduction

This chapter seeks to locate the developing role of leisure professionals in public sector leisure services within the framework of explanations of the state's changing role in leisure. It is ironic that in the early 1970s, at the moment of the state's addition of leisure to the welfare portfolio, the whole concept of the welfare state should be called into question. Thus, increasingly over the period since the beginning of the 1970s, leisure professionals have existed in a state of tension in terms of their own role in service provision, and also in terms of the legitimacy of the very services they have traditionally sought to provide. This has had an inevitable impact on the norms, values and goals of local government professionals and this chapter therefore outlines the trajectory of change, providing a foundation in Chapter 7 for analysis of the role of local government professionals in a specific local authority context.

The emergence of forms of 'new managerialism' in the public sector is well-documented in a variety of public sector settings in the UK (Farnham and Horton, 1993), and in developed welfare states more generally (Lane, 1995). Clarke and Newman (1997) seek to trace the development of generic public sector management from a traditional, bureaucracy-based, liberal-welfare professionalism to two forms of 'new managerialism', namely the culture of competitive management and transformational management. While their account captures the broad thrust of management change in the public sector, leisure services have some particularities in respect of the evolving management styles. Thus, while employing some of the features of their broader framework, this chapter will trace the specific development of management in public sector leisure services from the period of (the anticipation of) local government reorganisation which took place in most parts of England and Wales in 1974, and which resulted in the major growth of public sector facilities, to the beginning of the new century.

Table 5.1 is employed as an organising framework for the development of the argument. It identifies four types of managerial orientation over the time period, highlighting the periods in which they might be said to be the dominant orientations. Although these orientations reflect ideal types, and management practices may well draw on more than one such approach at any given time, nevertheless the framework is used here as an heuristic device to convey the nature of, and reasons for, management change in public sector leisure services.

From facility managers to liberal welfare professionals: public sector leisure management in the 1970s

The development of the welfare state in Britain was fostered through the establishment of a series of liberal-welfare, 'semi-professions' in the post-war period. These included, for example, teaching, nursing, social work, youth work, housing and planning, as well as the leisure profession, arguably the last substantial occupational group to seek this status. Each of these occupational groups sought to obtain and sustain its status as a professional group by following similar strategies and generating similar sets of values to be associated with their work. Each defined its commitment to its field of work as resulting from powerful motives of altruism, involvement with the work itself and with client groups, rather than resulting solely or primarily from economic motives. In each case 'specialist' knowledge was claimed by the group as essential to the addressing of a highly significant social problem. The work of the semi-professions was also redefined as the central and full-time concern of those in the occupational group, rather than as a subsidiary concern of those working in other fields. Each of the liberal-welfare semi-professions also sought to legitimate its status by the establishment of full-time education and training (usually of degree level or equivalent), and most struggled for political recognition of the sole right to claim professional expertise in their particular sphere of activity.

The history of the development of the public sector leisure professions illustrates these processes as effectively as other liberal welfare examples. Thus when local government reorganisation took

place in most parts of England and Wales, newly-unified departments of leisure services were established in many of the new
authorities (Veal, 1979). Just as the social work profession had
received an impetus towards professionalisation by the Seebohm
Report on personal social services in 1968, which signalled the
bringing together of the previously separate services for children's
welfare, the elderly and other special needs groups, so the Cobham
Report (House of Lords Select Committee, 1973) which informed
the process of leisure services reorganisation provided a similar
unifying force. The leisure occupational groups which had dealt
previously with parks, swimming pools, indoor and outdoor sports
facilities, and countryside recreation, were drawn together, for the
most part into shared departments in local government. The set of
concerns of this group prior to this amalgamation had been with
technical skills (horticulture, water treatment in swimming pools,
etc.), but with the advent of large-scale authorities and grouping
together of diverse facilities and responsibilities the skills required of
leisure managers were generic and related to the social project of the
welfare state, rather than specifically to physical structures.

A unified professional body (the Institute of Leisure and Amenity
Management, ILAM) was established in 1979 from the previously
disparate group of organisations (the Association of Recreation
Managers, the Recreation Management Association, the Institute of
Parks and Recreation Administration etc.) which had served many
of those working in this field. Librarians, and those working in the
fields of arts and museums, and to a lesser extent children's play,
retained their own identities and professional organisations, and one
organisation (the Institute of Sport and Recreation Management)
'stubbornly' refused pressures for amalgamation with ILAM, but in
the early 1980s the new Institute established a curriculum for
professional training and sought to use the associated membership
examinations as a means of controlling access to both the Institute
itself and to junior, middle and senior management posts in leisure
services. ILAM members were encouraged in placing job advertise-
ments to require, or cite as desirable, membership of the Institute.
Throughout the 1980s and 1990s the Institute sought to establish a
system of 'recognised' courses in colleges, polytechnics and universities, leading to exemption from some parts of its membership
examinations. In the three decades from 1972, the significance of

Table 5.1 *Changing management styles in public sector sport and recreation services*

Managerial Orientation	Facility manager/engineer	Bureau/liberal welfare professional		Competitive/contract manager	Transformational manager
Nature of the State	Maturing of the Welfare State		Economic realism	Disinvestment and the flexible state	In Search of the responsible market
Management Focus	Facility focus	Activity/group focus	Community focus	Market focus	Quality focus
Time scale	Early 1970s	Late 1970s/early 1980s	Mid-1980s	Late 1980s/early 1990s	Late 1990s
Objectives	Maximise income	Maximise participation	Maximise opportunities for 'problem groups'	Maximise revenue & economic efficiency	Maximise quality & achieve best value
Management Styles	Centralised	Decentralised	Decentralised, advocacy, catalytic role	Expert marketeer	Agent of organisational change
Mode of Consultation	Professional	Consultant	Partnership	Market sensitivity	Customer surveys
Attitude to Users	Regulation/control of users	Clients: encouragement of under-users	Clients: positive support of disadvantaged	Customers/consumers: identify appropriate market segments	Citizens: one among groups of stakeholders

		Service provision and delivery	Shared resources	Products to be designed to meet needs of target markets	Vehicles for achieving corporate goals
Perception of Facilities	Technical				
Programme Emphases	Reactive (e.g. clubs, schools, casual usage)	Informal, fun and sociability, élitism played down	Proactive, creative, developmental	Selling lifestyle, health and fitness	Meeting corporate goals through leisure
Key Govt. Initiatives	Local govt. reorganisation	White Paper Sport and Recreation	Urban Programme; Sports Council Areas of Special Need	CCT	Best Value

Source: Adapted from Haywood and Henry (1986a).

leisure, and therefore the importance of the leisure profession, had been redefined from that of a right of citizenship recognised in the early 1970s, to that of a central area for the combating of urban/ youth problems in the late 1970s to the mid-1980s, to one of establishing efficient (increasingly defined as 'commercial') management practice and subsequently demonstrating best value in the late 1980s and during the 1990s. Thus a fairly classic pattern has been followed by ILAM in attempting to strengthen the political recognition of its constituency albeit with a changing rationale for its own importance.

The two dominant perspectives on professionalisation in the literature have traditionally been Weberian and Marxist (Esland, 1980; Johnson, 1969), and more recently these have been either overlain or challenged by feminist and race theorists some of whom (White, 1988; Yule, 1992, 1997) have focused explicitly on the development of professional status in leisure services. Weberian accounts of professionalisation explain the emergence of professionalised groups in the workforce as a function of the development of rationality in industrialisation. As rationality has been applied to production processes (whether in the commercial or welfare sphere), 'rational' forms of organisation (bureaucracies) have been developed which incorporate a high degree of task specialisation. Specialist knowledge and skills are therefore required within these organisations, and professional groups are portrayed as providing such knowledge and skills in exchange for privileged status (in wage bargaining, job design and autonomy etc.). For Marxists, bureaucracies represent the administrative means whereby the interests of capital are represented in commercial or welfare organisations. Professionals enjoy privileged status as a function of their value in either maximising return on investment (industrial semi-professions) or securing social order (liberal welfare semi-professions).

Although Marxist and Weberian accounts may differ concerning the explanation of the underlying processes which have resulted in the emergence of the professions, they share aspects of their characterisation of the ways in which professionals should be viewed. The traditional professions (medicine and the law) have been very successful in establishing status and power in advanced industrial/capitalist societies, and the semi-professions are seen as attempting to achieve similar ends by emulating aspects of the strategies employed by the traditional professions, Thus both Weberians and Marxists argue that although professions may promote an ideology of altruism and service, they are essentially pressure groups operating in ways which assure their members of privilege. This is accomplished by establishing a monopoly over certain areas of work ('only qualified professionals need apply'), and through this monopoly position enhancing their own negotiating position *vis-à-vis* pay and conditions. Professional groups seek to maintain autonomy by operating their own supervisory bodies as, for example, ILAM did in establishing a panel to vet practice in the implementation of compulsory competitive tendering. Finally, professions off-load alienating work by distinguishing mental labour (conception) from physical labour (execution), claiming expertise in the former while downgrading the latter. Thus certain occupational groups (described as class fractions in Marxist terms) maintain their privilege and enforce social closure.

However, in addition to the concern with social class implied in these analyses, the process of professionalisation was subject to criticism from a range of other sources, most notably from feminist, race and disability perspectives but also from the consumer rights movement (Clarke and Newman, 1997). With reference specifically to professionalisation in leisure, accounts which have focused on gender and race in addition to class have emphasised the ways in which women and black workers have been excluded from managerial positions (Town and King, 1985; White, 1988), both by virtue of recruitment policies and the white/male-centred definition of appropriate professional and managerial skills, and consequently the types of activity promoted by such professionals have tended to reinforce the hegemony of patriarchy, race and class (Yule, 1997). Consumer-rights advocates have criticised the paternalist approach of professionals which disempowers consumers, defining them as 'clients' in the bureau-professional's discourse, implying a knowledge deficit in comparison with professional expertise (Coalter, 1990). At base in each of these critical approaches was the implication that professional status was a means of serving the interests of the occupational group rather than the interests of service users or the interests of groups excluded from access to the profession.

Professionalism in local government under pressure in the 1980s: from welfare ideology to new economic realism

In the period following the establishment of the leisure profession from disparate technical occupational groups such as horticulture and swimming pool management, there was a growing recognition through, for example, Sports Council-sponsored studies (Collins, 1979; Gregory, 1979; Grimshaw and Prescott-Clarke, 1978) that public sector facilities were failing to meet the needs of the general population, and specifically of disadvantaged groups. Thus the targeting and attraction of such groups came to be regarded as priorities. This implied a new set of skills more akin to community work than facility administration, and a range of schemes, delivered under the auspices of the Urban Programme and the Sports Council, fostered the adoption of new techniques and approaches in management. Community recreation approaches applied decentralisation of provision and of decision-making which had implications for the notion of the professional as 'expert', implying a partnership approach, making policy decisions in close cooperation with community groups, particularly those which might have felt alienated and unserved by centralised, 'expert', decision-making (Haywood and Henry, 1986a, b; Henry and Bramham, 1986). In the early 1980s this approach was further refined by the pressures associated with urban disorders to focus policy attention specifically on the volatile, 'troublesome' sectors (typically, unemployed, black, male, young inner-city residents) who might potentially be implicated in urban disorder.

The initial period of economic realism not only implied a particular focus on inner-city groups, it also implied a reduction of budgets and a pressure to generate income. Leisure services, as a revenue-generating set of activities, were thus placed under increasing pressure to maximise revenue in order to minimise the impact of budget reductions and to reduce costs. This in most instances ran counter to the requirement to effectively target disadvantaged groups.

Over the period from the mid-1970s to the mid-1980s, therefore, the role of leisure professionals was subject to severe tensions with implications for the changing nature of professionalism (facility administrator, bureaucrat, community worker, income generator), for the changing nature of the relationship between the professional and the public (patrons, clients, customers, revenue-generating market segments), and the relationship between the professional and politicians (from provider of relatively objective policy expertise and advice, to budget maximisers whose effectiveness had to be closely monitored) (Coalter, 1990). Thus the decade following the publication of the 1975 White Paper *Sport and Recreation* (Department of Environment, 1975) (which had declared the welfare policy goals of sport as a social service with its implications for leisure professionals as liberal welfare professionals) reflected what might be described as something of an identity crisis for the leisure professional.

Leisure management in the context of the flexible state and disinvestment: the New Right, new managerialism and competitive management

If the decade 1975–85 carried mixed messages in terms of the role of the leisure professional, the development of the ideology of Thatcherism carried clear implications for all forms of public sector management. The New Right recognised that 'rolling back the state' meant undermining the position of traditional public sector professionals. It was not that public sector management should disappear from the Conservative lexicon, nor that management should not have legitimating functions; a new rhetoric of public sector management would be required to redefine that function – one which was oriented to the market, employed an entrepreneurial discourse, and focused on competition as a key to success.

> The legitimacy of managerialism, like that of bureau-professionalism, also depends on its internal knowledge base and the sciences/technologies from which these are derived. Bureau-professionalism offers the pursuit of the 'public good' based on the application of forms of expert power which are service specific. These are substantive forms of knowledge about particular sorts of needs and interventions. By contrast managerialism promises the best use of public resources based on the deployment of calculative power. The knowledge of managerialism is 'universalist', applicable to all organisations rather than substantive and specific. It is presented as a rationality which transcends the differences of services or sectors. (Clarke and Newman, 1997: 66)

A single universal logic which was to be applied to all service areas was thus to be applied to public sector leisure services and the principal vehicle for that logic was to be Compulsory Competitive Tendering (CCT). Though it did not result in the widespread transfer of contracts to the private sector, it changed the way that public sector facility managers thought. If they were to avoid losing out in a competitive bidding process, they had to be certain of being at least as frugal in costs and as ambitious in revenue generation as their commercial counterparts.

The CCT process split public sector leisure professionals structurally between 'client' and 'contractor' roles, but also, potentially at least, could divide them ideologically since client officers were charged with drawing up contractual obligations in the pricing and programming of facilities. However, the financial space to draw up social goals was perceived as narrow given the squeeze on local government budgets, and the flexibility to specify social goals in contracts was limited. In these circumstances, minimalism and cost control and entrepreneurial management represented the policy approaches most likely to flourish.

The contract approach also brought into stark relief the nature of the 'core' and the 'peripheral' workforce in local government. Hard-edged 'macho' management styles were employed in imposing tough decisions on downsizing and flexibilising the workforce. The 'core' function of the local authority leisure system included client specification and contractor monitoring and control roles, with the peripheral workforce being employed on contracted-out and other forms of outsourced work. Direct service organisations or commercial companies winning contracts would make greater use of part-time, seasonal, casual and self-employed or sub-contracted staff. More females were coming into the workforce in the 1980s (Central Statistical Office, 1991) but, as with workers from ethnic minority groups, these tended to be overrepresented in the low-paid, less secure and often seasonal or part-time roles associated with the peripheral workforce. Indeed Escott and Whitfield (1995) argue that the goal of equal opportunities was undermined by CCT which was originally invoked as part of a movement to do away with bureaucracy and to 'let managers get on with managing', and as such was antipathetic to social interventions. Clarke and Newman point out the discourse of competitive management reinforces masculinist notions of management as an activity:

The dominant imagery of bureau-professional regimes was masculine – the depersonalised application of expertise and rules ... The competitive order takes this further. Its economic calculus depersonalises the provision of services in a different way – by insisting on the commodification of labour like any other resource. (Clarke and Newman, 1997: 74)

Life for the core workforce may be pressured, but life for those in the peripheral workforce was likely to be very much more difficult. Some operating in the periphery (e.g. some consultants) might benefit from the greater flexibility, but the experience for most would be one of increased insecurity and risk. The dismantling of CCT, however, would not do away with core–periphery distinctions and their implications.

In search of the responsible market: from contract culture to transformational management

The repeal of CCT and its replacement by the Best Value regime should not be seen simply as the replacement of a New Right policy approach; it also implied a modification of the approach to new managerialism, a rejection of the unidimensional nature of competitive management. Unlike competitive or contract management, corporate goals (social or environmental as well as economic) were said to be at the centre of the process of establishing which policy solutions had given best value. It is associated also with a form of new managerialism, but sits more comfortably with the transformational management of Tom Peters and his colleagues (Peters, 1987, 1993; Peters and Waterman, 1982), and with the process of the 'reinvention of government' promoted by Osborne and Gaebler (1992), which emphasise empowerment, partnership, participation and communication. New Labour policy statements are redolent of this without abandoning the need for market realism:

The Government is re-inventing Britain. We want all Government services to be of the highest quality, efficient, responsive and customer focused. We are working with the private sector through competition to achieve this. What matters to the citizen, and therefore to the government, is quality for the customer at the most reasonable cost to the taxpayer. If we are right, the distinctions between public and private are not so important. We want to encourage business to play a fuller role in providing public service. That is why we stress Public-Private Partnerships. (Cabinet Office, 1998a: 3)

It is not that the hard-edged capabilities associated with, for example, promoting worker flexibility in the peripheral workforce are not present in transformational management. (New Labour had no intention of repealing most of the Conservative trades union legislation – and competition is still one of the four cornerstones of Best Value.) However, such requirements are mediated (at least for those working in the core workforce) by the relational skills required to generate commitment and consensus, establishing partnerships between managers and employees, flattening structures and pursuing the related strategies of the transformational management mantra. Partnership rather than adversarial relationships are key.

Following Peters, Waterman and colleagues (Peters, 1987, 1993; Peters and Austen, 1985; Peters and Waterman, 1982), the gurus of transformational management stressed a shift from the masculinist values of traditional management, based on rational models of management, to social/relational approaches (see for example Chapter 2 of Peters and Waterman, 1982). The emphasis on 'masculine' skills of detached analysis, rational calculation, linear and compartmentalised thought and hard data, gives way to an emphasis on the 'feminine' elements of people and process concerns, qualitative judgements on style and image, and relationship building Because of this feminisation of management processes, women might have been expected to flourish more in managerial roles. However, conflict though underplayed does not disappear – individual targets and personal appraisal replace the collective bargaining and collective rewards system, and in this kind of individualised context the collective representation of gender, race or other interests is less rather than more likely. Furthermore, although the management rhetoric is about empowerment, individual responsibility can of course also imply punishment for failure.

While the adoption of market targets in disadvantaged constituencies is made possible by the acceptance of corporate goals which embrace such groups, as a potential cornerstone of the Best Value approach, it remains to be seen whether local authorities will so commit themselves given the need for financial targets. While the implications of Best Value for the relationship between professionals/managers and their client/customer groups is unclear and may vary from one local authority to another, the implications of Best Value for officer member relationships seem to be rather more apparent. The technical specificity of Best Value reinforces the role of the professional *vis-à-vis* the political actors in leisure policy. Professionals are required to define standards, to operate benchmarking systems, to identify appropriate performance indicators, and to operate the various quality systems (Quest, ISO, Investors in People etc.) that have proliferated in local government. Such 'technical' requirements render the professional officer rather more central to the process than perhaps was the case on those authorities where, in terms of CCT, the judgement of performance was a simple matter of the bottom line.

Management in the Best Value context exhibits a range of conflicting tendencies. It stresses the importance of adopting an enabling role and partnership, while also promoting competition and market testing. It advocates the promotion of greater flexibility in the market but the costs of flexibilisation are to be borne by the workforce. It promotes more clearly the desirability of social goals without necessarily furnishing the means to achieve them. At best, relational management approaches and New Labour's promotion of them may be seen as attempts to mediate some of the worst excesses of competitive management. At worst, New Labour's adoption of this approach to management might be regarded as a kind of 'feng shui' of discourse, ensuring that management and political statements are all appropriately ideologically aligned, without necessarily providing definitive guides for action.

Conclusion

We have sought in this chapter to trace the development of management styles across the period since the reorganisation of local government in the 1970s which resulted in the establishment of large-scale leisure departments. Table 5.1 represents a schematic account of these trends. The shift from bureau-professionalism to forms of new managerialism is about more than simply the value-sets of those responsible for the delivery of policy; it reflects changing relationships with service users, and with politicians and differing policy orientations. The specifics of local circumstances provide an important context for the playing out of these themes, and we therefore return to the interplay of professional roles and other factors in a case study of the development of policy in the city of Sheffield in Chapter 7.

6 The Commercial and Voluntary Sectors

Introduction

The preceding chapters of this book have sought to map out the changing role of the state in leisure policy, and to identify both the trajectory of, and influences affecting, such change. However, the state's response in policy terms does not take place in isolation from developments in the commercial and voluntary sectors. In particular, during the 1980s and 1990s, when attempts were made to reduce and restructure state spending, the commercial and voluntary sectors became, if anything, more significant. Any explanation of the nature of leisure policy and the role of the state will be required to take account of the process of mutual adjustment between the leisure sectors. An analysis of leisure policy cannot be neatly encapsulated in a discussion of the state machinery. This chapter will therefore provide an account of the contemporary significance, and historical development, of the commercial and voluntary sectors, as a precursor to the discussion in the final chapter of the state's role in a neo-Fordist or post-Fordist framework in contemporary Britain.

Limiting the discussion of leisure policy to distributive and redistributive policies (see Chapter 1) ignores the fact that there is a considerable proportion of state activity which goes, not only into direct provision (or into decisions *not* to provide for leisure), but also into the fostering or suppression of certain forms of voluntary or commercial activity. Some forms of leisure provision made by the commercial or voluntary sectors are licensed and subject to conditions (e.g. alcohol and tobacco) or simply forbidden (e.g. 'recreational' drugs, pornography). Clearly therefore an understanding of the nature of public leisure policy involves an understanding of state influence on, and reaction to, commercial and voluntary activity.

In an attempt to differentiate the nature of leisure activities promoted directly by the state from those provided by commercial and voluntary organisations, Haywood *et al.* (1996) employ a two-fold dichotomy. The first dichotomous relationship is that between active and passive leisure forms; the second between leisure forms produced by the participants for their own use, and those produced by others for the consumption of participants. Thus, it is argued, the *public sector* has been traditionally associated with fostering the *self-production of active leisure forms* through direct provision or through subsidy of voluntary organisations. Participation in sport, outdoor recreation, drama, music and the arts (outside the home) is fostered by direct provision (e.g. sports and arts centres) as well as through adult education programmes and financial and other forms of assistance to voluntary organisations. *Passive consumption* of activities and events has been traditionally associated with the *commercial sector* (e.g. cinema, night clubs, bingo, eating out, mass tourism). There are exceptions to this division of labour, however. Both the state and the commercial sector promote theatre and media, for instance, which might be categorised as consumption-based activities (notwithstanding arguments about the need for the audience to actively construct the messages they receive in such cultural contexts). However, the state's traditional concern has been with cultural élitism in the arts, and where this cultural élitist approach has been eroded (particularly in broadcasting) the state has begun to promote commercial activity in these fields. However, the relationship between the state, voluntary and commercial sectors is by no means static, it has been subject to change over time and it will be a feature of the argument of this chapter that we are at a crucial stage of readjustment between the three sectors.

The historical context of the development of the commercial and voluntary sectors in leisure in industrial Britain

The growth of the commercial and voluntary sectors in leisure, and the process of industrialisation, c. 1780–1840

Marxist analyses of the development of culture characterise the emergence of a commercial and a voluntary sector in leisure as a product predominantly of the process of industrialisation, a by-product of the process of developing industrial capitalism (Thompson, 1963; Williams, 1981a). In pre-industrial society, recreations, it is argued, were produced within the (rural, agrarian) community for its own diversion and amusement. Culture generally exhibited very little by way of a systematised division of labour with *production* and *consumption* of popular culture remaining largely unseparated. Sponsorship of traditional cultural; forms, whether music, traditional feasts and events, or folk recreations, was undertaken largely by the establishment of rural society, the local squirearchy in pre-industrial Britain. The major effect of such sponsorship was a reinforcing of community cohesion. Explanations of the role of leisure forms, whether Marxist (Malcolmson, 1973) or pluralist (Golby and Purdue, 1984), have tended to stress the function, even of apparently oppositional cultural forms, as one of cementing social solidarity providing a safety valve for the lower orders to let off steam.

However, such accounts are in danger of explaining away diverse cultural forms by reference to the singular functional requirements of the existing social order, and it seems clear that some commercial entrepreneurship predated industrialisation, with, for example, specialist entertainers travelling between hiring fairs (Cunningham, 1980). Nevertheless, it was the nineteenth century which saw both the proliferation and concentration of such individual entrepreneurs into circuses and performing groups. The increasingly widespread nature of commercial provision for leisure was indeed a reflection of the development of mass markets in urban locations with increased disposable time and income, but without the space and lengthy holidays of the rural calendar which had permitted the community to produce its own cultural events and attractions (Thompson, 1967). Thus the rise of state intervention in the leisure field in terms at least of distributive leisure policy was concomitant with the rise of the commercial sector in leisure. While the former was inspired by concerns for moral control and moral development of the new urban workforce, the latter was a response to the new market opportunities presented by the changing social structure.

The voluntary sector can also be said to be, in part, a product of the dissolution of the 'organic' ties of rural agrarian society amongst the displaced population, which, following the development of new agrarian technologies, enclosures and clearances, had flocked to the town. Where informal links within communities could generate many of the social and individual benefits associated with voluntary-sector organisations, the new urban society required more formal frameworks for certain types of social interaction (Tomlinson, 1979). This is not say that voluntary organisations did not exist prior to the onset of industrialisation (the political groups forming around coffee houses in the early part of the eighteenth century bear witness to this); however, as with the commercial sector the proliferation and growth of formal voluntary organisation in leisure is largely a feature of the nineteenth century.

One normally associates the voluntary sector with self-help and mutual aid groups. However, the initial impact of the voluntary sector on popular recreation was not associated with the fostering of recreation opportunities but rather the suppression of particular recreational forms. The Royal Society for the Suppression of Vice (to give it its briefer title) formed in 1802, and which spawned the Lord's Day Observance Society, was in particular concerned to control the breaking of the Sabbath, while the RSPCA and the Temperance movement also sought to curtail or control certain popular leisure forms (Harrison, 1971). However, although accounts vary in their conclusions as to whether the suppression of popular recreations was, or was not, successful (see for example Cunningham, 1980; Malcolmson, 1973) there is agreement that the attempted suppression was to be replaced by attempts to foster 'rational recreation' provision whether by the state, often in conjunction with the voluntary sector (e.g. museums and libraries), or by the voluntary sector itself (religious organisations such as Sunday Schools promoting educational day-trips, sports and so on, or mutual improvement societies). By the last third of the century the voluntary sector could, however, be represented as containing a significant proportion of mutual aid groups with a central interest in particular leisure forms, whether these be working-men's clubs, sports organisations or hobby groups (Bailey, 1987; Meller, 1976; Waters, 1990). Indeed the struggle to wrest control from middle-class reformers in certain leisure organisations illustrates the 'coming of age' of the male working-class workforce which won universal (male) suffrage in 1884. Bailey cites the case of the working-men's club movement, while Dunning and Sheard (1976) document the struggles over the control of rugby which led to the split between union and league codes. Thus the emergence of a mature voluntary sector parallels the development of the commercial and state sectors of leisure. The erosion of a *laissez faire* approach to state intervention, the emergence of commercial-sector provision, and the development of a mature framework of mutual aid or self-help organisations are both broadly contemporaneous, and shaped by the same factors of adjustment to the social dislocation of industrialisation and urbanisation. They reflect an adaptation to the emergence of a new urban mass market with increasing disposable income and time, and to the social confidence instilled by economic growth and the relative political quiescence of the British working class.

The commercialisation of leisure: mass markets, mass products, and market concentration c. 1840–1939

In their classic text *Monopoly Capital*, Baran and Sweezy (1968) promote the argument that industrial structure under capitalism follows an almost inexorable logic of development which begins with small-scale entrepreneurs in systems which may reflect the economic competition envisaged in classical economics, but continues through a process of mergers, take-overs and competitive struggle to domination by larger firms, and subsequently large-scale and even global corporations. The net effect of the process is, for Baran and Sweezy, the loss of consumer power as market structures become oligopolistic, that is, dominated by few and powerful companies which can shape the market rather than simply responding to it. The development of certain elements of the leisure industries provides examples of the processes identified by Baran and Sweezy, though recent tendencies towards disaggregation of capital and fragmentation of some markets must also be noted.

The development of the music halls in the nineteenth century, and their successors, provides some evidence of these processes at work. In the later part of the eighteenth century publicans as individual entrepreneurs also fostered trade by allowing performers to dance and play music for the drinking public. By the 1790s, tavern concerts had become known as 'free-and-easies' which incorporated visits from professionals as well as performances from the floor. At this stage the orientation of the publican was towards stimulating consumption of drink rather than the sale of entertainment (Summerfield, 1981).

Publicans sponsored a wide range of recreations, not simply music, and by offering this support attracted considerable middle-class opprobrium and opposition from the local magistracy. However, music was at least more respectable than some of the other attractions on offer, and after the 1840s, with the demise of Chartism and the subsequent lack of mass working-class political activism in Britain, the authorities began to relax their attitude to the granting of music licenses, the number of which grew rapidly to a peak in the mid-1860s at which point market concentration seems to have set in (Summerfield, 1981). However, alongside the provision of sing-song-type pub music grew a more capital-intensive form of provision, the music hall. It is estimated that by 1866 there were 33 large music halls in London alone, with average capital investment of £10 000 and average seating capacities of 1500 (Cunningham, 1980). Similar types of capital-intensive investment were becoming evident in other leisure spheres with, for example, fixed venues for circuses, heavy mechanical equipment for fair roundabouts and rides, and for seaside resorts (Bailey, 1987; Cunningham, 1980; Walvin, 1978).

While initially these capital-intensive investments were being made by individuals and partners, legislation introduced in 1856 permitted the forming of joint-stock and limited liability companies opening up the possibility for an increasing number and size of capital investments, fostering the process of market concentration. The nature of leisure investment in joint-stock companies did permit some widening of ownership as Waters (1990) illustrates by reference to the establishment of the Halifax Royal Skating Rink Company in the 1870s. £7500 was raised in £5 shares, with a relatively small number of large shareholders dominating (predominantly local textile industrialists purchasing more than 50 shares each) but with a sizeable number of shopkeepers, local professionals and clerks also taking up the investment opportunity. The first limited liability music hall company opened the Alhambra in 1866, and it seems clear that, in London at least, by this time the small-scale individual entrepreneur was losing ground to the larger-scale and latterly the corporate investor. Summerfield's (1981) evidence in relation to the licensing of small-scale pub music activity indicates that the number of venues (in the areas she investigated) were already declining by the 1870s under pressure from the larger music halls.

As the potential of the music hall as a form of mass entertainment was realised, and the industry became increasingly heavily capitalised, not only was competition squeezed, but the oligopolistic powers of the dominant companies were exerted on the performers.

Cunningham (1980) describes how music hall proprietors sought to maximise productivity and the return on capital by introducing two performances per day, and operating in syndicates introducing contracts which required performers to perform at a number of venues on the same night (also barring them from other competing venues). The significance of this move is in the application of the concepts of industrial capitalism beyond factory-based manufacturing to seek economies of scale from human, as well as material, resources. Thus in the leisure industries the application of scientific management techniques is, in a sense, prefigured in such developments.

The process of *market concentration* in certain areas at least of the leisure industries was therefore accompanied by a *standardisation of cultural products*. The mass market required the reproduction of increasingly standardised cultural products, and this appears to have been as strongly evident in the music hall as it was in the manufacture of leisure goods such as bicycles and sports equipment. Contemporary socialist commentators bemoaned the loss of local 'indigenous' working-class culture in the development of the mass appeal of the products of the music hall industry (Waters, 1990). Indeed by the end of the century there was also evidence of the internationalisation of the process of cultural standardisation. Products like the can-can had been imported from the continent, and by the turn of the century artistes appearing elsewhere in Western Europe were being recruited by British music hall proprietors to appear in Britain (Summerfield, 1981).

However, although by 1907 it was claimed that music hall attendance in London alone had risen to 1 250 000 per week (Waters, 1990), new technology was about to have a profound effect on the music hall following the appearance of the first cinematographic exhibitions in Britain in 1895. Both the cinema and gramophone industries offered far wider scope for the standardisation and internationalisation of cultural products, phenomena which would become increasingly evident as the twentieth century progressed.

With increasing competition in manufacturing, particularly from the United States and Germany, the leisure industries assumed greater importance in the national economy in the first half of the twentieth century. Employment in entertainment and sport provided a growing number of jobs, despite relatively troubled economic environments. In 1920, 101 700 were employed in this area, while by 1938 this figure had grown to 247 900, a rise which according to Beveridge's (1944) survey of employment was the third greatest increase of all industrial sectors, and, as Jones (1986) points out, by 1938 those employed in the manufacture of toys, games, sports equipment and musical instruments exceeded those employed in the fishing industry.

Tendencies towards standardisation of cultural products in the leisure industries were matched by standardisation of the physical infrastructure for leisure provision. The construction of facilities as varied as cinemas, football stadia, dance halls and holiday camps, with relatively uniform standards of comfort and service, was a feature of this period of competition for the discretionary income of those in work. Despite the economic depressions of the interwar years, those in work who constituted the majority enjoyed increased affluence, and leisure investors sought to capitalise on this source. The level of capital investment in leisure continued to increase with 1000 cinemas being built in Britain in the period 1924/5 to 1931/2, and 11 000 dance halls opening in the six years after the First World War (Howkins and Lowerson, 1979). Billy Butlin, with a back-ground in fairground entertainment, identified a market for stan-dardised holiday products and in 1938 invested £100 000 in the first of his holiday camps. Thomas Cook's, the travel company, also *diversified* into the holiday camp market investing in the setting up of British Holiday Estates with £250 000 in the same year.

Uniform holiday products, such as those at Butlin's camps, both guaranteed that the public knew what it was paying for when a holiday was booked, and also ensured that economies of scale could be achieved, for example in the training of red-coat personnel, as well as in the purchase of materials required. Economies of scale are more often associated with the production of goods, and Jones (1986) points to evidence to suggest that in larger firms in the leisure industries the output per person was greater than that in small firms. In 1935, cinematographic film printing companies employing be-tween 11 and 24 workers registered an average output of £452 per worker, while those employing between 100 and 199 workers had an average output of £708. In the manufacture of sports requisites the firms employing 50 to 90 employees had an average output of £165, while the figure for those employing 200 to 499 employees was £220. Similarly in the brewing industry, per capita output for the smallest firms was £538 while for the largest it was £905. Thus while output in the manufacture of sports requisites actually fell from £234 to £195 per head in the period 1924–35, this was partly attributable to falling prices during this period, while the reduction in output, where it was real, seems to have been more manifest in smaller firms.

The process of market concentration associated with increased productivity among the larger firms continued in the inter war years. Between 1920 and 1939 the number of breweries fell from 2889 to 885 with the larger breweries eliminating marginal producers through merger, buyout and price competition, as well as by ensuring outlets through the purchase of pubs as tied houses. By 1933 the cinema industry was dominated in Britain by three groups, the Gaumont British Picture Corporation, Associated Picture Houses, and the Odeon group. The speed of this process of market concentration in the new technology leisure industries is illustrated by the fact that although 40 companies were established in Britain in the gramophone and record industry in the period from 1927 to 1929; and by 1932 EMI (Electrical and Musical Industries) dominated the market (Howkins and Lowerson, 1979; Jones, 1986).

The growth of the voluntary sector and the formalisation of collective relationships, c. 1840–1939

In the same way as commercial activity was in part fuelled by the dissolution of informal extended family and community relationships, so also the development of the voluntary sector parallels this phenomenon. The processes of rationalisation and market concentration in some areas of the commercial sector in leisure were accompanied by a rationalisation process in the voluntary; sector; which resulted in large-scale national bodies emerging in the first half of the twentieth century, and was followed by their subsequent incorporation into the state and/or their emergence as lobbying interest groups.

As we have noted, the rationalisation process in the commercial sector; had two principal facets, the first involving the concentration of providers, the second the homogenisation of cultural products, of mass products for mass markets. The national profile of such; groups as the Council for the Preservation of Rural England, the National Playing Fields Association, the National Trust, the Youth Hostel Association, the Young Men's Christian Association, and the Central Council for Physical Recreation and Training, was in a sense made possible only by this homogeneity. Large groups of people with similar cultural aspirations are a prerequisite of the establishment of large-scale leisure organisations on a national basis.

Homogeneity of cultural aspirations, for example an interest in access to the countryside, does not, however, imply that organisational membership was not class- or indeed gender-based. When the rational recreation movement of the mid-nineteenth century petered out, it was in large part a reflection of working-class cultural independence. The working-men's club movement's break away from the goals and influence of its middle-class founders, the formation of the Rugby League (in a dispute over payment of players for broken time), the emergence of the working-class brass band movement, and the demise of middle-class-inspired innovations such as the mechanics' institutes, all provide examples of the ultimate failure of middle-class attempts at cultural control. Leisure activities pursued for extrinsic purposes of social or intellectual 'improvement' were replaced by those pursued for intrinsic purposes of enjoyment, even though the rhetoric of 'improvement' continued to be used well into the late nineteenth century often in support (sometimes in advertising) of recreations which were far from intellectual or improving in their appeal (Waters, 1990).

One does not have to support the stratified diffusion explanation of the changing nature of tastes to explain increased homogeneity. As Cunningham (1980) argues, the development of the music hall is a fairly prominent example of cultural interests of the *working class* growing 'upwards' across class boundaries. Indeed Bourdieu (1989) warns against understanding the participation of different class groups in a given activity as reducing the cultural space between class groups. (For example, participation in tennis may have grown in all classes in recent years, but, as Bourdieu points out, playing tennis on municipal courts in jeans and training shoes is, in an important sense, not the same activity as playing tennis in a private members club dressed in 'correct', fashionable attire.) Nevertheless, cultural homogeneity was in evidence as working-class groups strove to emulate the opportunities of more affluent groups for freedom of access to rambling, cycling and tourist environments, as well as to sport. Organisations such as the Clarion Cycling Club (associated with the Labour movement), the Cyclists' Touring Club and the National Cyclists' Union developed and flourished in the late nineteenth and early twentieth century, while holiday organisations such as the Workers' Travel Association, the Holiday Fellowship, and the Cooperative Holidays Association enjoyed large memberships by the 1930s (ranging from 28 000 to 48 000 each in 1938). The Youth Hostel Association membership grew from 6400 in 1930 to 79 800 by 1938.

The first half of the twentieth century saw rapid growth also in leisure organisations providing opportunities for women and girls. Women's Institutes offered a wide range of cultural and social activities, while the Women's League of Health and Beauty (166 000 members in 1939), the Young Women's Christian Association (27 000 members in 1934) and the Girl Guides (474 000 members in 1934) provide some examples of this growth. The growth of women's leisure organisations, although they did provide out-of-home opportunities for leisure, did not represent a serious challenge to the prevailing ideologies of gender. These leisure organisations were separate but usually smaller and often subordinate to their male counterparts. The activities for which they provided were also invariably restricted to those which were seen as being consistent with a traditional femininity. The 'liberating' influence of women's cultural organisations was thus limited.

Although much leisure organisation in the voluntary sector invariably took place at the local level, perhaps the most notable feature of the voluntary sector in leisure in the first half of the twentieth century was their organisation on a national level and the incorporation of some such organisations into government decision-making. The roles of the National Trust and the Central Council for Physical Recreation and Training were underpinned and underlined respectively by the National Trust Act of 1907 and the Physical Training and Recreation Act 1937. In addition, the National Playing Fields Association enjoyed royal patronage, while the mass trespass movement (coordinated nationally across a number of local organisations) was successful in pressing government to making legislation in the form of the (admittedly ineffectual) Access to the Mountains Act of 1939. The level of organisation and coordination of the voluntary sector in a mature industrial society was one which gave government the opportunity to meet public aspirations and/or pursue its own goals through this sector, while some voluntary-sector interests were provided with a leverage on government policy.

Thus, just as significant areas of the commercial sector had been organised into large units through the processes of market concentration, diversification and mass production, so also a significant feature of elements of the voluntary sector was their organisation at a national level, and their concomitant incorporation into policy discussion or national pressure group politics.

Britain in the international economy: post-war social and economic change as the context for the development of the commercial and voluntary sectors in leisure

Understanding the roles and mutual adjustments of the commercial, voluntary and public sectors in leisure over the period since the Second World War, and in particular the period since the early 1970s requires an understanding of Britain's changing place in the world economy. As the first industrial nation Britain had enjoyed a privileged position in nineteenth-century international trade and was to the fore in promotion of free trade, abandoning the protectionism of the mercantilist system (Chase-Dunn, 1989). However, Britain by the beginning of the twentieth century had already lost much of its economic and industrial lead. By 1900, Germany and the USA had overtaken Britain in levels of production, and although Britain still had 33 per cent of the world's trade in manufactured goods, German and American manufactured exports had caught up by the 1930s (Champion and Townsend, 1990a). Britain's strategy to sustain its industrial position was to employ protectionist policies in relation to its colonial holdings and subsequently the Commonwealth. However, its manufacturing performance continued to decline throughout the period 1933–69, masked only by the effects of post-war recovery and the growing invisible earnings from insurance and financial services (Allen, 1988; Ball, 1989).

By the 1980s Britain was clearly on the periphery of Europe, with disadvantaged regions and certain prosperous core areas, in a way analogous, for example, to the situation with Northern and Southern Italy. Prosperous regions or cities were those which held a central place in the new service industries, while regions and cities in decline were those which had been most heavily dependent on traditional primary or secondary sector industries. Britain's decline in the production and export of manufactured goods was part of a global restructuring process with labour intensive production being transferred by transnational corporations often to low wage economies with subsequent unemployment resulting in the developed economies, particularly those with lower rates of productivity (Ball, 1989).

The establishment of a Common Market in Europe was in large part influenced by the economic (as well as the political) concerns of Western European nation-states. However, when, following the Treaty of Rome, the Common Market was established in 1958, Britain opted to stay out of the new grouping in order to sustain her privileged position in the Commonwealth trading area. There were several reasons for this decision, the most important of which appear to have been the political uncertainty surrounding the new union, Britain's difficulties in adjusting its agricultural production to the requirements of the Common Market, and its related loss of protected access to Commonwealth markets (Champion and Townsend, 1990b; Wallace, 1990).

At the time the decision seemed sensible to many, since in 1958 Western Europe received only 13.7 per cent of Britain's exports while the sterling area and Canada received more than half. However, in the period after the foundation of the Common Market, Western Europe experienced rapid and prolonged growth while the trade levels of the Commonwealth remained stagnant. In 1973 Britain, following a referendum, successfully sought election to the European Community (with Ireland and Denmark), though membership was to remain a contentious issue. Nevertheless, Britain's economic performance over the period since the initial post-war economic growth had continued to decline. In terms of comparison with other countries, Britain's GDP per capita (adjusted for local purchasing prices) was surpassed by West Germany in the early 1960s, by France in the late 1960s and by Japan in 1972, though by the mid-1990s it had just about stayed ahead of Italy and had remained behind, but not lost ground to, the USA (Ball, 1989; Champion and Townsend, 1990b). Without the windfall of North Sea oil, the economic consequences of decline could have been even more disastrous.

However, the restructuring of Britain's economy was only one aspect of a more general restructuring process. This process generated polarised contrasts in Britain in terms of differences by region, gender and race in terms of unemployment, underemployment and wealth, and was associated also with increasing polarisation within and between the major political parties. As we have seen, growth in the British economy had been a function of growth in the service sector. Both *producer services* (i.e. intermediate services to end producers, such as banking, accounting, advertising, transport) and *consumer services* (services delivered direct to the final consumer, including 80 per cent of leisure services, Ball, 1989) had grown disproportionately in certain regions. Consumer services tend to grow in those areas where producer services have expanded most, fostered by the income which the producer services have generated amongst the workforce. In Britain, in the 1980s, most expansion took place in the South East of England. As Martin (1988) points out, two-thirds of the 840 000 new jobs generated in the early 1980s were located in the three southern regions (though Greater London itself experienced very low growth, and in that respect was more akin to the peripheral regions). Private sector service location decisions are made on the basis of profitability and efficiency, while public sector services are located on the basis of political decisions. However, the public sector had clearly been affected by both the recession and the antipathy of government, and public sector service employment did not grow even in the period up to the mid-1980s (Damesick, 1986).

While consumer service growth followed the affluent consumer, generated by producer service growth, producer services showed a tendency to remove from London itself because of high costs of land and labour, but to locate in close proximity to the city (Allen, 1988). This is to some extent explained by the importance of access to corporate headquarters of major companies which remained in or near the capital, and the growing demand for export of producer services. Thus the areas least affected by deindustrialisation and the loss of manufacturing jobs were those most likely to see growth in producer services. Furthermore, given that the location of hotels, theatres, restaurants, health studios and the range of private leisure consumer services in the areas of growth for producer services, the pattern of spatial inequality in the distribution of services and service jobs was reinforced. Nevertheless even within the south, stark contrasts had emerged between the core workforce in full-time permanent employment, and those who had worked part-time or on temporary contracts, and it was in the white-collar area that most of the new core jobs were created.

Regional disparities were reflected both in unemployment levels (see Table 6.1) and in income levels. Pond (1989) illustrates this disparity by pointing to the Council of Europe's 'decency threshold' which is calculated as 68 per cent of the average available earnings for all men and women. The threshold stood at £3.50 per hour or £135 per week in 1987 in Britain, and a number of regions had significant proportions below this level in 1987. The figure for the proportion below the decency threshold for the south-east for example, was only 23.1 per cent compared with 36 per cent in Wales, Yorkshire and Humberside, the South West and North East, and 37 per cent in Scotland. Intra-regional differences were, however, also clearly very important, with semi and unskilled manual labour, the young and the old more likely to experience unemployment.

Disparities between age groups grew in the 1980s, particularly in respect of the young who were more likely to experience unemployment and low income. In 1979, 16 to 17-year-olds earned 42 per cent of average adult earnings. By 1987 this had declined to 39 per cent and was going down, with the loss of social security rights and the

Table 6.1   *Unemployment by region*

| Region | \% unemployment rate | | | | |
	1979	1981	1986	1989	1998*
South-east	2.6	5.4	8.4	4.0	3.5
East Anglia	3.1	6.3	8.6	3.6	4.0 (East*)
South-west	4.0	6.8	9.5	4.7	4.3
East Midlands	3.3	7.5	10.1	5.7	5.2
London					7.6
West Midlands	3.9	10.0	12.9	6.6	6.1
Yorks and Humberside	4.0	8.9	12.7	7.6	6.3
North West	5.0	10.2	13.9	8.6	6.1
Northern	6.4	11.7	15.5	10.0	9.0 (North-east*)
Wales	5.3	10.6	13.8	8.3	6.8
Scotland	5.6	10.0	13.4	9.5	7.5

* Data for 1998 are for Government Office Regions.

Source: *Department of Employment Gazette* and *Labour Market Trends* (various years).

requirement to accept youth training. Women, meanwhile, continued to experience lower pay levels than their male counterparts. In
1979 women earned on average 73.6 per cent of male wages but by
1987 the figure had dropped to 73 per cent despite a decade of equal
opportunities legislation (McDowell, 1989). There are few official
data available in respect of the employment of black Britons,
though a Policy Studies Institute study (Brown, 1982) indicated
that Asian and Afro-Caribbean males were likely to earn 15 per cent
less than the average white Briton's pay, and, as Sarre (1989) points
out, the situation was likely to be worse for young black males and
for black women when compared with white males.

Perhaps the most striking feature of the restructuring process is
the reversal of the narrowing of the gap between rich and poor in
Britain. In the 1980s, for the first time since records were kept, the
relative gap between rich and poor in terms of earnings actually
grew (Table 6.2).

Table 6.2   *Gross household income as a percentage of mean household
income*

	bottom decile	*bottom quartile*	*top quartile*	*top decile*
1970	31	60	141	194
1979	30	52	148	204
1989	25	46	164	233
1998/9	21	. . .	. . .	231

Source: Family Expenditure Survey Reports for 1970, 1979, 1989, 1998/9.

Although during the 1990s, Britain's economy enjoyed something
of a revival with unemployment dropping sharply from a high of
12.4 per cent for the UK in 1983, through 8.9 per cent in 1991, to 4.3
per cent in 1999, and inflation remaining very low, nevertheless as
Table 6.1 illustrates significant regional differences persisted. Income differentials also remained stubbornly high. Analysis in
Eurostat (1998) cites the 'general rule' that societies with high
income economies have low levels of income polarisation, with the
UK (and to a lesser extent Ireland) proving the exceptions to the
rule in terms of member states. Income polarisation in 1996 was

only greater in Greece, Portugal and Ireland. Of EU member states these were the only ones to have greater proportions than the UK of households earning less than 60 per cent of median household income.

The leisure and the commercial sector in Britain at the beginning of the twenty-first century

Given the growing significance of services in the British economy, the leisure sector has gained recognition as a much more significant feature of economic activity, though, as we have noted, its contribution to employment was not negligible even in the period prior to the Second World War. Across the 1990s, modest growth has been seen in most areas of leisure service employment but with significantly greater growth in the café and restaurant sector, and in tourism accommodation (see Figure 6.1)

It is not intended in what follows to provide a detailed analysis of the nature of economic activity in the commercial sector, but rather to highlight key features which reflect trends in the shaping of the

Figure 6.1   *Employment in leisure services*

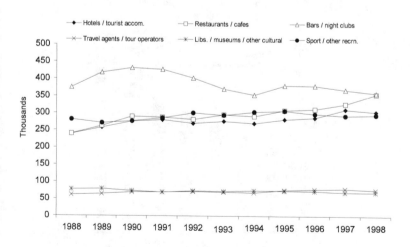

Source: Department for Education and Employment.

contemporary commercial sector and its relationship to the voluntary and public sectors. Outlined below, therefore, are factors
relating to the *demand* for leisure and its *supply* in the commercial
sector. Under the heading of demand, discussion will be linked to
four themes: the distribution of disposable income and disposable
time (the prerequisites of leisure demand); the nature and volume of
expenditure on leisure; polarisation in leisure behaviour and expenditure; and some key features of contemporary leisure behaviour
which can be identified in developing commercial leisure demand.

Changing leisure demand

Given the nature of Britain's economic context at the beginning of
the current decade, with sustained economic growth since the mid-
1990s, and low levels of inflation (below 2–3%) and low interest
rates (and therefore low mortgage rates), most of the population
could enjoy growing disposable income. As Figure 6.2 indicates,
although consumer expenditure increased significantly over the
1990s, savings increased at a greater rate. This tendency has been
taken by some to signal a more cautious consumer and may reflect a
growing concern to save in anticipation of expenditure on services in

Figure 6.2 *Disposable income growth, 1990–96 (actual)
1998–2002 (projected)*

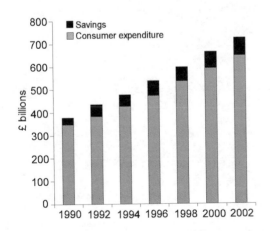

Source: Mintel (1998).

areas such as health, education and pensions once dominantly the preserve of government.

While discretionary income and savings rose in the 1990s, the data relating to discretionary time are ambiguous. Average annual holiday entitlements for full-time employees grew from 4.5 to 6.5 weeks over the period 1971–95; however, as Holliday (1996) points out, the average hours of full-time employees, despite falling from the mid-1970s to the mid-1980s, rose significantly in the 1990s. (Male hours of work for full-time employees stood at 46.2 in 1975, 40.2 in 1984 and 46.8 in 1995, while hours of work for females were 41.7 in 1975, 38.5 in 1984 and 39.8 in 1995.) Indeed, Gratton (1996) argues that the British labour force is the 'overworked labour force of Western Europe'; it has suffered significantly longer working hours than its EU counterparts. In 1992, for example, 16 per cent of the workforce worked more than 48 hours per week, with only Ireland among the member states exceeding 8 per cent, and an EU average of only 7 per cent. There is evidence to suggest that much of this work beyond the norm is undertaken by workers in the higher socioeconomic groups; that is, among professionals and managers with attendant impacts on the quality of working life (Charlesworth, 1996; Holliday, 1996).

Time free from work was also unevenly distributed throughout the population, and though unemployment had fallen in the 1990s, it was nevertheless the case that, for many, additional 'free' time was an unwelcome resource. The position of women had also been affected by the fact that traditional gender roles in terms of the household division of labour which have remained stubbornly unequal despite some amelioration (Sullivan, 2000), and yet many more women had become active in the paid workforce, particularly in the part-time sector. The number of women in employment grew from 8.4 million in 1971 to 11million in 1996, though most of this increase reflects growth of numbers of women in part-time employment which grew from 2.8 to 5.1 million across the period (Office for National Statistics, 1997).

Consumer expenditure grew in real terms over the period 1971–96 for most categories of leisure activities and products. Among the trends to note from the data in Figures 6.3 and 6.4 are increased consumer interest in *health and fitness* (sports expenditure grew by 193 per cent over the period while alcohol consumption, for example, though still of considerable significance, reduced in overall

180   *The Politics of Leisure Policy*

share of consumer expenditure). *Privatised* leisure forms in the home also show through in the figures in the form of increased spending on home entertainment (computers, records, tapes and audio equipment) with new opportunities produced by new technology, growth was highest in this segment of the market at 676 per cent in real terms from 1971–96. In out-of-home entertainment there was perhaps a tendency towards greater *individualisation* or market segmentation (the resurgence of cinema through multi-screen complexes, and the growing variety of restaurants for eating out provide examples of this). The range of tastes in relation to food, with most towns having restaurants representative of a variety of nationalities, has been fuelled in recent years less by a colonial heritage (Indian and Chinese restaurants) than by tourist experience (Greek, French, Italian, Spanish outlets). Indeed it is tourism which provides one of the most significant features of the data in Figures 6.3 and 6.4, with spending on accommodation for domestic holidays increased form 1971 to 1996 by 126 per cent while expenditure on holidays abroad grew by 282 per cent over the same period.

Figure 6.3 *Volume of leisure expenditure, 1996*

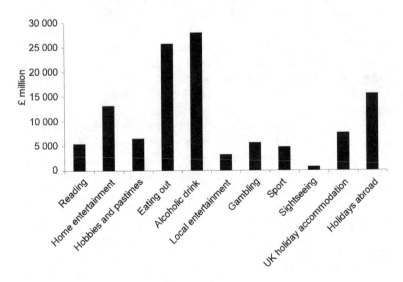

Source: Office for National Statistics (1999).

Figure 6.4 *Selected leisure markets: % growth, 1971–96, in real terms*

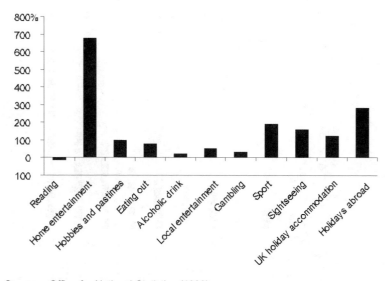

Source: Office for National Statistics (1999).

Individualism is also evident in the sports participation data (Mintel, 1998b), with participation in sports either alone or with one or two others growing by some 11 per cent over the 1982–96 period, while other sports participation remained stable across the same period. Gender differences also persist across virtually all categories of leisure activity although they have declined in respect of the major leisure pursuits cited (Mintel, 1998b). However, though leisure expenditure has grown, leisure expenditure differentials remain high. Figure 6.5 illustrates this point, with the lowest decile in terms of household expenditure spending less than one-eighth of the amount spent by the top decile, while Figure 6.6 indicates how, across a wide range of activities, higher socioeconomic groups are more frequent participants.

What emerges, then, in terms of the demand for commercial leisure at the beginning of the new century, is a pattern of uneven distribution of free time and money. This has given rise to a four-fold typology of groups, used by consultants as a basis for developing some ways of segmenting the leisure market (Martin and Mason, 1998). The four types are those who are:

Figure 6.5 *Expenditure on leisure goods and services by households from lowest income decile to highest*

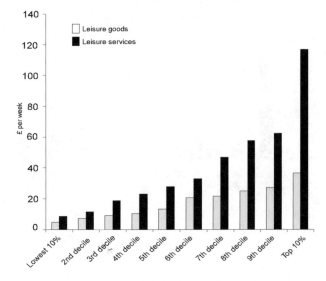

Source: Office for National Statistics (1999).

- time rich and money rich (e.g. the affluent retired);
- time poor and money rich (e.g. full-time core workers; executive mothers);
- money poor and time rich (e.g. many part-time workers; unemployed and enforced early retired; some single parents; retired on stated benefit);
- money poor and time poor (e.g. working mothers in poor families; single parents with large families).

Income differentials are reflected in differing patterns of expenditure such that lifestyle differences remain significant and are reflected in the market segmentation strategies of commercial providers.

Leisure supply

The discussion of developments in leisure supply in the commercial sector will incorporate four themes. The first is the development of the health and fitness area of the market which reflects some subtle responses to changes in the nature of demand. The second is a brief

Figure 6.6   *Participation in selected leisure activities in the last 12 months by social grade, 1996*

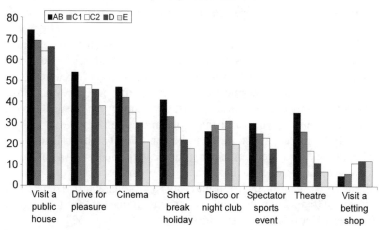

Source: Leisure Tracking Survey, *Henley Centre for Forecasting, cited in Office for National Statistics.*

review of the market for leisure goods. The third theme relates to developments in market structure with the ongoing oligopolistic tendencies of particular areas of the market. The final theme concerns the development of transnational strategies of leisure companies, reflecting the globalised context of leisure businesses at the beginning of the twenty-first century.

The health and fitness market
The growth in the health and fitness sector provides a good example of response to (and stimulation of) changing demand. The growth in 'individualisation' of leisure pursuits and the concern for health have been identified by the market in the health and fitness area, and pursued as a market opportunity both by private sector investment and management initiatives, and by private sector management of public sector provision (see Chapter 4).

Heath and fitness clubs tended to polarise in terms of size with approximately 60 per cent under 10 000 square feet in size and approximately 20 per cent over 20 000 square feet (Mintel, 1996). Figure 6.7 shows the fee levels for membership at health and fitness clubs as at 1994. These were not inconsiderable sums, though the introduction of direct debit payment, spreading the cost across 12 months, seems to have stimulated the market. Nevertheless, although the commercial product appeals to both sexes, and to a relatively wide age range, there is evident economic exclusion of certain groups.

The volatility of leisure markets, and in particular the vulnerability of discretionary spending to market conditions, is reflected in Figure 6.8 which illustrates the impact on the market in real terms of the antipathetic economic conditions of the early 1990s. Thus market commentators warn against the impact on leisure service revenue of any downturn in the economic cycle (Key Note, 2000).

By 1999, there was estimated to be some 2500 clubs in Britain, of which one third were modern and well-equipped, with approximately half of these in the ownership of major operators, that is about 15 per cent of the total market (Key Note, 2000). These clubs were able to appeal not simply to the general market, but to position themselves in relation to specific market segments:

> To differentiate themselves in a competitive market place, the branded chains are developing distinctive USPs [unique selling points]. For example, Virgin Active is targeting children

Figure 6.7 *Annual membership fees in private health and fitness clubs, December 1994*

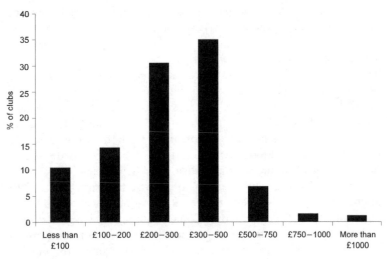

Source: Mintel (1996).

Figure 6.8   *The UK market for private health and fitness clubs, 1990–95*

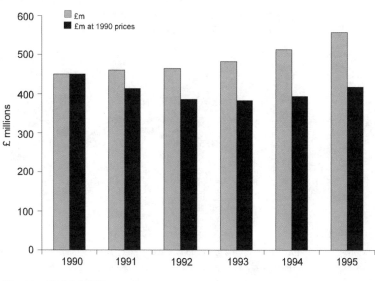

Source: Mintel (1996).

(PlayStation facilities, cartoon cinema), New Generation and Invicta are majoring on racquet sports, Holmes Place (in the City of London) is offering a 'prestige ambience', and Fitness First is promoting 'affordable fitness'. (Key Note, 2000: 48)

The development of individualised forms of offering within mass markets via careful segmentation is an evident feature of such leisure markets.

Manufacture of leisure goods
The leisure industries are not simply service industries, and though manufacturing in Britain has been in decline, the situation is far from uniform in respect of leisure manufacturing. Four areas of leisure manufacturing for which data are given in Figure 6.9 illustrate the point (see also Gratton and Taylor, 1991). Exports in terms of alcoholic drinks have been in continuous net surplus in terms of trade balance over the period since 1980 (largely accounted for by whisky exports), while electronic consumer goods have generated a continuous net deficit. The situation in respect of

186   *The Politics of Leisure Policy*

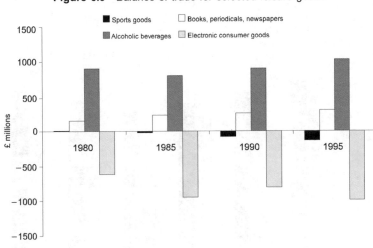

Figure 6.9 *Balance of trade for selected leisure goods*

Source: Overseas Trade Statistics (1981, 1986, 1991, 1996).

consumer electronics had improved slightly in the late 1980s, in part because of market saturation in respect of video and colour television, and in part because of the decisions of transnational corporations to relocate production plants in the UK (Ball, 1989), but net imports had begun to grow again in the 1990s.

The sports goods market has experienced a steadily worsening situation in terms of its import:export ratio, with a positive balance of trade in the late 1970s being converted into a significant net deficit of £135 million by 1995. With the growing market penetration of brands manufactured by transnational corporations such as Nike, Adidas and Reebok, and their diversification across a range of sports equipment and clothing markets, combined with the growth in significance of consumer spending on sport and fitness, this represents a serious leakage from the UK leisure economy. The figures for sports equipment exclude trainers and clothing and thus the situation is considerably worse if these items are included. Britain's only net export in terms of sports equipment is fishing equipment (with a positive balance of £2 million in 1996), with golf equipment and gymnasium equipment having negative balances of £45 million and £57 million respectively in 1996 (Department of Trade and Industry and Sports Industries Federation, 1999).

Finally, books and periodicals show a significant balance of payments surplus continuously throughout the same period. The hegemony of the English language gives the UK a structural advantage in all media sectors.

Thus in terms of leisure goods, the situation is variable depending on the specifics of the particular leisure good. At the beginning of the new millennium Britain still faced the (political and economic) conundrum of whether and when to join the Single European Currency. A strong pound and a weak euro made export difficult, and because of a lack of convergence in value between sterling and the euro, made joining the single currency more problematic. The stability of leisure markets (which deal largely in stylistic rather than use-value) is subject to the vagaries of fashion. For them also to be subject to the vagaries of currency markets makes them even more vulnerable to fluctuations in demand.

Market structure in the leisure industries
In terms of market structure, oligopoly (the dominance of a small number of firms) is the norm in many areas of leisure as in other sectors of British industry. Oligopolies may result in either intense competition between competitors or in price fixing cartels. Two cases dealt with by the Monopolies and Mergers Commission in the late 1980s and early 1990s illustrate this contrast (Gratton and Taylor, 1991). The acquisition of the Horizon Holiday Company by the Thompson Group in 1989 gave it almost 40 per cent of the package holiday market, but the acquisition was approved by the Monopolies and Mergers Commission on the grounds that the market was subject to intense competition and therefore unlikely to affect the interests of the consumer negatively. Continuing, occasionally fierce price competition across the 1990s has borne this decision out. By contrast, aspects of the brewing industry were also investigated by the Commission in the 1980s and 1990s, which ruled that the practice of operating tied houses adversely restricted consumer choice, and ruled that brewers should both reduce the number of tied houses held, and introduce beers from other breweries into the tied houses which were retained. This ruling effectively enhanced consumer choice, and was in tune with increasingly differentiated tastes in the beer market. In 1997, Bass disposed of its 1500 tied public houses, and subsequently developed a wide range of pub concepts for different market segments, from, for

example, city-centre continental café bars, through O'Neill's Irish pubs, to Harvester family restaurant pubs.

There are essentially two types of major operator in the leisure sphere – those operating in specialist market niches, and diversified leisure companies. Of the latter, Bass, the Rank Group, the Granada Group and Whitbread are the most significant (Key Note, 2000). Specialist niche operators are, however, vulnerable to pre-datory acquisition by the major diversified operators – as for example when in 1995 Whitbread purchased David Lloyd Leisure immediately acquiring market leadership in a particular niche (Eaton, 1996). The big four mentioned here number among their investments hotel and catering outlets, brewing, gambling and entertainment, attraction management, and media interests. All of these areas are subject to intense scrutiny and investment/divest-ment strategies as these companies seek to maximise profits while controlling risk (Henry and Spink, 1990).

Most leisure markets are more subject to the vagaries of fads and fashions than markets for more clearly staple goods. Often the stylistic value of leisure goods and services is more significant than its use value, and they may be employed by social groups in their search to generate stylistic differences thereby culturally distancing them from other groups (Bourdieu, 1989). Thus change is an inherent feature of many areas of leisure investment for consumers and therefore also for the successful producer. This is reflected in the fact that in the 1990s expansion and contraction of the major operators was a feature of leisure market activity. Rank, for example, the UK's biggest operator and owner of commercial leisure properties and services, with a turnover of £2 billion in 1999 and a pre-tax operating profit of £108 million, disposed of its holdings in Rank Amusements, Shearing's Coach Holidays, Butlin's Holiday Hotels, four holiday parks, Pinewood Studios, its night-club interests, and in 2000 sold its Odeon cinemas, while in the same period increased its investment in themed restaurants (including Planet Hollywood) and in casino and gaming activities.

At the other end of the spectrum of commercial leisure investors there is very little data relating to the role of small-scale local capital in leisure investment. Small firms are less evident in individual terms in their impact on leisure markets and may be more transient, particularly in periods of economic retrenchment (witness the rate of business failures in the early and late 1980s and into the early

1990s). However, it does seem clear that much of the investment in sport and recreation facilities, in for example health and fitness clubs, in squash clubs and in golf courses, was, initially at least, the product of local capital. Volatility of markets and market niching seem likely to promote a continued role for small firms in this type of market, while sustained profitability and potential economies of scale make such businesses subject to the predatory interests of larger companies. However, as Collins and Randolph (1991) recognised in their pilot study of small firms in Leicestershire, there remains a considerable need for further work in this field, particularly given the importance of small firms for employment growth (Mason and Harrison, 1990).

Global market strategies
One of the features of the last two decades of the twentieth century in respect of leisure markets was the increasing impact of globalisation on leisure markets. Just two examples will be employed here to illustrate this phenomenon, those of media and sports interests, and the sports clothing market.

Television has proved to be the global medium par excellence, and the advent of satellite and digital TV has reinforced this status. However, with the new technology came additional suppliers and additional competition for both audiences and programming. Sports programming has proved crucial in this competition. That Rupert Murdoch's BSkyB was able to transform itself from a company haemorrhaging badly in financial terms in 1989, to one of Britain's 50 most profitable companies by 1995, was largely a result of its capturing of the exclusive contract to show matches from the English Football Premiership in 1992. The market position of non-terrestrial television is to a considerable degree dependent on the ability to negotiate exclusive rights to show major sporting events. In a market research panel of 1066 respondents, access to sports coverage (cited by 38%) was the third most significant influence on the decision to subscribe to satellite or cable, after films (55%), and access to additional channels (52%) (Mintel, 1997). The rights to broadcast were gained at a price – the five-year deal in 1992 was won for £191.5 million, and the 1997 contract was also won by BSkyB for £670 million compared with the £44 million it had cost ITV to win the four-year 1988 contract (Gratton and Taylor, 2000).

Given the competition for the broadcasting contracts and the possibility of new European-level competitions emerging involving the leading clubs, BSkyB was anxious to ensure that it was close to the sporting market and sought to enter into a merger with Manchester United. This was disallowed following a report of the Monopolies and Mergers Commission in 1999, but between September 1998 and January 2000 BSkyB had bought 9.9 per cent stakes in Manchester United, Chelsea, a 9.08 per cent stake in Leeds United and a 5 per cent share in Sunderland, while NTL had purchased a 9.9 per cent share in Newcastle United with a 9.99 per cent share in Aston Villa. Granada also purchased a 9.9 per cent share in Liverpool. The figure 9.99 per cent was the maximum permitted share for a media company, and in most cases the investment (from £84 million in the case of Manchester United to £4.65 million in the case of Sunderland) also bought the rights to act as TV rights agent to the club (Rice, 2000).

Football, though the main sport, was by no means the only one to be affected by television investment. In the mid-1990s the launching of the Rugby League Super League, funded by money from a BSkyB contract, saw the British game switch from a winter to a summer season to synchronise with the Murdoch News Corporation's interests in Australian Rugby League. Merging of some clubs followed, as it had done in Australia, and the nature of the peripheral product (e.g. pre-match entertainment) changed radically. This new set of arrangements and source of funding has significantly altered the nature of governance in these sports with major clubs, and the media companies which have provided them with a degree of additional financial power, having a considerable influence on the nature of the game and its competitions. Thus, for example, clubs have felt able to discuss breaking away from their national leagues to play in new European competitions despite opposition from their own national governing bodies.

In addition, the new arrangements have had significant implications for sports spectatorship via television. The range of penetration and access of satellite and cable to British households is considerable (estimated at 6.8 million households in 1997), and the take up of this form of television by socioeconomic status is revealing, with C2 and D groups dominating satellite and cable respectively. However, the low level of access for benefit dependants and socioeconomic group E reflects clear concerns for exclusion, both from spectating via television in the home and in terms of more public social contexts. Of the social grade E households, 50 per cent had no access to satellite television and only 4 per cent accessed this through pubs and clubs, while for welfare dependent households the figures were 56 per cent and 1 per cent respectively, with the national average being 34 per cent and 10 per cent (Mintel, 1997). Access to major sporting events is potentially limited by the exclusive contracting of broadcast rights, a point addressed by the European Union in its revision of the *Television Without Frontiers* directive (1997). According to the directive, national governments may reserve for free-to-air television the broadcasting of a limited number of sporting events deemed by national governments to be of particular national importance. The rationale here is that sport is more than simply a product, and that all broadcasting rights cannot therefore be simply sold to the highest bidder. Sport is, in effect, part of a nation's cultural heritage and may be subject to protectionism. Thus in the 'search for the responsible market', governments may be forced to regulate at transnational level in order to counter global strategies of commercial-sector leisure operators.

The second example relating to the globalisation of the commercial leisure sector, is that of the sports clothing sector and in particular the case of Nike. Nike is a company that specialises in sportswear design and marketing and has been spectacularly successful in generating sales, keeping costs low in production (Gratton and Taylor, 2000), and liberating revenue to be spent on promotion via individual sports stars, such as Michael Jordan, or major teams such as the Brazilian soccer team. Costs of production are kept low by the shifting (or threat of shifting) of contracts between competing (usually Asian) economies. This has led to accusations of worker exploitation and the sanctioning of child labour (Bigelow, 1997; Boje, 1998; Donaghu and Barff, 1990). However, short-term contracts, keeping suppliers on their toes in respect of quality and price, and strong marketing and design, mean that the company has been spectacularly successful. In 1996–97 alone its revenue exceeded $9 billion compared with its nearest rival Adidas with a turnover of $5 billion. Thus flexibilised production via short-term contracts, and distribution via franchise operations, means that a small core organisation can generate huge growth without risk of investment in production and distribution capacity. The notions of a core and a peripheral workforce are thus superimposed across national boundaries, with profits expropriated to core economies.

The leisure and voluntary sector in Britain in the 1980s and 1990s.

Given the growing divide in Britain between the 'beneficiaries' and 'victims' of economic restructuring, it seems clear that for many the role of active consumer in the leisure market is either restricted or unavailable. With state-provided services also being reduced or being required to operate on a more commercial basis, the significance of voluntary sector provision for the less affluent became even greater in the 1990s. However, research relating to the roles and activities of the voluntary sector at the level of small-scale local organisations, like that for small firms (and for similar reasons), is lacking.

There are some indications of trends which emerge from a review of national data on voluntary organisation membership. The two areas in which growth in membership on a national scale might have been expected to be most significant from the 1980s were in membership of environmental organisations and in organisations serving the elderly. Three organisations representing elderly memberships, Pensioners' Voice, the Royal British Legion, and Age Concern, had a combined membership of 2 million by the mid-1980s, a 50 per cent increase on their membership in 1971, but their membership had begun to fall away considerably in the 1990s. Table 6.3 cites the membership for some environmental groups, clearly reflecting the growth of a green consciousness.

Voluntary organisations in decline included women's organisations associated with traditional female roles such as the Mothers' Union and National Federation of Women's Institutes (see Table 6.3). Significantly women's organisations associated with the business community or the role of business woman (Soroptimists, Inner Wheel) enjoyed some growth. Uniformed youth groups also appear to have declined in significance from the 1970s to the 1990s (Central Statistical Office, 1990; Office for National Statistics, 1998).

At the local level generalisations are much more difficult to support. The only major funded study of voluntary-sector leisure organisations to be published was undertaken in the 1980s by Hoggett and Bishop (1986). This study, however, was limited in scope since it identified only a limited proportion of those organisations which met leisure needs, excluding those which did not constitute 'mutual aid' organisations and restricting itself to two small area studies. One of the few attempts at a detailed and

Table 6.3 *Membership of selected voluntary organisations (in thousands)*

Organisations	1971	1981	1988
Environmental Organisations			
Civic Trust	214		249
Council for the Preservation of Rural England	21	29	32
Friends of the Earth	1		65
National Trust	278	1046	1634
Ramblers' Association	22	37	65
Royal Society for Nature Conservation	64	143	204
Royal Society for the Protection of Birds	98	441	540
World Wildlife Fund for Nature	12	60	147
Women's Voluntary Organisations	*1971*	*1981*	*1988*
Mothers' Union	308	210	180
National Federation of Women's Institutes	440	378	335
Association of Inner Wheel Clubs	31	34	35
Soroptimists' International of GB and Ireland	13	14	17
Young People's Voluntary Organisations	*1971*	*1981*	*1992*
Cubs (incl. Beavers)	265	309	349
Scouts (incl. Ventures)	215	234	191
Brownies (incl. Rainbow Guides)	376	427	418
Guides (incl. Ranger Guides)	316	348	2243
Duke of Edinburgh Scheme	122	160	. . .
National Federation of Young Farmers			
(male)	24	28	16
(female)	16	23	14
Other Voluntary Organisations	*1971*	*1981*	*1992*
Age Concern			180
Pensioners' Voice	600	113	25
Royal British Legion	750		679
Rotary International	50	59	65
National Assoc. of Round Tables	250	475	350
PHAB (Physically Handicapped and Able Bodied)	2		20
Royal Soc. for Mentally H'cap'd Children and Adults	40	55	55
British Red Cross Society	172	112	90
St John's Ambulance brigade	91	77	50

Source: Central Statistical Office (1991); Office for National Statistics (1996).

wide-ranging inventory of voluntary organisations including those for leisure is Newton's (1976) study of voluntary-sector political activity in Birmingham. Although the study predates the time period on which we are focusing here, two points are worth emphasising from the findings of Newton's study. One is the sheer volume of voluntary organisations in a major city such as Birmingham (he identified some 3000); the second is the large proportion of those organisations (more than half) which had a primary or subsidiary leisure function.

The structure of the voluntary sector in leisure involves more than those hobby, arts or sports organisations through which individuals cater for their own leisure interests. It incorporates a range of organisations which, for example, have primary goals other than those relating to leisure (e.g. the scouts and guides) or which may exist to provide leisure for people other than the organisation's own members. Such organisations might be characterised as falling into one of the following five categories (Haywood and Henry, 1986a, b):

1. *Organisations developed around a particular leisure form*: typically sports or arts organisations
2. *Mutual aid groups and community service groups* where the group is 'client centred' and its membership is involved in providing a service;
3. *Community development groups*, where the theme of 'self-help' is central;
4. *Community action groups*, which focus their activities on a particular 'cause' acting as a pressure group, often in relation to the activities (or inactivity) of a public body;
5. *'Social' groups*: those with 'socio-emotional' goals, but for which recreation forms an important element in their activities. Such groups may initiate community recreation projects. Working men's clubs, for example, not only promote leisure opportunities within the confines of their own premises, but also generate sports teams, hobby and interest groups, competitions, trips to events etc.

What research has been carried out on voluntary leisure organisations has tended to treat voluntary organisations as an undifferentiated homogeneous group, or, like Hoggett and Bishop's study, to focus exclusively on mutual aid organisations. Voluntarism has traditionally had an appeal to both the political left (which has seen it as an alternative to state paternalism) and the political right (which sees it as both cost-saving and a bulwark against budget-maximising bureaucrats). Nevertheless, reliance on the voluntary sector to provide services or opportunities suffers from the class, gender and location-specific nature of the interests such organisations might serve. Hoggett and Bishop's (1986) review of voluntary sector provision contrasted two locations, one a predominantly suburban and relatively affluent area on the outskirts of Bristol, the other an inner-city location in Leicester. Their review was limited to research concerning the activities of mutual aid organisations, but, for example, highlighted that the inner-city area in Leicester had relatively many fewer voluntary organisations, and these tended to have shorter histories, be less well-resourced, and were more likely to have been supported in some way through public funding. Nevertheless, these authors regard the range and diversity of the voluntary sector as its major strength, and argue that to maintain such diversity, or 'fragile pluralism', public sector support should where possible be avoided.

Both the Hoggett and Bishop study and those of Limb (1986) and Henry (1987) predate the shift in government policy concerning the use of urban aid for support of voluntary-sector leisure organisations (see Table 3.3 and associated commentary). Limb and Henry's studies highlighted the incorporation of voluntary organisations into local policy often through special finding schemes such as the Urban Programme. These forms of limited corporatism were severely weakened by the later 1980s when government sought to promote sponsorship as an effective alternative to some forms of state funding though sponsorship is of limited value in the arts or sport for those organisations providing low-profile, local opportunities (Beck, 1990; Mintel, 1994). Thus sponsorship, on the whole, tends to support those organisations which are viable and have a popular appeal, that is those least in need.

Similarly, the advent of the Lottery as a source of funding for voluntary sector leisure organisations in 1994 reinforced the weaknesses of the declining pattern of public sector investment in leisure since it brought with it a bidding culture that favoured more affluent and well-resourced communities and organisations. The requirements for a successful bid included knowledge of how to bid, professional services (e.g. in finance, architecture or business planning) and financial resources (to provide a contribution to capital and to contribute to the revenue costs of running a facility once it had been constructed or developed). The government had recognised this difficulty and introduced Priority Area Grants which required lower levels of financial contribution from bidding organisations, and which allowed for some revenue funding in some cases. It remains to be seen how successful this will be in redressing the difficulties of funding those most in need.

Conclusions

In the opening chapter of this book, Table 1.1 characterised the post-1997 period as that of a 'search for the responsible market'. It is described as a period in which the commercial sector has sought global strategies and partnerships to exploit profit opportunities in the leisure industries. The transnational interpenetration of media and professional sports club ownership represents, for example, such a strategy, with the commercial sector increasingly commodifying sport and thereby changing the nature of the relationship between clubs and their supporters. Just as globalisation is reflected in the activities of the commercial sector, so transnational activity is evident in the voluntary sector. High-profile environmental groups such as Greenpeace and the World Wildlife Fund are perhaps obvious examples. However, in the sporting sector in the mid-1990s we saw organisations such as ENGSO (European Non-Governmental Sports Organisations) and the Central Council for Physical Recreation lobbying the European Union, the former advocating and the latter opposing EU action in the field of sport (see Chapter 8). ENGSO and other sporting organisations sought the inclusion of an article in the Treaty on European Union revised at Amsterdam in 1997 to provide the EU with the competence to intervene in the field of sport. Although this was not wholly successful, the Treaty did incorporate a Declaration on Sport, signalling the EU's recognition of the importance of this field and indicating a willingness to consider the matter further (Henry and Matthews, 1998). The whole lobbying process, however, reflects a recognition of the need to intervene at transnational level if the commercial sector in particular is to be effectively regulated, and the voluntary sector to be protected from 'over commercialisation', and this is a matter clearly under review at the time of writing by the EU in the field of sport (European Commission, 1998). Transnational commercial strategies imply a need for transnational forms of regulation and control on the part of states, and often further imply a transnationally active voluntary sector. Thus the relationship between local, national and transnational policy provides the focus for the final two chapters.

7 Social Regulation and the Governance of Leisure

Introduction

The discussion of the role of leisure professionals in leisure policy in Chapter 5 focused on the 'internal' workings of the local authority, and on the roles of professionals involved in policy development. However, one should recognise that though policies may be *effected* by the actors involved, they are likely to be *affected* by other factors, including those external to the authority itself. The potential for action of the actors involved is a function of the context of the framework of strategic relations within in which they find themselves. Thus, the structural location of local governments in Britain *vis à vis* central government, the European Union and the international economy, are important factors in defining the resources for, and limitations of, the action of local government politicians and professionals. In this chapter we therefore return to a discussion of the wider political, economic and cultural context of leisure policy decision-making, before going on to consider the development of new policy responses to the changing context of local government in the last two decades.

In Chapter 3 a strategic relational explanation of the nature of the state was promoted, arguing that the nature of the state was a function of the outcome of past struggles between interest groups, and represented the context of future contests. The British state during the 1970s and 1980s was clearly involved in a series of overt power struggles. Anti-rate capping campaigns; social disorder associated with opposition to the community charge; battles between government and groups as diverse as miners, teachers and the medical establishment; the failed prosecution of civil servants under the Official Secrets Act and the rendering of civil servants as accountable not to Parliament but to the government of the day; these all represent examples of such struggles. Although in the 1990s such confrontational tactics were eschewed by John Major's administration, nevertheless, at a national level, the legacy of these battles provide the strategic context for policy and politics in local government under both the governments of John Major and of Tony Blair. However, it is important to recognise that the outcomes of *transnational* interaction, such as the changing position of Britain in the world economy, in an important sense, provide the resources for intra-state struggles. Thus explanations of the development of policy should take account of the pressures and opportunities generated by such transnational phenomena.

Social theory in the 1980s and early 1990s manifested two apparently contrasting trends. The first, most notably represented in the 'regulation school' of political economy (Aglietta, 1979; Boyer, 1986; Lipietz, 1987) and by cultural theorists of postmodernity (Featherstone, 1995; Lash and Urry, 1987, 1994; Urry, 1990), emphasises the aforementioned need to locate discussions of local, regional or national phenomena within a wider discussion of transnational economic, political and cultural processes. The second, mirrored in, for example, the work of Cooke and his colleagues (Cooke, 1989b) was to re-emphasise the significance of place, the contingent and local outcomes of social, political and economic processes. These two trends are not mutually incompatible (both strategies are evident in Cooke's own work and that of his colleagues, Cooke, 1989a). Similarly this chapter will seek to illustrate the interaction of the transnational and national context with local agency in the form of local leisure policy development. Perhaps the most useful framework for providing such an account is provided by regulation theory which, though Marxist in its origins and with considerable variations in its expression (Jessop, 1990a, b; 1995a), has attracted a considerable amount of attention in respect of its explanatory power in relation to changes in the welfare state (Jessop, 1995b) and in local government specifically (Christopherson, 1994; Mayer, 1994).

Regulation theory: explanations of the changing global political economy

The structure of regulation theory explanations of politico-economic development hinges on the articulation of the relationship between 'regimes of capital accumulation', which are forms of economic activity, and the 'modes of regulation', the social, political and cultural arrangements which sustain such forms of economic accumulation. Thus, as the nature of capital accumulation changes in a society – for example, from the individual entrepreneurialism of the early nineteenth century, through the emergence of corporate capitalism in the late nineteenth and early twentieth centuries, to the global strategies of capital in the late twentieth century – so the social arrangements which accompany such economic organisation are also likely to be subject to change. Although certain socio-political arrangements may be said to be consistent, or compatible, with particular regimes of accumulation, the former should not be regarded as 'functional requirements' of the latter. Most articulations of regulation theory seek to avoid the reductionist weaknesses of both functionalist and structuralist Marxist accounts of political economy (Jessop, 1990b). The establishment of new forms of capital accumulation should not be regarded as mere historical accident, since it does not take place without the contingent efforts of political actors to establish an environment which will foster new forms of economic activity. In the form of the Thatcherite Conservative governments of the 1980s, a group of actors existed which sought to foster not only the restructuring of the British economy, but also of the social and political culture of Britain, and any explanation of leisure policy since the mid-1980s must take account of the nature and success (or failure) of such changes. Thatcherism, as the most radical and most significantly actioned ideological programme of the last quarter of a century thus provides the context for the contemporary struggles in local and central government, and at one level at least the policy directions subsequently followed by John Major and Tony Blair represent extensions of, or responses to, this programme.

The key contemporary shift in developed capitalist economies identified by regulation theorists, is the move from a Fordist to a post-Fordist regime of accumulation. A Fordist regime of capital accumulation is one in which mass, standardised production of uniform goods is achieved largely through the rationalisation of production tasks, typically in assembly-line techniques. The archetype for such production processes was the development of the assembly line production of the 'model T' Ford car, hence the sobriquet 'Fordism'. Such production processes generated alienation in a workforce which was deskilled by virtue of the application of scientific management thinking which broke down work tasks into simplified repetitive routines thereby maximising productivity. In order to ensure worker co-operation in production, some of the benefits of the economic gains to capital were to be shared with the workforce as mass consumption of consumer goods was underwritten by increases in real wages, generated by substantial national economic growth. This had the added benefit of generating a mass market for the mass-produced goods developed under Fordism.

The Fordist system of production was, however, to be underpinned by more than simply wage increases. Industrial labour in post-war Britain, organised within unions, achieved real gains not only in private standards of living but also in the 'social wage' sustained by public expenditure as part of the social democratic settlement between labour and capital. Although regulation theorists' claims concerning the level and extent of 'Taylorism' (application of scientific management principles) and attendant deskilling in Britain have been subject to debate (Allen, 1992; Peck and Tickell, 1994), nevertheless, it is clear that the British state in the post-war period adopted a Fordist approach to state intervention, managing demand by Keynesian methods, developing an infrastructure to sustain production and improve productivity, and increasing collective consumption thereby 'ensuring' the compliance of both capital and labour in the system of production. The state's role in accommodating the interests of capital and labour was sustainable so long as economic growth provided the resources to undertake the role, and the legitimacy of the state was underpinned by the incorporation of the major interest groups in decision-making on economic and social issues. However, economic decline exposed the inadequacies of the Fordist regime of accumulation and the social democratic framework which supported it. The corporatism of the post-war settlement became increasingly fragile and was to be dismantled largely in the period of Conservative rule under Mrs Thatcher.

In the period of growth after the Second World War, Fordism was underwritten by the US dollar, the value of which was tied to gold reserves. US military supremacy also provided a stable framework for world trade among the capitalist economies of the developed and developing worlds. However, the US carried a considerable balance of trade deficit over an extended period, in part to finance its military supremacy, with troops in Europe and Asia, and with expensive military hardware. This severely weakened the US economy. At the beginning of the 1970s it became clear that the financing of the US dollar's trade deficit by gold holdings was no longer viable and the US abandoned the policy. The value of the dollar which had been sustained at a falsely high position fell sharply, and American domestic demand was severely reduced. Given the size of the American domestic market there was an immediate negative impact on world trade. Currencies went onto the unprotected market and the value of sterling fell. The quadrupling of oil prices in 1973–74 accelerated the world recession, and Britain was also further affected by having to meet the costs of entry into the European Community. The cornerstone of social democratic economics, the Keynesian economic policy of demand management failed in such circumstances and no longer offered the opportunity to trade off inflation against unemployment. As the world recession deepened domestic demand management appeared powerless to alleviate either inflation or unemployment; both continued to grow alarmingly, while the economy stagnated.

In such circumstances it is hardly surprising that the legitimacy of social democracy seemed bankrupt. The two major means of mobilising consent in twentieth century parliamentary politics had been, either by popular vote and parliamentary leadership, or through corporatist strategies of accommodating interests within the machinery of government decision-making. In the 1970s, as Gamble (1988, 1993) points out, social democracy failed to realise either of these sets of circumstances. The majorities gained by governments in the 1970s were thin, and the industrial strife which contributed to the demise of the Heath and Callaghan governments was considerable. Social democracy was called into question as the failure of economic management eroded the political legitimacy of the central state. Thus, politicians of all parties were beginning to reassess Fordism in a changed international economy in the 1970s. Consensual politics was replaced by an authoritarian state strategy in which state-imposed solutions to social, economic and political problems were developed. The government's imposition of spending limits in 1976, and the battles with public sector trade unions in the 'winter of discontent' of 1978–79, constituted elements of this authoritarian style. This strategy was, however, manifestly unsuccessful, and the state's legitimacy further weakened. The Right under the leadership of the new Tory Party leader, Margaret Thatcher, was thus able to appeal to an anti-collectivist disaffection when it came to develop an alternative project to social democracy.

Thatcherism as a hegemonic project, post-Fordism and urban leisure policy

The mere fact of a crisis in Fordist economic organisation and socio-political regulation does not of itself explain the development of a new post-Fordist accumulation regime. Regulation theory represents an attempt to escape the notion that capitalism has a single inevitable logic of development. Politico-economic systems develop their own trajectories influenced by the political, economic and ideological actors and historical alliances within those systems (Jessop, 1988), and the emergence of a New Right-led Conservative government with an ideologically driven political programme provides a major element in the impetus to seek a new set of economic and social relations (Gamble, 1988, 1993).

Some writers have explicitly rejected the notion that Britain has already moved into a post-Fordist accumulation regime, suggesting that the continuities between the post-1970s and the dominantly Fordist period are more significant than the contrasts. These writers prefer to refer to a neo-Fordist (Stoker, 1990) or after-Fordist (Peck and Tickell, 1994) accumulation regime. It is certainly the case that despite radical changes in the industrial structure of post-war Britain and of other industrialised nations, together with the loss of US economic hegemony, no new accumulation regime is as dominant as the Taylorist US post-war regime. The Japanese, German and US economies therefore continue to strive for dominance (Lipietz, 1987), and the development and restructuring of state socialist economies in Eastern Europe will play a crucial part in the formation of a new system of politico-economic relations. Nevertheless, despite the disputed nature of claims that Britain has moved into a post-Fordist era, there is good evidence (as illustrated in Gamble, 1988; Jessop, 1991; Stoker, 1990) to support the claim that Thatcherism constituted a hegemonic project which sought in the 1980s to establish elements of a new accumulation regime, in large part by establishing elements of a new approach to socio-political regulation. Hegemony in Gramsci's terms relates to the struggle to provide moral and political leadership which usually reflects, and is a vehicle of, class dominance although he allows for the development of alliances beyond solely class-based groupings. Gramscian analysis highlights the need for political leadership to win the active popular support of civil society, providing the ideological prerequisites for successful hegemonic leadership and political practice. Leisure has been one of the sites of ideological and economic activity on which the political leadership has alighted as a means of shifting the nature of accumulation and its legitimation.

A brief consideration of the main policy thrusts of the Conservative governments after 1979 illustrates the nature of the attempts to dismantle Fordist structures and discredit their support amongst the electorate. The government abandoned the corporatist practices of its predecessors, which had been a key feature of the political compromises underpinning Fordist regulation. The monetarist attacks on welfare spending sought to reduce spending on services such as health and education, and though public spending in revenue terms was not significantly reduced, these attempts were seen as consistent with the aim of reducing, restructuring, and ultimately dismantling the apparatus of the welfare state. A major deliverer of welfare services, local government was also subject to intense pressure by central government.

By tackling one of the cornerstones of collectivism, the power of the trades unions, the government sought to sweep away a major barrier to the restructuring of accumulation. Thus, in the 1980s it introduced legislation to require ballots for strike action, to limit numbers of pickets, to prevent secondary picketing, to require union leaders to subject themselves to regular elections, and to require authority from the membership via a ballot for the use of union funds for support of political parties. In addition the government successfully took on public sector unions, most notably the steel workers, the miners and (less successfully) the teachers in major strikes which illustrated the strength of government in opposing worker organisations.

In abandoning Keynesian economic management, Conservative governments, employing monetarist tactics, accelerated the restructuring of British industry. Under Thatcherism there were some heavy losers, most notably heavy engineering and chemical production, while other areas of capital enjoyed growth throughout the recession of the early 1980s, including banking and finance, food, oil, and the protected sectors of defence and agriculture. The substantial revenues from North Sea oil were consumed in funding benefits during periods of high unemployment, and substantial tax cuts, rather than long-term investment in collective consumption goods, as was the experience of other European oil producers. The dramatic loss of manufacturing industry was complemented (though not compensated for) by the increased growth of the service sector. In the early days of the Thatcher government, between 1981 and 1984, 700 000 new jobs were claimed to have been created in the service sector, of which 230 000 were in the banking, finance sector and related areas, and were predominantly located in the south of England (Cooke, 1989b).

The traditional class divisions of Fordist industrial organisation do not disappear under a post-Fordist regime but are reshaped and deepened. 'Core workers' in the new industries are recruited and retained with packages of inducements, both monetary and in terms of enhanced conditions and other perquisites. Those in the 'peripheral workforce' to whom work is sub-contracted and for which job security is therefore low, are subject to insecurity, poor conditions and low wages. Often such jobs involve part-time work. The dissolution in the 1980s of the Wage Councils which had guaranteed minimum wage rates was a crucial feature of this overall strategy, as was the need to educate young workers into the realisation that past practices would 'price them out of employment'. The peripheral workforce and those outside the workforce, the low paid, the underemployed and the unemployed, would invariably feel the loss of welfare services most keenly. They would be unable to avail themselves of the new rights of consumer choice in welfare services – since they do not live in those more salubrious areas where schools would have the resources (parental and financial) to maximise the benefits of local management. They would be unable to avail themselves of leisure services in contracted-out leisure centres because of the price levels implied by the limits set in charge-capping by central government. They would not be able to afford the health insurance premiums required by private medical companies. Thus a two-tier welfare system is implied in the post-Fordist mode of accumulation, with consumer choice for flexibly provided and managed welfare services (including leisure services), and 'safety net' provision (with low levels in volume and quality) for those without the resources to benefit from the enhanced consumer choice.

In the process of industrial restructuring in Britain, the manufacturing investment which was lost was predominantly that which required labour-intensive production. Many of these jobs went to low-wage economies. Automation of production, which may save on costs, also loses jobs, but may allow more flexibility in production. The technology of robotics and the speed and accuracy of market intelligence thus allows mass marketing to be superseded in these areas by the identification and servicing of market segments, production for market niches. Cultural theorists of postmodernism underline the highly differentiated lifestyles in contemporary society. Indeed, traditional work and 'working-class culture' become stylised and consumed in idealised forms in industrial museums, such as Beamish and Wigan Pier, which package and sell our industrial past to our postmodern present (for those who can afford such consumption).

The evolving industrial structure of British industry is not, however, self-generating. The government across the 1980s aided restructuring directly. As Gurr and King (1987) point out, it was political choices which left some cities to decline and others to stagnate. There is nothing inevitable or natural in permitting market forces to decide the fate and futures of UK cities. In addition, government activity aided certain sectors of industry and certain geographical areas indirectly, with, for example, the case of the financial services sector which was given a considerable boost by the government's programme of privatisation. The various privatisation programmes resulted in short-term gains for some investors, as well as wider share ownership, blurring traditional class divisions and drawing larger numbers of the electorate into the world of enterprise and finance.

However, as the concept of hegemony implies, the Thatcher governments' programme operated on more than simply the economic plane. Ideological change is more than a mere byproduct of economic change, in that the government sought to put moral and political values on the agenda in an overt way, opening up debates about values which had been seen as virtually beyond politics in the period of social democratic consensus. Few areas of social relations were left untouched by this new discourse and leisure proved to be no exception. Individualism (or the emphasis on the individual within the family unit) was used in justification of the reduction of welfare provision, and of policies such as the placing of those in institutional care within the community. The state was no longer to be the final arbiter and guarantor of income support in old age. The shift away from statutory state provision, represented for instance in community care initiatives, introduced a tension in that because of traditional gender roles 'community care' usually means 'care by women', and yet flexible employment of women was seen as one of the major changes in employment patterns which would aid economic regeneration.

Law and order and the strong state were also key ideas in the government's ideological programme which were used to justify the considerable strengthening of police powers, and the protection of police pay. The legitimation crisis of the state in the 1970s and 1980s found its expression most clearly in the importance of race and race relations on the political agenda. Throughout the 1980s there was growing racism and racist violence within inner-city areas. Positive discrimination to redress disadvantages experienced by racial minorities became unfashionable as a policy option, and good race relations were seen to demand tighter controls on immigration and growing fears that multiculturalism would dilute the English tradition and heritage (Thrift, 1989). This appeal to nationalism which invoked such a strong positive reaction from the electorate following the Falklands conflict was used to justify the position taken by Mrs Thatcher in, for example, her Bruges speech and her subsequent resistance to joining the European Monetary System.

However, the conflicting ideological messages of Thatcherism (of the strong state and the free economy, and the freedom of the individual and the return to 'traditional family values') were not solely to be communicated by the medium of political pronouncements but also through, for example, the reshaping of the education system. A range of initiatives were taken in this field in the 1980s, such as the 'enterprise in the curriculum' scheme designed to infuse entrepreneurial approaches into higher education courses, and the development of a core curriculum with, for example, its attendant encouragement to study 'British history', and the denigration or marginalisation of critical areas of social analysis (in for instance the restructuring of the Social Sciences Research Council, and attacks on Peace Studies). The significance of ideology in establishing a new hegemony was clearly, therefore, not lost on the Conservatives in the 1980s.

Table 7.1 presents an idealised form of the Fordist–post-Fordist regimes of accumulation and their associated modes of social regulation. The first four headings relate to the 'industrial' dimensions of the distinctions drawn in the literature. The next two relate to the different cultures and concepts of citizenship, while the remaining headings contrast the nature of local–central relations, of local government and of leisure policy under the respective regimes.

Table 7.1 *Ideal typical representation of the Fordist/post-Fordist distinction and its implications for local government leisure policy*

	Fordism	Post-Fordism
ECONOMIC RELATIONS		
Manufacturing/markets	Mass production Deskilled labour Mass consumption	Flexible production Skilled labour Market niches
Organisation types	Mechanistic, 'tall', bureaucratic	Organismic, 'flat', flexible
Management type	Corporate management, centralised control	Deconcentration, autonomous roles to section/division managers within organisations
POLITICAL RELATIONS		
Politico-economic system	Corporate policy-making, involving business, unions, and government	'Strong state, free economy'
Central–local relations	Local responsibility for service provision; central responsibility for economic planning	Service provision, taxation levels, economic development, centrally decided
Local government	Large-scale, bureaucratic, corporate, policy-making	New flexible forms of management and control
CULTURAL RELATIONS		
Social impacts	Worker alienation	Two tier workforce, 'core' and 'peripheral'
Dominant culture	Welfarism	Enterprise culture
Rights of Individual	Universal rights of citizenship	Dual system; consumer rights, and 'safety net' welfare provision
LOCAL GOVERNMENT LEISURE POLICY		
Orientation of leisure professionals	Bureaucratic, liberal welfare professional	Entrepreneurial, 'industrial' professional
Leisure policy emphasis	Social democratic, leisure as a right	Leisure as a tool of economic (or social) regeneration
Leisure policy rationale	Largely social with some economic benefits (externalities)	Largely economic with some social benefits

As we have seen, the ideological agenda of Thatcherism saw as central the need to break down welfare dependency and to instil entrepreneurial spirit. Rights of citizenship were to be replaced by consumer rights since commercial organisations were seen as responding to dynamically changing needs more quickly, efficiently and ultimately effectively. Large-scale bureaucratic provision whether in production (the nationalised industries) or in consumption (public sector health, education, housing, leisure services) were regarded as invariably inferior. The inevitable consequence of such a move towards private provision for such services is that those who could not afford to take advantage of these more flexible forms of commercial provision would be reduced to receipt of a residual, low-level, safety net form of state provision. The divisive nature of post-Fordist regimes is evident in the deepening divisions between core and peripheral workforces, between affluent and depressed regions, and within cities.

The post-Fordist city therefore requires a very different form of local government strategy and central-local relations from that implied by the social democratic structures of Fordism. Under Fordism there was a tendency to separate production concerns which were dealt with predominantly by central government through corporatist structures, and consumption issues which were largely consigned to local (though not necessarily pluralist) politics, or to quangos. This has given way to a much greater concern with controlling local spending levels, local service delivery structures, and aspects of local planning. Local government itself was encouraged to scale down its activities, to divest itself of some responsibilities, and became much more tightly constrained. In this new environment local government professionals, particularly in the leisure sphere, are more likely to adopt a view of efficiency and effectiveness which draws from the ideology of the industrial professions (accountancy, marketing) than the liberal welfare professions.

The disintegration of social democracy impacted upon central government policy on the leisure quangos in the 1980s. The Sports Council's role, under the Thatcher and Major governments, far from promoting access to recreation as a right of citizenship gave way to an emphasis on a residual social policy role in the inner city and a health promotion role. The Arts Council was not to be seen as a politically disinterested body promoting critical evaluation of the nature of life in contemporary Britain, but was to be charged with weaning arts organisations onto commercial sponsorship. The Countryside Commission's position in the 1980s was also marginalised by the granting of quango status, reducing its opportunities to defend recreation or conservation interests from within government. The restructuring of the Nature Conservancy Council and its responsibilities was viewed by many as a direct attempt to dilute conservation policies which interfere with producer policies. Local government was no longer to be the arbiter of, and provider for, the 'community's every day needs'. It was central government which was to determine the spending needs of local authorities and distribute the nationally determined business rate. Within this context the aims of leisure policy more generally shifted from a dominant emphasis on achieving social benefits, to one which stressed an economic rationale for leisure policy.

The Thatcher era may have ended at the beginning of the 1990s, but the influence of Thatcherism was still clearly evident across the decade. This is not simply because many of the institutional changes invoked under Thatcher remain in place (e.g. trade union reform, the stringent controls on local government, and the introduction of market mechanisms), but also because the Major administration, while modifying the style of government, continued many of the policy programmes begun under Thatcher. Even the policy themes which were most publicly associated with the demise of Mrs Thatcher as Conservative leader, the poll tax and Europe, were areas in which a clean break from Thatcherism was not sought. This was evident in the struggle to exclude aspects of the Social Charter from the Maastricht Treaty and the opposition to the imposition of a single currency, aspects of the Major government's approach to Europe, and in the new Council Tax retaining the element of personal responsibility of the Community Charge which it replaced, with those in areas of high-spending local authorities being directly affected by higher taxation. Thus the impact of Thatcherism had, in an important sense, defined the strategic, post-Fordist relations which were to exist in post-Thatcher government throughout the 1990s, and in particular the strategic relations between local and central government.

The Blair government in its first three years in office up to 2000, seemed also to be convinced of the need to keep in place many of the principal elements of the Thatcher programme for constraining trades unions, fostering business interests and suppressing public expenditure demands, though, in the leisure field, it did reinstate the rhetoric of sport for all, and did place access and social inclusion on the agenda. At the time of writing, the government had also just announced a doubling of central government support for sport and for the arts. This was seen as part of a not uncommon strategy of relaxation of public expenditure targets in the approach to a general election (which would have to be held by 2002). However, the reality up to 2000 had been one of tying down public expenditure, and limiting Lottery support (by adding new demands on Lottery resources such as the New Opportunities Fund). Thus this constituted a moderation, rather than replacement, of the market-based approach of its predecessors.

Post-Fordist local government and leisure policy

The response of local authorities in leisure policy terms, as in other policy areas, to economic and political restructuring, should not be seen as an automatic consequence of the restructuring process. Restructuring can be resisted, promoted or reshaped in varying degrees by local government, and it is important therefore to identify the strategic choices available to local authorities, and to explain why, in specific contexts, particular strategies have been adopted. Significant differences have emerged within and between local governments as to the appropriate direction of leisure policy and these can perhaps best be characterised under three main headings: left Fordist strategies, left post-Fordist strategies, and right (or mainstream) post-Fordist strategies. We will consider each of these before going on to review how each approach is evident in turn in the history of leisure policy in a single city, Sheffield, over the period from the reorganisation of local government in 1974 to the beginning of the new century.

'Left Fordist' strategies of resistance

One of the problems local government had during the 1980s while defending local services in the social democratic mould, was that these welfare services tended in many instances to reinforce, rather than to redress, certain forms of inequality. These forms of inequality were features not simply of services delivered (since in many instances the disadvantaged were underrepresented among users of services), but were also reproduced by the ways in which local government organisations operated, with hierarchically ordered structures dominated by white, male, middle-class professionals and incorporating Taylorist control of an alienated workforce. Nevertheless, left Fordist strategies sought to oppose the attack on welfare services and Keynesian planning by resorting to, or modifying, traditional Fordist approaches. In terms of economic development, for example, Geddes (1989) cites the West Midlands Enterprise Board as adopting a typically left Fordist strategy since it sought to combat deindustrialisation by substituting public sector capital for 'missing' private investment.

In the leisure sphere, however, perhaps the most obvious form of 'left Fordism' was in the planned response of a number of authorities to the requirement to put leisure services out to competitive tender in the early 1990s. A typical Fordist strategy here was to construct tendering packages which were so large that it was unlikely that any commercial concern would have the resources to compete effectively to win the contract or meet its requirements. Where virtually the whole of a local government department's work was put out to a single contractor, the existing council management was likely to retain this work. Although winning the contract may place on management the requirement to achieve a specific return on investment, management practices in respect of the workforce were unlikely to be significantly altered. Indeed, management was likely to have both to cut costs and to generate increased revenue in ways which were likely to damage the interests of both the workforce and the less-affluent market segments served by leisure services. Thus the strategy of constructing large-scale contracts to stave off commercial interest, even where it was allowed by the Secretary of State (who had to approve such tenders documents) was likely to reinforce existing inequalities in welfare service provision.

'Left post-Fordist' strategies and leisure policy

The rejection of a traditional social democratic model of the local state as neither efficient nor democratic led some members of the left to adopt a more positive approach to the opportunities offered by post-Fordist regulation and accumulation. The Greater London Council's challenge to Thatcherism was particularly influential here

in inspiring alternative agendas to that framed by central government. In particular, the cultural industries strategy of the Greater
London Council generated considerable interest on the left, in cities
such as Sheffield and Manchester.

The thinking underpinning this approach to development was
influenced by critical theory in the tradition of the Frankfurt School
(particularly Adorno's aesthetics) and the analysis of the political
economy of the culture industries undertaken by Garnham (1983)
on behalf of the Greater London Council. Because ownership in the
cultural industries in terms of both production and distribution is
highly concentrated, these industries have been dominated by the
production of mass products, and cultural diversity and critical art
have been stifled. The aim of municipally provided training, production and trading opportunities in the cultural industries was therefore to foster opportunities for cultural minorities, particularly
those disadvantaged by race, class or gender, without the market
requirement of the immediate adoption of mass appeal. However, as
Garnham argues, market survival should be an important goal for
the groups supported, and the traditional public sector approach of
providing continuing revenue subsidy should be abandoned. This
strategy is post-Fordist rather than Fordist in that it provides
resources for disadvantaged groups without seeking to manage or
control those resources directly through managerialist methods, and
because it represents public investment not as a replacement for the
private sector, but as a stimulus for new forms of market niching.
Examples of left post-Fordist strategy were rare, even in the mid-
1980s before the demise of the anti-rate capping campaign. Where
they were evident, they might co-exist with economic regeneration
strategies of the right in the same authorities.

A further element in left post-Fordist thinking is the recapturing
of city space through cultural development of unused city areas
(Bianchini, Fisher, Montgomery and Worpole, 1991; Chambers and
Curtis, 1983). Following the experience gained in Western European
cities, particularly in Italy with the staging of feminist torch-lit
processions to 'reclaim' certain areas of the city, and the 'estate
romana' promoted in Rome by the PCI (the Italian Communist
Party) administration, there has been a realisation on the left that
cultural animation and development can bring night life to under-
used city centres, rendering them potentially safer, particularly for
women, to use at night (Bianchini, 1989). This approach was evident

in Glasgow's campaign to redress its reputation as a city of macho violence, drunkenness and poverty. Glasgow Action was a public–private coalition which sought to update the city centre environment, to improve the image of the city, and to develop Glasgow's tourism potential. The first of these aims represents an element of left post-Fordism, using the reconstruction of the city to challenge the spatial expression of oppressive structures.

A third aspect of left post-Fordism is evident in the attempts of a number of Labour-controlled authorities to introduce decentralisation of service decision-making and delivery. Decentralisation was adopted by the left as a means of overcoming problems of insensitivity to local needs and alienation of the workforce in large-scale bureaucratic local government organisations. The benefits of decentralisation were said to be a more flexible response to local needs, greater opportunity for community involvement, and the generating of opportunities for the workforce for job enrichment, involvement in decision-making and reduced alienation from the public. Among the more publicised decentralisation schemes in respect of leisure were those developed in Hackney, Middlesborough and St. Helens in the mid-1980s. However, though the thinking behind these approaches may have been influenced by a radical critique of the professions, the practice of design, implementation and control of decentralisation was dominated by professionals, the top tier of such local government organisations not having been decentralised. The 'dispersal' of the workforce may have made the organisation of labour more difficult but the dominance of decision-making by professionals remained (Hoggett, 1987). In a sense, then, decentralisation, despite the intentions of Labour politicians, may have represented a managerialist tool strengthening professional autonomy (Geddes, 1989).

'Right post-Fordism' and leisure policy

The momentum of post-Fordist strategies, in public sector leisure services as elsewhere, has of course received greatest support from the New Right. Flexible units of production were encouraged through the introduction of compulsory competitive tendering, of urban development corporations, and of local management of schools. These units of production broke with the corporate management approaches of the early 1970s and mirrored management styles introduced in the private sector (Peters, 1987, 1993; Peters and Austen, 1985; Peters and Waterman, 1982; Quinn, 1980). Thus in many instances, even where local authorities won their own contracts to manage existing services, they would do so through new mechanisms such as management boards (analogous to boards of directors) with managerial autonomy to act within the parameters laid down by the contracts concerned.

Locally managed schools were given control over education facilities outside school hours, a valuable leisure resource in many communities. Urban Development Corporations were organisations freed from the constraints of local democracy to plan (through meetings which initially could be held in camera) the future of the areas under their control. Development Corporation plans invariably included significant leisure elements, particularly when such elements implied economic development. Thus London Docklands and the Merseyside Development Corporations used waterside leisure developments to render housing attractive to an affluent market, and as an incentive for capital investment in profit-making facilities, as well as facilitating direct investment in profit-generating leisure facilities such as the Docklands Arena. Consequently, such bodies were restructured and populated with 'right minded' individuals essentially committed to a new discourse about economy and efficiency rather than social effectiveness. The work of Myerscough (1988) in relation to the arts, and the Henley Centre (1986) in relation to sport, suggests that aesthetic and social concerns had given way to these concerns of economy and efficiency, even in public sector arts and sports subsidy.

Much cultural provision in cities, by the early 1990s was a function of policy-makers' assumptions about the nature of industrial location decisions for the new service industries. Whereas manufacturing industry traditionally had had to locate itself close to sources of raw materials or skilled labour, the new service industries, it was assumed, were able to locate in cities which would provide the cultural infrastructure likely to attract and retain geographically and socially mobile core workers, such as financial services and information technology personnel. Allied to this strategy of facilitating the recruitment of key personnel to the new industries was the development of an infrastructure for tourism, generating business opportunities for small and large-scale capital in, for example, hotels and themed attractions. In Bradford, for example, the refurbishment of the city centre incorporated the development of the National Museum of Film and Photography (with an estimated annual attendance of 750 000), the renovation of the St George's Hall (a major concert venue), the modernisation and redevelopment of the Alhambra Theatre, together with proposals to develop the West End area of the city. The West End proposals included a major private investment in a tourist facility, with discussions, for example, focusing on an 'electronic theme park' or adventure facility.

The Bradford example is an interesting one since it was an authority which had not only been subject to changes in party control during the period of redevelopment, but also the Conservative group which assumed power in 1988 was one dominated by a new right leadership. In fact the Conservative administration in the city introduced one of the most highly publicised programmes of radical cuts in jobs and spending in 1988, but continued to support the programme of cultural provision as broadly developed under previous administrations controlled by both Labour and Conservative parties. There were different nuances of policy; for example some members of the Labour group originally sought to use the West End development to celebrate the city's multicultural background by incorporating an eastern bazaar into the new shopping element of this development. But the plans of both political parties for restructuring of the city in other respects were remarkably similar. In Liverpool also, following the disqualification of the majority of the Labour group, its successor cooperated with the Merseyside Development Corporation in the redevelopment of the city's cultural facilities including the Albert Dock project, and the development of a tourism package based on the city's pop music heritage.

Although by the late 1980s economic development constituted the major new state interest in leisure; consumption or service provision issues were of significance in a post-Fordist scenario. The dislocation implied in restructuring the accumulation regime means that some care must be taken to provide for those who had lost out in the restructuring process. Provision for sport and recreation had traditionally been seen as a means of reinforcing social order (see Chapters 2 and 3). The continued financing by the Sports Council and its successor bodies of schemes such as Action Sport in the early 1980s and Sports Action Zones in the late 1990s, during times of pressure on public sector service budgets reinforces the notion that this is an important function of leisure policy. Thus a two-tier notion of leisure provision was fostered, with local authorities encouraged to either sell off facilities or to run them in ways more akin to commercial operations, while at the same time making residual provision in areas of high social need.

Leisure policy in Sheffield: the journey from left Fordist to right post-Fordist strategy

Sheffield is an interesting context within which to review policy change. It is a city whose political and economic roots lay in the steel industry, and the Labour Party had had control of the City Council for all but a very brief period from the 1930s until 1999. Over the period from 1974 until the end of the 1990s, there were major shifts both in the nature of the local Labour Party and in the nature of the local economy. In the period from 1974 to the beginning of the 1980s, Sheffield was controlled by a 'traditional' Labour group on the Council, generally older, male members, drawn from predominantly manual occupations and often with a background in the trade union movement (Seyd, 1990, 1993).

This group, which we will describe as 'Traditional Labour' was supplanted in terms of its leadership of the local Labour Party by a group of younger members, generally with more experience of higher education and of white-collar roles whose prominence was symbolised in the capturing of the Council leadership by David Blunkett. The rise to prominence of this group reflects similar trends in other British cities (Gyford, 1985). In Sheffield as elsewhere, this group was referred to as the New Urban Left. The emergence of this new type of Labour politician was contemporaneous with the decline of the steel industry as an employer, from which Labour traditionally had drawn much of its support. In 1971 almost half of the workforce was engaged in manufacturing industry, but this had fallen to 24 per cent by 1984, with job loss in the metal-based manufacturing sector between 1981–84 being double the rate for the UK generally (Sheffield City Council, 1984).

The New Urban Left which sought to foster a 'radical' edge to local policy was itself supplanted by a group (which we shall term 'Labour Modernisers') in the later 1980s which sought to put an end to antipathetic relationships with local business and to establish partnerships with industry. This approach was based on the realisation that government acting alone, especially local government, could no longer be expected to achieve significant political and economic objectives, and thus a system of local governance which brought together in partnership a variety of public, private and third-sector interests together with local government would be essential in order to achieve meaningful change.

These three groups, Traditional Labour, the New Urban Left and the Labour Modernisers who succeeded one another in dominating the controlling Labour group in Sheffield across the 1970s, 1980s and 1990s, tended to reflect each of the three strategies we have outlined.

Left Fordism: a strategy of resistance to the rolling back of the state

As we noted in Chapter 2, the reorganisation of local government in England in 1974 heralded a rapid expansion of public sector investment in sport and leisure. However, during the 1970s, in contrast to other local authorities, the Traditional Labour Group in Sheffield sought not to expand its stock of sports facilities. Provision was very much 'community oriented', with facilities concentrated in many traditional working-class housing areas but heavily reliant on an ageing stock of sports facilities (Sheffield City Council Recreation Department, 1984; Taylor, 1990).

The generic concerns of the local authority were with maintaining social service provision, sustaining low charges for municipal services, including public transport, and protecting public service employment in the face of attacks from central government on local government spending levels. As a consequence, sport and some other forms of leisure provision were de-prioritised. Furthermore, the dominant mode of delivery of council services in the city was through local government departmental bureaucracies with little wider involvement of voluntary organisations in the city. This was a common feature of service provision not simply in Sheffield but in most of the large-scale local government units established in the reorganisation of local government (Hambleton, 1988). As a consequence of this approach to service delivery, provision was seen as inefficient (because of bureaucratic waste) and ineffective (the most disadvantaged groups in society were not well-targeted by such provision). This was as true in sports provision as it was in other service areas (Audit Commission, 1989). Thus in Sheffield, leisure services were seen as low in priority and ineffectively delivered (Taylor, 1990).

In 1976, the first years for which comparative data are available for the reorganised local government system, Sheffield, with 14 swimming pools and three sports halls spent a total of £1.85 per head of population on indoor sport and recreation, ranking 27th out of 36 metropolitan districts in England (CIPFA, 1976). By contrast, in the same year it spent £1.61 per capita on cultural services, ranking second equal. This level of cultural expenditure reflects the city's traditional commitment to improving civic intellectual capital, which had left it with a heritage of traditional museums, theatres and art galleries, many of which also dated from the previous century. As the figures for 1980/1 provided in Table 7.2 indicate, the situation had changed little by the end of the period of Traditional Labour control.

In the later 1970s, Traditional Labour had opposed central government's attempts to squeeze local government expenditure, and the Sheffield Labour group under New Urban Left leadership in the early 1980s pursued this policy aggressively. As central government introduced more and more legislation to curb local government spending, Sheffield City Council sought ways to circumvent this legislation and to continue to resource local services and public sector employment. This eventually brought the City Council into direct confrontation with central government as it refused to set a budget in line with the legal limits introduced by the Conservative government. Faced with the threat of personal bankruptcy for local councillors, the Council eventually backed down in 1985 and resistance to central government's reduction of local government financial resources and policy powers was effectively ended in Sheffield (Stoker, 1991).

Thus, in general, the strategies and outcomes of this period were negative in relation to investment in sport. In the period of control by Traditional Labour, the implicit strategy was avoidance of the opportunity costs of investing in sporting or other infrastructure, focusing instead on investment in core social services, and resistance to cuts in services, public sector employment and local systems of

Table 7.2 *Comparison of Sheffield expenditure on sport and culture with all Metropolitan districts for selected years, 1980/1–1991/2*

	Net expenditure on indoor pools		Net expenditure on indoor sports halls/leisure centres with and without pools	
	Sheffield	All met. districts	Sheffield	All met. districts
1980/1				
Total expend (£000)	1 046	24 895	562	14 418
per capita expend (£)	1.92	2.14	1.03	1.24
1982/3				
Total expend (£000)	1 246	29 709	665	22 251
per capita expend (£)	2.29	2.55	1.23	1.91
1987/8				
Total expend (£000)	1 740	37 899	1 851	50 720
per capita expend (£)	3.2	3.25	3.41	4.36
1991/2				
Total expend (£000)	1 267	38 779	6 695	104 497
per capita expend (£)	2.33	3.33	12.32	8.11

	Outdoor sports facilities		Cultural facilities (e.g. theatres, museums)	
	Sheffield	*All met. districts*	*Sheffield*	*All met. districts*
1980/1				
Total expend (£000)	29	3 187	1 242	11 380
per capita expend (£)	0.05	0.27	2.29	0.8
1982/3				
Total expend (£000)	38	3 123	1 706	16 310
per capita expend (£)	0.07	0.27	3.14	1.4
1987/8				
Total expend (£000)	380	6 947	2 579	29 298
per capita expend (£)	0.7	0.6	4.75	2.51
1991/2				
Total expend (£000)	1 318	11 501	3 034	50 047
per capita expend (£)	2.43	0.99	5.58	4.30

Source: CIPFA *Leisure and Recreation Statistics Estimates* (various years).

subsidy. However, although the New Urban Left group continued with the policy of opposition to government cuts, in other crucial respects, by the beginning of the 1980s, it had begun to drive policy in a different direction.

The New Urban Left: attempts to use restructuring positively

With the arrival of the New Urban Left on the local political scene from the early 1980s, there was a continued policy of opposing government cuts. However, the Traditional Labour focus on core social services, the protection of public sector employment and support for traditional industries was to be called into question (Benington, 1987; Sheffield City Council, 1983). The New Urban Left group sought new ways of promoting the interests of the local community. If economic restructuring could not be effectively resisted by governments, local or national, then how could that restructuring process be used positively to promote the needs of local people? The answer to this question favoured by the New Urban Left in Sheffield had few implications for sport but did signal important developments in respect of culture, when the Council, following the lead of the Greater London Council, developed a cultural industries strategy involving in particular the development of an Audio-Visual Enterprise Centre incorporating a municipal recording studio and video and film production capacity (Betterton and Blanchard, 1992).

The Council promoted cultural production within the local community with three principal rationales. First, the value thus implicitly placed on local culture (the culture of local communities and of disadvantaged groups) was intended as a boost to the morale of those groups, particularly those hard hit by the impact of the decline of the steel industry. Second, the cultural industries were part of the new service sector in which jobs were seen to be growing, and thus was a potential source of employment. And finally, by improving the cultural infrastructure of the city it was intended that it should become more attractive to inward investors. Thus within the leisure sphere, investment in the city continued with an emphasis on culture rather than sport. As Table 7.2 indicates, sports expenditure remained stubbornly low and little policy change was evident (Taylor, 1990). The cultural industries strategy itself was

Table 7.3 *Per capita expenditure on sport and recreation and on the arts excluding debt charges for Sheffield and for all Metropolitan districts*

	Indoor sport and recreation	Outdoor sport and recreation	Arts
1994/5			
Sheffield	£8.12	£9.96	£4.76
All Met Districts	£10.09	£11.42	£4.08
1998/9			
Sheffield	£5.36	£6.83	£2.82
All Met Districts	£8.32	£14.16	£4.14

Source: CIPFA (1995, 1998).

subsequently subject to criticism as providing too little impact either in terms of employment or in relation to the cultural life of the city, and with a change of political leadership, political enthusiasm was attenuated.

Right post-Fordist strategy: the World Student Games and city imaging – Labour modernisers seeking partnership with business

After the debacle of the Council's climbdown in its confrontation with central government, and with a deepening of the crisis of the steel industry and the continuing squeeze on local government finance, Sheffield's Labour politicians acknowledged that finance and other resources had to come from sources other than local taxation (which had been effectively capped by central government legislation) or from financial transfers from central government. Partnership with local capital provided one of the few ways forward. As the Labour Chair of the Finance Committee expressed it, most were initially reluctant to cooperate with business; there had been:

a continuing and underlying suspicion within Labour Group against developing too close a relationship with the private sector ... For many, if not all, Labour councillors, partnership was a marriage of convenience, even a shotgun bond, rather than the union of natural soul mates. (Darke, 1992)

The partnership process was facilitated by a change in leadership within the Sheffield Labour group as David Blunkett had departed to the national political scene, and leadership of the Council was taken up by Clive Betts who was associated with a much more pragmatic and less ideological approach to politics. Formalisation of partnership arrangements came in December 1986 with the establishment of the Sheffield Economic Regeneration Committee in the City Council's Department of Employment and Economic Development (Seyd, 1990; Strange, 1993). This committee brought together representatives of the City Council, the business community, trades unions, higher education institutions, central government agencies and local organisations. The aim of the group, as stated in the principal planning document it produced, *Sheffield 2000* (Sheffield Economic Regeneration Committee, n.d), was to develop a long-term economic regeneration strategy for the city, with a particular focus on the Lower Don Valley in which most of the old steel plants had existed and which was now largely derelict.

As part of the regeneration process and following the recommendation of commercial consultants that a flagship project was required to spearhead the drive for regeneration, the city developed a successful bid over the period 1986–88 to stage the 1991 World Student Games. This project, as described below, stemmed from the partnership process (business and civic leaders together put forward the bid to the governing body of the World Student Games), and further contributed to partnership activity. However, the Games were also the source of divisions which began to appear in the partnerships established as the Games approached.

If partnerships were to be the way forward and one of the new vehicles for partnership was to be the city's bid for the World Student games to be held in 1991, how was sport and leisure policy affected in this context? The staging of the Games had several objectives. First, it was intended to reorient the image of Sheffield from 'City of Steel' to 'City of Sport'. Second, the bid was to promote tourism in the city. Third, the use of partnership with business was thought likely to erode central government antagonism to the city and thus to improve the city's financial standing with central government. Fourth the Games were intended to generate a range of new and exciting facilities for local people to use after the Games, and which would allow in the post-Games era the staging of international sporting events. Fifth, the building of new facilities in the Don Valley would enhance the environment, given that the Valley had been decimated by the closure of steel-related plants and factories and was an eyesore, a large swathe of highly visible derelict land.

The policy redirection instigated by the Labour Modernisers had a profound effect on sports policy in a number of ways. It determined the strategy to be adopted which was in effect an event-led planning approach, focused on the requirements for staging the World Student Games (Foley, 1991; Roche, 1992), rather than one which began with an analysis of local needs. In tandem with this was a strategy in terms of management of sports facilities which involved the 'debureaucratisation' of sports services, with the formation of private companies and trusts to operate some of the facilities opened for the World Student Games in particular. The medium for achieving this strategy was partnership. The outcomes can be summarised under four main headings: financial; sports development; environmental; and political.

In financial terms there were significant hidden costs in running the Games. In November 1986, the City Council had approved a bid, believing that the cost of running the Games would be met by generated income, and the capital costs of the facilities would be met by government grants, charities and private sources (Foley, 1991; Roche, 1992). However, by 1988, new central government legislation constrained the City Council's capital borrowing and spending. The city faced a critical dilemma, and at the time estimated that at least £110 million was needed to develop the facilities for the World Student Games. A private trust was created to run the facilities and to access private funding. This private trust, the Sheffield Leisure and Recreation Trust (SLRT), was established in March 1988 to provide the facilities and manage their future use. The capital was raised through foreign bank loans with a 20-year repayment period (Seyd, 1993).

Subsequently, two subsidiaries of SLRT were established with different roles: firstly, Universiade (GB) Ltd to administer and raise finance for the Games, and, secondly, a joint public–private board, Sheffield for Health Ltd to manage the World Student Games and three of the major facilities (Ponds Forge Swimming Pool and Sports Centre; the Don Valley Athletics Stadium; and Hillsborough Sports Centre); the fourth major new facility, the Sheffield Arena was put in the hands of an American company, SMGI subcontracted to Sheffield For Health.

The World Student Games involved the largest sports facilities construction programme which had then been seen in Britain with a total cost estimated at around £180 million. Construction of the new facilities accounted for nearly £150 million, with £27 million required for the running of the event itself (Middleton, 1991; Seyd, 1993). Except for Sheffield Arena which attracted some commercial-sector investment, the rest of the construction was underwritten by the Council. By mid-1990 only £500 000 had been raised and the company Universiade (GB) Ltd was forced to cease trading and wind up with debts of nearly £3 million. Thus in June 1990 the city was compelled to take direct responsibility for the running of the Games.

As a result, the city's commitment to the World Student Games was criticised as a high-risk strategy, being financially questionable (Roche, 1992). It was also criticised as being the product of a lack of consideration of alternatives (Critcher, 1991). Due to the escalation of the facilities costs from £110 million in 1988 to £147 million, the payment of debt charges commenced in 1992 and was rescheduled to end in 2013, with every adult paying an additional £25 annually in local tax (Seyd, 1993). Table 7.2 shows that Sheffield's expenditure on sport had moved by the end of the 1980s to significantly above the national average, having trailed for most of the rest of the period. Although Table 7.3 suggests that Sheffield's expenditure reverted in the 1990s to below that of the national average, this is misleading in that the rescheduling of Sheffield's debt repayments and the ongoing revenue costs of running the new facilities are not taken into account in this budget heading because of the establishment of an independent trust to run the new facilities.

In political terms the strategy also appears to have been problematic. Labour's vote locally diminished significantly against the national trend, and though it may be difficult to attribute this wholly to the Games issue, this was certainly a salient and hotly debated issue. A group calling itself the 'Stuff the Games Group' campaigned heavily locally against the staging of the Games and had political support within the Labour Party as well as from other local community and political groups.

While the Games were financially a disaster for the city (council taxpayers will be paying £25 each in local taxes up to the year 2013 simply to service the rescheduled debt for building the facilities), and politically a problem for the Labour Group controlling the city, they did leave a legacy of facilities which have allowed the attraction of a programme of events of international sporting significance (Gratton, 1998; Kronos, 1997). In addition they had a positive effect on the environment, the sporting facilities in effect creating a sport and leisure 'corridor' through the Don Valley, the area of the city most affected by de-industrialisation. However, in terms of meeting the social needs of the local population the Games legacy has been problematic. The management of the new facilities was placed by the local authority in the hands of a division of a City Trust established for the purpose, namely Sheffield International Venues Limited. This Trust was, however, contracted by the local authority to meet certain standards of financial performance, but had no significant social goals specified by the contract. As a result of this, social goals were de-prioritised and contractual standards of financial performance given prominence. The policy of centralising swimming provision in a large city-centre facility of international competition standard has also radically affected those neighbourhoods which lost their swimming pool to permit this centralisation. As Taylor (1998) has shown, participation in swimming in the city has actually declined since the introduction of the new facility, against the national trend.

The overall outcome in terms of sport policy might be characterised, therefore, as a two-tier policy, with an increase in consumer rights for those who could afford to pay private sector or near private sector rates, with some lower-level welfare rights (e.g. subsidised sports development, use of more basic facilities) for others who do not have the financial resources to benefit from consumer choice. This two-tier situation is structurally represented in the organisational arrangements for sports facility management in the city in Figure 7.1. The management of prestige facilities and events (the shaded areas in the diagram) are operated by arms-length bodies such as Sheffield International Venues Ltd, reflecting commercial pressures and therefore charging much closer to market rates, while older facilities remain in the traditional management structure of the Leisure Services Department incorporating a lower level of provision.

It is ironic that Sheffield, a city regarded as having had an implacable socialist spirit, should preside over the construction of facilities which because of the financial context may be out of reach for a significant proportion of the local population. Right post-

Figure 7.1   *Management of sports facilities and services in Sheffield*

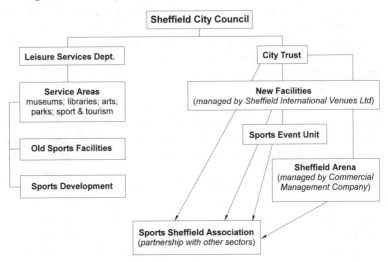

Fordism as a policy approach is normally based on the assumption that restructuring is inevitable and should therefore be hastened (getting the pain over quickly), but that there will be a 'trickle-down' effect in terms of benefits even to the lowest socioeconomic strata. The problem with this approach is that it is not clear that such a trickle-down process will always eventually operate.

Conclusion: some comments on local, national and transnational influences on leisure policy

We began the review of the politics of leisure policy in this book by promoting the argument summarised in Table 1.1, that the development of leisure policy can be effectively portrayed as a series of developmental stages. This chapter has sought to illustrate the nature of the contemporary stage in which public sector leisure policy now finds itself, in particular at local government level in Britain. It is worth emphasising, however, that the influences which mediate leisure policy are transnational, as well as national and local. Although such influences do not require (in some functionalist manner) particular policy responses, nevertheless nation-states with developed economies can be expected to feel many of the same pressures as those which we have identified as influential in the British context. Thus, for example, world recession may be reacted to differently by different political groups in different cities and countries, but will nevertheless have impacts across national boundaries, as will the investment and disinvestment decisions of multinationals, major cultural shifts, political changes and so on. We have stressed the impact and heritage of New Right thinking in fostering structural changes in the British economy and the implications which this has had for the forms of leisure policy promoted in Britain. It is worth, therefore, considering the nature of policy responses in leisure adopted by other nation-states with governments of differing ideological complexions. We will select for brief review here three European Community governments with contrasting political histories.

Dutch governments since the Second World War have tended to be coalition governments, and therefore supposedly less subject to the 'extremes' of left and right than majority, single-party governments. Notwithstanding this and the very different nature of the cultural context and historical development of Dutch society, the trajectory of Dutch leisure policy manifests some remarkable similarities with that of British leisure policy. Van der Poel (1993) describes a state of affairs in the 1950s and 1960s which has significant parallels to the traditional pluralism we have described in British leisure policy in the post-war period up to the mid-1960s, with government recognising the externalities which accrue from investment in sport and the arts, but avoiding direct provision. Instead, provision was to be fostered by funding through the 'confessional and non-religious pillars' (Catholic, Protestant and non-religious) voluntary organisations which, though now in decline, were a characteristic feature of the pluralist nature of Dutch society. Funding grew rapidly for the voluntary organisations from 14.5 million guilders in 1950 to 150.9 million by 1960, and 933.6 million by 1970 to 4477 million guilders by 1980.

During the 1960s and 1970s, van der Poel detects a shift towards the acceptance of leisure policy as an area of legitimate welfare provision, with, amongst other policy initiatives, the establishment of a new Ministry of Culture, Recreation and Social Work. Public spending on leisure increased across the 1960s and 1970s, and cultural policy was reshaped emphasising cultural democracy rather than cultural instruction as a key principle.

The 1980s and early 1990s saw a move away from the welfare-based rationale for leisure policy in the Netherlands. The Ministry of Culture, Recreation and Social Work was disbanded and responsibility for recreation (outdoor recreation in the Dutch context) lodged predominantly with a 'production' ministry, that of Agriculture and Fisheries, with aspects of cultural policy organised within the Ministry of Health, Well-Being and Culture. The scheme of public subsidy, administered by municipal government, for artists was abandoned in 1986 to be replaced by a smaller, central government-administered fund which aimed at subsidy for low-income consumers rather than subsidy of artistic producers. Although this continued as a programme of public subsidy, it represented a policy aim of extending consumer sovereignty to a wider constituency, rather than funding producers of art forms which have 'little or no market appeal'. However, the major growth area in government concern with leisure over the 1980s was in the field of tourism as a potential source of revenue. The concern with social tourism of the late 1960s was no longer visible in the policy priorities of government in the 1990s, and cities and central state have both focused on the economic benefits of public sector provision.

The example of the Netherlands is one of a predominantly conservative, Christian Democrat-led coalition (in particular in the 1980s) invoking a similar policy direction to that of its Thatcherite equivalent in Britain. The move from indirect state involvement through voluntary associations, to direct expenditure on leisure as welfare, to a concern with supply-side economics, which van der Poel illustrates, is one that mirrors the direction of policy change in Britain over a similar period. Perhaps more surprising, however, is the trajectory of leisure policy in two other western European countries, led by Socialist administrations.

The accounts of French leisure policy provided by Hantrais (1989) and by Poujol (1993) demonstrate the difficulties the Socialist administration experienced in its period in power from 1981 in introducing leisure policies which were led by social (rather than market) needs. The Socialist administration inherited a highly centralised policy system, one in which cultural, rather than leisure, policy was seen as significant. De Gaulle's Minister for Culture, André Malraux, had for example dismissed the significance of leisure and pursued an élitist policy of the democratisation of culture in the 1960s. Although Pompidou inaugurated a strong link between the presidency and culture with his personal support for the Pompidou Centre, the central state under the Fifth Republic had done little to promote state activity in the leisure sphere other than to reduce working hours, and, in the Fourth Central State Plan, to promote the construction of 'maisons de la culture', and 'maisons de la jeunesse'.

Amongst the first actions of the Socialist government were, however, the establishment of a 'ministère du temps libre', André Henry, in 1981, and the appointment of Jack Lang as Minister of Culture. In 1982 the socialists introduced legislation to decentralise responsibility for many aspects of planning and social provision, including that for leisure, and experiments were initiated in areas of urban problems aimed at countering the alienation of young people in such settings. Public spending was rapidly increased as France sought to spend its way out of the recession by increasing public expenditure, in particular on social projects. However, this Keynesian strategy practised by France in virtual isolation dramatically affected France's fiscal position and balance of payments, with the resultant threat of a run on the franc. In 1983, to forestall this economic disaster, the Socialist administration had to reverse its Keynesian strategy and impose stringent limits on public expenditure. The impact of this squeeze was felt at local level where the decentralisation of responsibilities was swiftly followed by policies of fiscal stringency. However, as had initially been the case in Britain, spending by local government on social and cultural facilities was not necessarily successfully inhibited. Other policies in the late 1980s also seemed to owe more to new right than to socialist thinking. The ending of the state monopoly on television and the commercialisation of television channels, together with a reduction in state investment in sport and the fostering (through fiscal incentives) of sports sponsorship as an alternative source of revenue for sport, led critics to claim that the government's approach was far from socialist.

One of the few areas of leisure to continue to receive growing central government funding was that of cultural policy. Cultural spending by central government more than doubled in the period 1979–83, and although its growth was less spectacular in the later 1980s it continued to remain high, with presidential works at the Musée d'Orsay, the Louvre Pyramid and l'Opéra de la Bastille accounting for significant sums in public investment. The rationale for such expenditure was less an aesthetic rationale than a reflection of right post-Fordist thinking. Mitterrand's intention was, at least in part, to demonstrate the forward-thinking nature of French cultural policy (Looseley, 1995; Wachtel, 1987), generating postmodern symbols of France's receptivity to new ideas and new values and promoting the image of a fertile ground for the knowledge-based post-Fordist industries. Nevertheless, the French government's wooing of Euro Disney demonstrated the state's willingness to compromise French culture and to modify French taxation, planning and employment law to attract inward investment.

In contrast to the French Socialists' initial attempts at introducing socialist policy reform through Keynesian spending programmes in the early 1980s, Felipe González's PSOE government following its initial election success in 1982 did not seek to achieve a socialist transformation of the Spanish economy. Rather, González's government sought to modernise the Spanish economy and to rid Spain of its isolationist stance. In these endeavours it met with some limited successes in the 1980s. In 1982 the PSOE inherited a growth rate of 1%, which they had boosted to 5 per cent by 1987; inflation was cut at the same time from 14 per cent to 5 per cent; foreign debt was reduced and the trade balance improved. However, the cost of this restructuring was to be felt largely in the form of unemployment, particularly among the young, with Spain recording twice the OECD average. Not only were there more unemployed people, but the socialists failed in their avowed goal of extending social security payments to more than half those unemployed, and by 1987 only 30 per cent of the unemployed were in receipt of such payments. In the early 1990s attempts to reduce in real terms the value of unemployment benefits met with considerable trade union resistance.

Under the Socialist government social spending did rise, from 3.3 billion pesetas in 1982 to 6.3 billion pesetas in 1987, but education spending fell behind military spending; a proposal for a national health service was abandoned in favour of a much less ambitious scheme; and previous policies such as withdrawal from NATO were dropped. Wage restraint agreed with the unions in the mid-1980s was beginning to be seen by trades unionists as a pointless concession since unemployment grew inexorably, and government schemes for the unemployed were limited in number and generally temporary in scope. By the early 1990s the PSOE had lost the support of the union movement in Spain, and was in 1992 faced with threats of serious industrial disorder. The economic priorities of preparing Spain initially for entry to the European Community in the early 1980s and subsequently for entry into monetary union, left the Socialist government sacrificing social to economic priorities, for which they paid the electoral price when defeated in the parliamentary elections of 1996.

In their analysis of the development of leisure and policy Spain, in González and Urkiola (1993) stress the importance of understanding the developments in Spain as influenced by a reaction to the period of Franco's dictatorship. During the dictatorship a unitary culture was stressed, with the promotion of leisure forms as either vehicles for affirming national unity or as providing an alternative focus for political energies. By the 1990s they cite in relation to sport evidence of the individualisation and segmentation of tastes, and increased concern with health and lifestyle, and a drop in demand for collective, community sports. The growth activities included water sports, cycling, jogging, adventure sports and outdoor pursuits. In the production of literature, music and the plastic arts, they identify an increasing transnational influence and a subsequent diminution of national cultural influences. These trends are fairly typical symptoms of the disaggregation of tastes identified in postmodern cultural theory.

Although encouragement to local government to increase sports provision through the construction of municipal sports centres (polideportivos) bore fruit in Spain in the form of increased provision, in many other respects the leisure policies promoted by the socialists reflected economic goals. In the cultural sphere, promotion of professional training and artistic education was motivated by the need to generate jobs to counter high unemployment levels. In the tourism field there was a concern to combat the erosion of the (Fordist) mass-market package holiday by diversification of the tourism product in Spain (e.g. folklore, gastronomy, archaeology and history). However, the most spectacular feature of Spanish leisure policy in the early 1990s was the promotion of city marketing through world-scale cultural events (World Expo in Seville, the Olympics in Barcelona, and Madrid, European City of Culture), all of which took place in 1992. The vast sums spent on these projects, when social projects had been faltering, illustrate the degree to which economic development goals had displaced those of social or community development.

If there are similarities in the pattern of leisure policy at the level of the nation-state between Britain and other EU member governments of differing political persuasions, the same case can be made for the limited studies which exist of sport and leisure policy at European city level. Studies of Birmingham (Arnaud, 1999), Grenoble (Dulac, 1996), Lyon (Henry, 1997) and Bilbao (Henry and Paramio-Salcines, 1998) suggest that urban entrepreneurial approaches are evident among local authorities of differing political persuasions, though with local variations and nuances evident in each case. These characterisations of policy change in different political contexts, illustrate how policy approaches have been adapted to prevailing economic circumstances. There is a real need for more detailed analysis in this area and for evaluating the interplay between economic, political and cultural change at the transnational as well as the local level (Henry, 1999).

Our primary focus in this book has, however, been the politics of leisure policy in Britain. In the British context, the response of local government to the pressures experienced across the last two decades is illustrated by the case of Labour-controlled Sheffield. The restructuring of the global economy with the attendant loss of traditional manufacturing industry, the need to secure alternative sources of local wealth creation and the exertion of ever-more effective controls on local government throughout the 1980s meant that the freedom for manoeuvre for local government had been much reduced. In strategic relations terms, the access to strategic resources had been reduced by changes in the global context beyond the control of local government itself. Indeed, with the progressive squeezing of financial resources, local authorities were left with few significant sources of additional public funding. Though European funding had grown in importance it did not compensate for the parsimonious financial settlements for local government provided by Conservative and Labour governments across the 1990s. The case study of Sheffield was not selected as necessarily typical (indeed, it is atypical in respect of leisure in that it was the first, and one of only four cities to gain the Sports Council designation of National City of Sport, but, nevertheless, the right post-Fordist approach exhibited in Sheffield is to be found in other prominent

British cities. However, the opportunities and constraints for policy change are often a product of the international rather than simply the local or the national context, and in respect of some policy domains it is only really feasible to achieve change through action at the international or transnational level (take, for example, policy on satellite broadcasting). Thus it is the discussion of transnational policy and the strategic relations and alliances which produce it that provides the principal focus for the final chapter.

8 Leisure Politics and Policy: Strategic Relations in the Global Context

To date in this book we have focused largely, if not exclusively, on the domestic context, and in particular the English context. Anglo-British political, economic and cultural history over the last few decades has formed the primary context for this discussion. In Chapter 7 we focused more broadly on the changing politico-economic context as political actors at national and city levels reacted to the decline of Fordist systems of economic organisation and social regulation, and promoted alternative leisure policy approaches. An ideal-typical representation of Fordist and post-Fordist scenarios was provided in order to highlight ways in which groups of actors have sought to foster change. The claim was made, not that the Fordist to post-Fordist shift was an inevitable consequence of structural changes and was therefore taking place ubiquitously, but rather the characterisation of an ideal-typical model of leisure policy in post-Fordist social regulation was employed as a useful benchmark against which to conceptualise and evaluate aspects of actual policy change which have taken place in particular contexts.

In Chapter 3 we argued that a strategic relations approach to the analysis of leisure policy invited empirical evaluation of how policy change (or stasis) was effected, by whom, and reflecting which sets of interests. The strategic relations view as developed by Jessop (1990c) was intended by its originator to provide a Marxist orientation which would avoid determinist notions that the state invariably acts in the interests of capital.

> State power is capitalist to the extent that it creates, maintains or restores the conditions necessary for capital accumulation in a given situation. It is non-capitalist to the extent that these

conditions are not realised. This view radically displaces our theoretical focus for the search for guarantees that the state apparatus and its functions are necessarily capitalist in all aspects to a concern with the many and varied contingent effects of state power on accumulation in specific conjunctures. (Jessop, 1990c: 354; quoted in Kelly, 1999)

Claims of pro-capital, class, gender, or race bias of the strategy and selectivity of a state are to be decided on the basis of empirically informed analysis, rather than built into theoretical premises. However, Jessop proceeds with his argument to suggest that although outcomes are contingent, they do ultimately tend to favour dominant group-related interests by virtue of the fact that those interests are able to exert hegemonic influence given their structural advantages which are the product of past history. Thus, as Kelly argues, this approach suggests that in capitalist states:

Policy is best understood as being moulded around particular hegemonic projects, as expressed mainly by dominant political parties, whose relationship to the dominant regime of accumulation is crucial. Therefore the nature of the state form, its particular structural and strategic selectivity, problematises its functions. Again there are no theoretical guarantees. Power and policy are executed through various contingent mechanisms that form part of the dialectic of structure and strategy. (Kelly, 1999: 111–12)

The achievement of hegemony is never complete and the effects of strategies can never be wholly predicted. Thus empirical analysis of strategies in relation to leisure (or any other policy domain) is required. Indeed, the extent to which commentators give emphasis to the incomplete nature of hegemony might be regarded as the fault line between neo-Marxist and neo-pluralist explanation.

Approaches such as regulation theory not only invite analysis of links between the state's role in social regulation and the economic spheres, but underline the fact the such relations are set in a *global* context. Thus the analysis which follows considers strategic relations at three levels, the local, the national and the transnational, with particular emphasis on the last of these.

Strategic relations and policy: the city and the nation-state

The 'demise' of the nation-state in the face of globalisation may of course be overstated. While it is the case that in economic terms a nation-state's room for manoeuvre has been significantly eroded by the globalisation of the economy, this does not mean that the role of the state in economic terms is insignificant. Even, for example, in cases such as the establishing of a single European currency, individual states may opt in or out of such arrangements. Economic sovereignty may thus in some cases be ceded, but it is ceded by nation-states themselves and they should not therefore be dismissed as insignificant actors. Legal sovereignty for a European Union member state may also be ceded in certain instances. Where majority voting takes place and a member state is outvoted, European Directives or Regulations may be imposed on all member states despite the opposition of one or more states. But here again, though in political terms bodies such as the United Nations or the European Union exert influence beyond national boundaries, they do so by virtue of the agreement of nation-states.

In cultural terms, the 'nation' remains a strong source of identity for many. Nevertheless, although we may argue that the influence (and sometimes the means of exerting influence) of nation-states have changed, they have not necessarily been wholly eroded. The ability of actors within the nation-states to influence policy may be regarded as simply being more clearly a product of a wider set of strategic relations which, while they may also allow more policy space at the local (particularly the city) level and the transnational (e.g. EU) level, these strategic relations also define the potential for nation-states to mark out their own particular approaches. Similar policy lines may be adopted by particular nation-states (see, for example, the cases cited in the preceding chapter) and may be fostered by similarities in the strategic context of each such state, but they are not 'required' by such contexts.

How then can we draw together these related strands in the context of leisure policy? We cite below three sets of examples dealing with local governance, the nation-state and the European Union. The first two levels are dealt with relatively briefly since they have been the subject of discussion in earlier chapters. Strategic relations at the European level of policy-making is treated rather more fully.

We turn first to the local level of policy-making. How can the shifts related to changing forms of social regulation be explained within a network of global–local strategic relations? In the last chapter we considered in some detail aspects of the 'local' with our case study of Sheffield. Here, shifts in the global economy, and in steel production technology produced a set of circumstances which fostered policy change. Strategic relations between local (Labour Party) and central (Conservative) governments, and an extended squeeze on local government expenditure, promoted a rift within the local Labour Party between 'traditionalists' who advocated an entrenched Fordist position, and 'modernisers'. Modernisers were local Labour politicians who advocated abandoning traditional policy goals and promoting partnership with local capital in the form of the City Chamber of Commerce, to promote Sheffield's candidacy for the World Student Games. Shifting strategic relations and strategic alliances resulted in the adoption of an urban entrepreneurialism which reflects a post-Fordist characterisation of leisure policy. Certainly key local actors were influential, but their potential to effect change, and the limits of what could be achieved, can be characterised as a feature of this configuration of relations.

At the national level, perhaps one of the best illustrations of strategic selectivity in relation to leisure policy is provided in the circumstances surrounding the publication of the Conservative policy document *Sport: Raising the Game* (Department of National Heritage, 1995b) in the run-up to the 1977 general election (which are described more fully in Chapter 3). *Raising the Game* was the first major policy statement on sport in Britain for 22 years. The importance of sport for key actors in the government was underlined by the fact that the Prime Minister himself chose to write a preface to the document outlining the significance of sport. The document and in particular the preface, are fairly unequivocally nationalistic, if not jingoistic. John Major for example writes:

Sport is a central part of Britain's National Heritage. We invented the majority of the world's great sports and ... Sport is ... one of the defining characteristics of nationhood and of local pride. (Department of National Heritage, 1995c: 2)

The document focuses policy interest in sport on two areas, youth and national performance, and indicates the then government's

intention of investing £100 million in the establishment of a
National Academy of Sport. The policy statement came at a time
when the Conservative Party had reached a low ebb of public
support and when the Party itself was manifesting deep and
electorally damaging divisions on the issue of Europe and the
erosion of national sovereignty by the growing power of the
European Union (Black, 1992). The traditional proximity of interest
between the interests of (particularly large-scale) capital and the
Party were undermined by the split in opinion in the business world
in respect of Britain's opting out of the Single European Currency.
Sport was one policy area in which the government could demonstrate, at least in symbolic terms, its affiliation to the protection of
national identity in a way which was likely to have a wide appeal.
Attempts to rectify the decline of Britain's national performance
would almost invariably attract cross-party support from among
the electorate.

Thus, although the policy paper was in part the product of the
personal predilections of the Prime Minister, it has also to be seen in
the light of relations within the Conservative Party between Euro-
philes and Europhobes; of the salience of those damaging relations
in the context of a pending election; of Labour's perceived (at least
by some Conservative commentators) weakness in this area in
relation to popular fears about the surrender of sovereignty; of
Conservative problems in denigrating European integration having
been signatories to the Maastricht Treaty on European Union; and
so on. This network of relations provides the context both enabling
and constraining the promotion of the sports policy statement
which is underpinned by and further reproduces a strongly nation-
alist ideology.

Strategic relations and leisure policy: the European Union

Beyond strategic relations at the local and national level, and their
impact on leisure policy, is their significance for policy at the
international or transnational levels. For this illustration we will
consider the nature of European Union intervention in sport, its
means and rationales for intervention and how such intervention
can only be fully understood in the context of the network of
relations within and between European polity and civil society.

Central to a concern with understanding EU intervention in any policy area is an understanding of the concept of subsidiarity. Vertical subsidiarity is the principle by which decisions are taken at the lowest level of government possible. Decisions about, for example, whether to teach in minority languages are a matter for local decision-makers, while policy relating to the monitoring and control of pollution can only really be effective if agreed at the transnational level since pollution produced in one country may potentially affect many others. Horizontal subsidiarity is the principle by which matters of policy are only decided by government if they cannot be effectively displaced on to the voluntary or commercial sector.

Which policy domains then lend themselves to 'governmental' intervention at the European or supranational level? There are some obvious candidates such as environmental policy or trade policy, and some contested areas such as defence and foreign policy. But what of cultural and leisure policy – at what levels are decisions best taken for this policy domain? There are some aspects, such as broadcasting policy, which clearly require supranational regulation because broadcasts cannot be restricted by national boundaries. Nevertheless, other areas of cultural policy, such as sport, at first glance seem likely to lend themselves to the application of the principles of vertical and horizontal subsidiarity. Such a suggestion is, however, at odds with the fact that the Maastricht Treaty defined a new competence for the EU in respect of culture, and its revision at Amsterdam in 1997 incorporated a Declaration on sport effectively laying down a marker for future definition of the EU's legitimate interest in sport. Thus, despite the Declaration, the formal powers for intervention in sport on the part of the European Union are limited, and the rationales for and means of intervention in this policy area therefore need to be clearly spelled out. The commentary which follows therefore identifies the five principal rationales for, and forms of, European Union intervention in sport.

Sport as trade

While the European Union may have no clear and unambiguous competence in matters of sport, it certainly does in respect of trade. Policy in respect of trade provides one of the *raisons d'être* of the European Community, and sport is an increasingly significant area of trading activity representing an estimated 3 per cent of gross domestic product for all Council of Europe member states. Intervention in the sports field in the early years of the European Community was restricted solely to that justified by policy relating to trade as the 1973 decision of the European Court of Justice (ECJ) in the Walrave and Koch case illustrates, when the court declared that:

> the practice of sport is subject to Community law so far as it constitutes an economic activity in the meaning of article 2 of the Treaty.

The economic rationale for intervention in sport also underpins the Heylens decision of the ECJ in 1986. Heylens was a Belgian football coach employed in France who was taken to the French courts for practising his trade without obtaining a French football coaching qualification. He did, however, hold a Belgian qualification which the ECJ accepted was of equivalent standing. In this case the ECJ overruled the French court's ruling that a specific French qualification could be required. This decision, although made on the grounds of restraint of trade, has clear implications for vertical subsidiarity in sport. 'Local' decisions in this case cannot be made which conflict with European Union decisions about qualification equivalence.

While the Heylens case illustrates the erosion of vertical subsidiarity, the Bosman case, which began in 1990, illustrates the clear erosion of horizontal subsidiarity in respect of sport. Professional sport could no longer, after Bosman, be regarded simply as a matter for voluntary or commercial-sector interests.

The Bosman case related two significant elements. The first was freedom of movement of professionals at the end of their period of contract with clubs, and the second to Bosman's successful appeal against a UEFA and French Football Association ruling which limited the number of foreign nationals playing in professional teams in domestic or European competition. This element of the Bosman appeal was based on the argument that such quotas of foreign players restricted freedom of movement of professionals within the EU. The Bosman ruling has important implications for the production of 'local' talent in that free movement of players may mean that the best and cheapest players flood local markets (Chelsea FC have famously played matches without a British player on their team sheet). If this is permitted, then the opportunities for potentially good English players to develop within the English Premiership will be greatly reduced. Thus, if an economic rationale is applied to professional sport (as implied by the Bosman ruling), then a likely consequence would be a major decline in the local production of sporting talent for some member states. A national or regional economy can, of course, survive without a capacity to produce cultural products such as cars, but can a national culture survive without a capacity to produce cultural products such as sporting stars, when sport is a strong feature of national identity?

If the rationale that sport is an industry like any other, and should therefore be treated in exactly the same manner, is that which underpins the Bosman case, a different type of argument has been mobilised in the revision of the *Television Without Frontiers* directive (1997). According to the directive, access via television to selected sporting events for the general population can be protected by national governments which may reserve, for free-to-air television, the broadcasting of a limited number of sporting events of particular national importance. In other words the rationale here is that sport is more than a mere product, and that therefore its broadcasting rights cannot simply be sold to the highest bidder. Sport is, in effect, part of a nation's cultural heritage and may be subject to protectionism. This provision of special treatment for sport stands in stark contrast to the thinking behind the Bosman ruling. There seems to be a contradiction here which the European Union may be forced to consider in the future.

Sport as a tool of economic regeneration

The development of the Structural Funds (including the establishment of the European Regional Development Fund, which was targeted principally at lagging and deindustrialising regions, and the expansion of the European Social Fund, which aimed to combat unemployment) have been used in the funding of sport and leisure on a quite significant basis (Bates and Wacker, 1993). Though there are considerable *social* gains for regions and target groups, the rationale for such funding has to be one of economic development in order to conform to funding regulations. The competitive position of lagging regions is deemed to be a product of a mix of factors including physical, service, education and cultural infrastructures, and regional policy. Thus, improvement of cultural infrastructure to make regions more effective in attracting capital is legitimately funded for economic development purposes. Nevertheless, there are significant potential gains claimed by applicants for much of this funding in respect of reducing inequalities.

However, as commentators such as Harvey (1989) and Lash and Urry (1994) point out, much of the sporting or cultural infrastructure developed for economic regeneration purposes, targets groups such as service class professionals who will need to be retained in lagging or deindustrialising regions, and the investment in such cultural provision may reinforce rather than challenge social inequities in leisure. The examples of Sheffield in the UK and Bilbao illustrate this point. Sheffield attracted ERDF funding for some of the facilities required for the World Student Games which it staged in 1991. The intention of the local authority, as we have seen, was to use the Games as a vehicle for reimaging the city and providing new 'state of the art' facilities. However, the Games provided a huge financial burden for the local authority, and though the facilities inherited have allowed the staging of a programme of international sporting events in Sheffield, prices for ordinary members of the community using these new sports facilities rose considerably, militating against their use by some of the least affluent groups in the city (Henry and Paramio Salcines, 1999).

Similarly, the Guggenheim project in Bilbao represented an attempt to put Bilbao on the global cultural map. Although redevelopment of the riverfront has attracted European funding, the scheme attracted criticism that local culture was being sacrificed to pander to the tourist market, and that cultural budgets on behalf of local governments were totally absorbed by the prestige project (Henry and Paramio-Salcines, 1998). Thus the use of sport and leisure for economic regeneration purposes is not unproblematic since it may well privilege the interests of the more affluent users.

Sport and social integration

Ironically, however, sport may be used as a tool to combat social and economic exclusion. Although the initial phase of development of the European Community was dominated by economic concerns to set up an area of free trade, a common market, the implications of this process for the social as well as economic exclusion of some of its citizens were well-recognised. Expenditure on sport as an aspect of combating social or economic exclusion has therefore developed over time.

A budgetary line in relation to sport was first inserted in the EC budget in the early 1990s in response to the expressed interests of members of the European Parliament (interview with John Tomlinson MEP, Chair of the EP Sports Intergroup February 1996). The budget represented a small amount, but was not without controversy. Initially its inclusion was rejected by the European Commission and only reinserted in the budget at the insistence of the European Parliament. The original sports budget incorporated the European Awareness Budget (to which we return below) and funds directed at young people and socially excluded groups, particularly disability sport. The budget was consolidated into the Eurathlon Programme in 1996, with broadly the same objectives. However, there were worries that there was no legal justification for expenditure on sport *per se*, since sport had not been incorporated as a competence in the founding treaties, and there was some concern on the part of officials that the justification of expenditure was rather tenuous. Apparently as a result of this, the Eurathlon Programme was abruptly discontinued in 1998, when a number of the European Commissioners came under investigation and subsequently resigned over other issues relating to inappropriate use of funds.

In the period 1995–97, some of the key actors in the European sports scene had been involved in lobbying member states and European Commissioners to establish a competence in the field of sport in the revisions of the Treaty on European Union at Amsterdam. The support for such a move was by no means universal. UEFA, for example, and some of the other European bodies representing professional sports were very wary, having been profoundly, and (as they saw it) adversely affected by the EU through the Bosman decision. This and issues such as the ban on tobacco sponsorship made a number of people in the sports world nervous about increasing the powers of the EU to intervene in sport. Nevertheless, the amateur sports group were broadly supportive. In the end the lobby was not entirely successful, a competence was not incorporated in the Amsterdam Treaty, but a Declaration on Sport was adopted which dealt specifically only with amateur sport, but which was seized upon by interested MEPs who subsequently called for a full review of the EU's role in sport (Pack, 1998). (A 'Declaration' is of lesser significance than an article. The latter defines the EU as having legal competence, in a policy field, the latter simply declares the EU's intention to act in particular ways.) However, even the inclusion of the Declaration at Amsterdam was only secured after the personal intervention of Juan Antonio Samaranch, President of the International Olympic Committee, with Chancellor Kohl. Samaranch was wheeled in by supporters of the Declaration to use his personal influence and standing; a deal was struck such that Chancellor Kohl would propose the inclusion of a Declaration and support it, but only if it was accepted without discussion by all parties to the Treaty.

Sport as an ideological tool

The role of sport in helping to construct a European identity was recognised by the European Union explicitly in the 1980s (Shore, 1993). By the 1980s it had become widely acknowledged that progress with the European project was likely to be impossible without a strong element of financial and political integration. Political integration itself could not be achieved without winning over the consent and the commitment of European citizens; that is, it could not be achieved without citizens of the member states relating to a European identity. This concern exercised the minds of the European Council of Ministers when it received the Adonino Report *A People's Europe*, in 1985. The report highlighted ways in which a cultural identity for European citizens might be developed, such as the adoption of a European anthem, a European Union flag, and the promotion of EU policy in the cultural sphere.

Among some of the ideas rehearsed in the Adonino Report were the establishing of a pan-European Games, the entering of a European Olympic team, and the provision of support for sporting events which promoted European identity. Some of the more radical ideas have not been acted upon but others have found their way into EU policy. For example, the EU has funded the establishment of sporting events such as a European Clubs Swimming Champion-ship, and supported the European Ryder Cup team (even though that represents more than simply the EU states). It also supported, during the 1990s, developments such as the European Yacht Race which was routed to join various European ports, and the extension of the Tour de France into other countries (Netherlands, Belgium, Germany, UK and so on).

This symbolic use of sport to 'unite' the territory, has precursors in the premodern and the modern eras, at the levels of the local and the nation-state respectively. In the premodern era marching or riding the bounds, for example, in Scottish border towns was a means of annually reasserting the extent of the boundaries of the township and expressing civic community. Similarly the Breton *pardon*, the tradition in Catholic parishes in Brittany of procession round the boundaries of the parish on the feast day of the saint after whom the parish church had been named, reaffirmed the sense of religious and political community of the parish. Phillip Dine has illustrated how in the modern era in the early twentieth century, the Tour de France was inaugurated partly as a means of asserting the unity of the French nation, formed as it had been out of diverse regions, sometimes with aspirations for separate identity (Dine, 1997). In the late modern or high modern period of the late twentieth century, it may be argued that the EU support for the European Yacht Race seeks to perform in symbolic terms much the same function, of publicly asserting a symbolic unity of a political entity. Indeed the funding of this event in the early 1990s came from a European Commission budget line entitled the European Awareness Budget.

Whether one accepts this assertion or not, it is difficult to deny that sport has an ideological function. Culture and sport and identity politics are intrinsically interrelated and there is a tension in the period of late modernity between its use in promoting national, supranational or local identities (Roche, 1998).

Sport as a tool of international relations

The use of sport by nation-states as a tool for cementing international relations is well-established from the Berlin Olympics of 1936 to the ping-pong diplomacy of Richard Nixon reestablishing relations with China. A number of nation-states employ sports development aid as part of a wider programme of international relations. For example, Britain in 1989 signed a Memorandum of Understanding with Saudi Arabia incorporating the provision of sporting advice as part of a wider deal between British Aerospace and the

Saudi Arabian government to supply military aircraft. UK Sport (formerly the Sports Council) also has a programme of aid for Southern Africa and Eastern Europe.

Although sport has been used by nation-states in such a manner, it is interesting to note that in the mid-1990s when Nelson Mandela visited Europe, members of the European Parliamentary Sports Intergroup sought to ensure that the provision of sport aid was included in a package to be discussed by representatives of the EU and President Mandela. Sport as a tool of diplomacy was clearly an issue for development for certain parties in the EU arena.

In contrast to the nation-state, then, the focus of leisure policy at the European level is even more clear on regulative approaches than on direct provision. The strategic relations here relate to the network of interests, alliances and counter-alliances which run across the political sphere and into the commercial and voluntary sectors of civil society. Powerful sets of interests are, for example, at play in the relationships emerging between sport and the media, and powerful forms of regulation are thus required to mediate or control these. The five areas of sport-related policy at the EU level cited above illustrate different aspects of the implication of strategic relations and alliances:

1. The Bosman case illustrates the ability of the individual to draw on wider structural configurations to challenge the hegemony of the sporting bodies (his club, the Belgian Football Association, UEFA and FIFA), while the Heylens case demonstrates the implications of ceding aspects of legal sovereignty by the nation-state. Bosman in particular casts into stark relief the relationship between the organisations of civil society and government, and of capital and labour. Officers of the Commission had entered into a 'gentleman's [sic] agreement' to accept the exceptional treatment which had previously been accorded to professional sports contracts of the type held by Bosman. The strategic alliance between the football authorities and the European Commission was essentially nullified by the legal context underwritten in the Single European Act which guaranteed the freedom of movement of workers, which, ironically, had been constructed with little thought given to sporting contexts.

2. The funding of sport and culture through the ERDF in Bilbao and Sheffield provides an illustration of how the availability of

European funds can be used to legitimate some visions of the city and its culture and to marginalise others.

3. While the Bosman case provides an illustration of the use of the legislative framework to 'control' the activities of voluntary and professional bodies in sport, the success of lobbying bodies in countering political opposition to the incorporation of the Declaration on Sport in the Treaty of Amsterdam illustrates how influence can flow in the other direction given an appropriate strategic context and intelligent use of tactical resources. Although ENGSO (the European Non-Governmental Sports Organisations) and EOC (the European Olympic Committee) were unsuccessful in persuading the Council of Ministers to include a competence for the EU in respect of sport in the Treaty, the inclusion of a Declaration may be seen as a 'foot in the door' in relation to achieving the longer-term goal.

4. The use of sport to generate European identity reflects the importance of sport at a symbolic level as well as the significance of symbolism in terms of legitimising aspirations towards greater political integration. Cultural relations can thus be of strategic significance in political arenas.

5. Finally the use of sport in international relations is clearly a means of opening up cultural flows which may facilitate the development of political and economic interests.

Thus at the European level, as at the level of the nation-state or the city, policy outcomes are contingent on actors' use of the wider strategic networks of relations within which they are implicated, rather than determined by the structural context. Nevertheless, the nature of the strategic context and the abilities of individuals and groups to draw from their positioning within it will both constrain and enable actors to achieve their goals.

Conclusion

What this book has attempted to do is to highlight the key trajectories of policy change in relation to leisure; to explore the relationship between such trajectories and core political ideas; and to highlight ways in which ideas about leisure and culture reflect broader aspects of social, political and economic context. Finally the book, and in particular this last chapter, has sought to illustrate how the direction which such policy trajectories take are a reflection not simply of strategic alliances, but of the resources available to groups of actors in the wider strategic context.

Although the broader trajectories of policy change are sketched out, there is inevitably an element of selectiveness about the *level of government* at which analysis is conducted, the *policy areas* selected and the *policy issues* discussed. In terms of the level of government at which analysis has been conducted, primacy has been given to national and local government in part because of the indirect responsibilities held at the European Union level for sport, and for pragmatic reasons of space. Tourism is also a whole area of leisure policy which is not given prominence in this book. This is not because tourism has a largely economic and a lesser cultural significance for some governments (although for some this is indeed the case), but rather, again, on the pragmatic grounds of retaining a tighter focus for the commentary. However, many of the ideas rehearsed in the book in terms, for example, of the use of leisure for economic development, to combat social exclusion or to pro-mote national and local identity, might have been usefully explored in the context of tourism. Writing at the end of 2000 one might well also have considered the significance of a policy issue such as the Millennium Dome to have attracted comment and analysis. As a project it is reflective of New Labour's propensity for embracing popular culture, for economic purposes, for hedonistic associations for the Party, and for the establishing of an appropriate emblem of the age, and it is also illustrative of the dangers of such approaches. Iconic though the Dome may be both as an image of the era and a reflection of the New Labour government's difficulties after a protracted honeymoon period, it is likely to be a transient feature of the leisure policy landscape.

What is not likely to be transient, however, is the significance of leisure as a policy domain. As the historical context provided in the earlier parts of this book sought to illustrate, leisure had clear economic, cultural and political saliency, and hence was a signifi-cant area of state activity in the emergence of modern industrial society. However, in the post-, late- or high modern context, with the decline of traditional modernist industrial structures and the reshaping of cultural boundaries, the salience of leisure as an area of policy seems set to grow given its place in the reshaping of economies and cultural identities. For cities, nation-states and for transnational bodies such as the European Union, leisure policy is significant: in *economic* terms it is important for local, national and European economies; in *cultural* terms it is important for local, national and even European identities; and in *political* terms leisure and culture provide the context of, and resources for, strategic battles in relation not only to leisure policy itself, but also to other policy areas (e.g. education, national sovereignty and so on). In such circumstances, leisure and cultural policy might be anticipated to assume a higher profile.

Guide to Further Reading

While the leisure studies literature has continued to burgeon since the appearance of the first edition of this book, leisure policy *per se* has received rather less attention, and even where materials have been produced they are perhaps most strongly concentrated in sports or arts policy. This broadly in the field of policy analysis in relation to sport Barrie Houlihan's work (Houlihan, 1991), and in relation to the arts (and the activities of the Arts Council) work by Hewison (1994) and Witts (1998) represent useful starting points. In relation to economic analysis of policy Gratton and Taylor (2000) provide material which has the rare mix of analytic depth and accessibility for the non-specialist in the discipline.

In relation to local government, literature on leisure policy tends to be fragmented and episodic, focusing on generic issues and their implications for leisure policy. The two key such policy initiatives in the period prior to and following the election victory of New Labour were Compulsory Competitive Tendering (Centre for Leisure Research, 1993; Coalter, 1995) (which arguably changed the face of local government service delivery in a range of service areas) and more recently Best Value (Williams, 1999). The contribution of the arts to urban regeneration (Griffiths, 1995; Williams, Shore and Huber, 1995; Wynne, 1992) and of sport and the arts to social inclusion (Department of Culture Media and Sport, 2000) or of sport to wider social, economic and political urban agendas (Gratton and Henry, 2001) also represent significant policy debates.

Analysis of policy at the transnational and comparative levels is also limited in volume. Bramham *et al.* (1993) provide a review of leisure policy in a number of European states, while Barrie Houlihan's (1997) comparison of policy in Britain, Australia, Ireland and Canada, though limited to sport, is a rare comparative study. Also in the sports field is a useful comparative analysis of sports legislation systems has been published by the Council of Europe (Chaker, 1999).

Much of the material cited above relates to policy rather than to politics (though clearly there is some overlap) and the literature on the *politics* of leisure continues to represent a relatively disparate field in which political analysis is often a secondary concern. There is of course some very useful and insightful analysis 'out there' on much of which this book has drawn, so that further references may be pursued in relation to topics of particular interest to the reader by reference to the appropriate section and the bibliography.

References

Aglietta, M. (1979) *The Theory of Capitalist Regulation: The US Experience* (London: Verso).

Alexander, S. (1990) 'Women, Class and Sexual Differences in the 1830s and 1840s: Some Reflections on the Writing of a Feminist History', in T. Lovell (ed.), *British Feminist Thought* (Oxford: Blackwell).

Allen, J. (1988) 'Towards a Post-industrial Economy', in J. Allen and D. Massey (eds), *The Economy in Question* (London: Sage).

Allen, J. (1992) 'Post-industrialism and Post-Fordism', in S. Hall, D. Held, and T. McGrew (eds), *Modernity and Its Futures* (Cambridge: Polity/ Open University Press).

Allison, L. (1994) 'Sport for the Best, Not All', *Guardian*, 29 September: 24ff.

Amery, J. (1946) *The Conservative Future: An Outline in Policy* (London: Conservative Political Centre).

Amis, K. (1979) *A Policy for the Arts?* (London: Centre for Policy Studies).

Andrew, C. and Goldsmith, M. (1998) 'From Local Government to Local Governance – and Beyond?' *International Political Science Review*, 19(2): 101–17.

Arnaud, L. (1999) *Politiques Sportives et Minorités Ethniques* (Paris: L'Harmattan).

Arts Council (1974) *Research and Information Statistical Reports*, (nos. 2–4) (London: Arts Council).

Arts Council (1984) *The Glory of the Garden: Strategy for a Decade* (London: Williams Lea).

Arts Council of England (1999) *Annual Report* (London: Arts Council of England).

Atkins, R. (1990) Open Letter to the Chairman of the Sports Council, December.

Audit Commission (1984) *The Impact on Local Authorities' Economy, Efficiency and Effectiveness of the Block Grant Distribution System* (London: HMSO).

Audit Commission (1989) *Sport for Whom? Clarifying the Local Authority Role in Sport and Recreation* (London: HMSO).

Audit Commission (1990) *Preparing for Compulsory Competition* (London: HMSO).

Audit Commission (1999) *Best Value Performance Indicators for 2000/2001* (London: Audit Commission).

Bachrach, P. and Baratz, M. (1970) *Power and Poverty* (New York: Oxford University Press).

Bacon, R. and Eltis, W. (1978) *Britain's Economic Problem: Too Few Producers* (London: Macmillan – now Palgrave).

Baggott, R. (1999) 'Reforming Welfare', in B. Jones (ed.), *Political Issues in Britain Today*, 5th edn (Manchester: Manchester University Press).

Bailey, P. (1987) *Leisure and Class in Victorian England*, 2nd edn (London: Methuen).

Bains, R. (1972) *The New Local Authorities, Study Group on Local Authority Management Structure* (London: HMSO).

Baldry, H. (1981) *The Case for the Arts* (London: Secker & Warburg).

Ball, M. (1989) 'Perspectives on the British Economy: Contemporary Social and Economic Change', in M. Ball, F. Gray, and L. McDowell (eds), *The Transformation of Britain* (London: Fontana).

Baran, P. and Sweezy, P. (1968) *Monopoly Capitalism* (London: Penguin).

Barlow, J. (1995) 'The Politics of Urban-Growth – Boosterism and Nimbyism in European Boom Regions', *International Journal of Urban and Regional Research*, 19(1): 129–44.

Bates, J. and Wacker S. C. (1993) *Community Support for Culture*, a study carried out for the Commission of the EC (DGX) (Brussels: European Commission).

Baudrillard, J. (1988) *Selected Writings* (Cambridge: Polity Press).

Beck, A. (1989) 'The Impact of Thatcherism on the Arts Council', *Parliamentary Affairs*, 42(3).

Beck, A. (1990) 'But Where Can We Find a Heineken?' Commercial Sponsorship of the Arts on Merseyside, *Political Quarterly*, 61(4).

Bell, D. (1960) *The End of Ideology: The Exhaustion of Political Ideas in the Fifties* (Glencoe: The Free Press).

Bellamy, R. and Warleigh, A. (1998) 'From an Ethics of Integration to an Ethics of Participation: Citizenship and the Future of the European Union', *Millennium-Journal of International Studies*, 27(3): 447 (23 pages).

Benington, J. (1976) *Local Government Becomes Big Business* (London: Community Development Project Information and Intelligence Unit).

Benington, J. (1987) 'Sheffield – Working It Out, an Outline Employment Plan for Sheffield City Council', *Local Government Studies*, 13(3): 103–4.

Benn, T. (1979) *Arguments for Socialism* (London: Penguin).

Benn, T. (1982) *Arguments for Democracy* (London: Penguin).

Betterton, R. and Blanchard, S. (1992) *Made in Sheffield: Towards a Cultural; Plan for Sheffield in the 1990s* (Sheffield: Sheffield City Council, Sheffield Hallam University, Yorkshire and Humberside Arts Board).

Beveridge, W. (1944) *Full Employment in a Free Society* (London: Allen & Unwin).

Bevins, A. (1994) 'Heseltine Changes Grants into Prizes', *Observer*, 29 May: 3.

Bianchini, F. (1987) 'G.L.C. – R.I.P.: Cultural Policies in London 1981–1986', *New Formations*, 1(1).

Bianchini, F. (1989) 'Cultural Problems and Urban Social Movements: The Response of the "New Left" in Rome (1976–1985) and in London (1981–1986)', in P. Bramham, I. Henry, H. Mommaas, and H. van der Poel (eds), *Leisure and Urban Processes: Critical Studies of Leisure Policy in Western European Cities* (London: Routledge).

Bianchini, F., Fisher, M., Montgomery, J. and Worpole, K. (1991) *City Centres, City Cultures* (Manchester: Centre for Local Economic Strategies).

Bigelow, B. (1997) 'The Human Lives Behind the Labels – The Global Sweatshop, Nike, and the Race to the Bottom', *Phi Delta Kappan*, 79(2): 112–19.

Black, C. (1992) 'Conservatism and the paradox of Europe', (pp. 54–74) in (ed.) Robertson, P. *Reshaping Europe in the Twenty-first Century* (London: Macmillan – now Palgrave).

Blackie, J., Coppock, T. and Duffield, B. (1979) *The Leisure Planning Process* (London: Social Sciences Research Council/Sports Council).

Blair, T. (1996) *New Britain: My Vision of a Young Country* (London: Fourth Estate).

Blunden, J. and Curry, N. (1985) *The Changing Countryside* (London: Croom Helm).

Boddy, M. and Fudge, C. (1984) *Local Socialism?* (London: Macmillan – now Palgrave).

Boje, D. M. (1998) 'Nike, Greek Goddess of Victory or Cruelty? Women's Stories of Asian Factory Life', *Journal of Organizational Change Management*, 11(6): 461 (21 pages).

Bourdieu, P. (1989) *Distinction: A Social Critique of the Judgement of Taste* (London: Routledge).

Boyer, R. (1986) *La Théorie de la Régulation: un Analyse Critique* (Paris: Éditions de la Découverte).

Braden, S. (1977) *Artists and People* (London: Routledge & Kegan Paul).

Bramham, P., Haywood, L. and Henry, I. (1982) 'Recreation Versus Vandalism: A Rationale for the Profession?' *Leisure Management*, 2(12).

Bramham, P. and Henry, I. (1985) 'Political Ideology and Leisure Policy', *Leisure Studies*, 4(1).

Bramley, P., Henry, I., Mommels, H. van der Poel, H. (1993) *Leisure Policies in Europe* (Wallingford: CAB International).

Brindley, T., Rydin, Y. and Stoker, G. (1989) *Remaking Planning* (London: Unwin Hyman).

Brohm, J.-M. (1978a) 'Sport: An Ideological State Apparatus', in J.-M. Brohm (ed.), *Sport: A Prison of Measured Time* (London: Pluto Press).

Brohm, J. M. (1978b) *Sport: A Prison of Measured Time* (London: Ink Links).

Brough, C. (1978) *As You Like It: Private Support for the Arts* (London: Bow Publications).

Brown, C. (1982) *Black and White Britain: The Third PSI Survey* (Aldershot: Policy Studies Institute/Gower).

Bruce, M. (1968) *The Coming of the Welfare State* (London: Batsford).

Burke, E. and ed. C. Cruise O'Brien. (1969) *Reflections on the Revolution in France* (London: Penguin).

Butler, J. (1990) *Gender Trouble: Feminism and the Subversion of Identity* (New York: Routledge.

Cabinet Office. (1998a) *Better Quality Services: A Handbook on Creating Public/Private Partnerships through Market Testing and Contracting Out* (London: HMSO).

Cabinet Office (1998b) *Service First: The New Charter Programme* (London: Cabinet Office, Service First Unit).

Caillois, R. (1961) *Man, Play and Games* (New York: Free Press of Glencoe).

Callaghan, J. (1990) *Socialism in Britain Since 1884* (Oxford: Blackwell).

Carr, M. S. Weir, S. (1986) 'Sunrise City', *New Socialist*, 41: 7–10.

Casanova, P. G. (1996) 'Globalism, Neoliberalism, and Democracy', *Social Justice*, 23(1–2): 39–48.

Castells, M. (1976) *The Urban Question* (London: Edward Arnold).

Central Statistical Office (1990) *Social Trends* (London: Central Statistical Office).

Central Statistical Office (1991) *Social Trends* (London: HMSO).

Centre for Leisure and Tourism Studies (1992) *The Nationwide impact of CCT in the leisure services* (London: Centre for Leisure and Tourism Studies, University of North London).

Centre for Leisure and Tourism Studies (1996) *A Survey of Local Authority Service Budgets in England and Wales 1995/6* (London: Centre for Leisure and Tourism Studies, University of North London).

Centre for Leisure Research (1993) *Sport and Leisure Management: Compulsory Competitive Tendering; National Information Survey Report* (London: Sports Council).

Chaker, A. (1999) *Study on National Sports Legislation in Europe* (Strasbourg: Council of Europe).

Chambers, I. and Curtis, L. (1983) 'Italian Summers', *Marxism Today*, July.

Champion, A. and Townsend, A. (1990a) *Contemporary Britain: A Geographical Perspective* (London: Edward Arnold).

Champion, A. and Townsend, A. (1990b) *Contemporary Britain: A Geographical Perspective* (London: Edward Arnold).

Charlesworth, K. (1996) *Are Managers Under Stress? A Survey of Management Morale* (London: Institute of Management).

Chase-Dunn, C. (1989) *Global Formations: Structures of the World Economy* (Oxford: Blackwell).

Christopherson, S. (1994) 'The Fortress City: Privatized Spaces, Consumer Citizenship', in A. Amin (ed.), *Post-Fordism: A Reader* (Oxford: Blackwell).

CIPFA (1976) *Leisure and Recreation Statistics 1976–7 Estimates* (London: Chartered Institute of Public Finance and Accountancy).

CIPFA (1982) *Leisure and Recreation Statistics 1982–3 Estimates* (London: Chartered Institute of Public Finance and Accountancy).

CIPFA (1984) *Leisure and Recreation Statistics 1984–5 Estimates (London: Chartered Institute of Public Finance and Accountancy)*.

CIPFA (1988) *Leisure and Recreation Statistics 1988–9 Estimates (London: Chartered Institute of Public Finance and Accountancy)*.

CIPFA (1995) *Leisure and Recreation Statistics 1995–6 Estimates* (London: Chartered Institute of Public Finance and Accountancy).

CIPFA (1998) *Leisure and Recreation Statistics 1998–9 Estimates* (London: Chartered Institute of Public Finance and Accountancy).

CIPFA (1999a) *Leisure and Recreation Statistics 1999–2000 Estimates* (London: Chartered Institute of Public Finance and Accountancy).

CIPFA (1999b) *Leisure and Recreation Statistics Estimates 1999–2000* (Croydon: The Chartered Institute of Public Finance and Accountancy).

Cixous, H. and Clément, C. (1987) *The Newly Born Woman* (Manchester: Manchester University Press).

Clark, R. (1980) *The Arts Council* (monograph) (Salford: Centre for Leisure Studies, University of Salford).

Clarke, J. and Critcher, C. (1985) *The Devil Makes Work: Leisure in Capitalist Britain* (London: Macmillan – now Palgrave).

Clarke, J. and Newman, J. (1997) *The Managerial State* (London: Sage).

Coakley, J. (1990) *Sport in Society*, 4th edn (St Louis: Mosby).

Coalter, F. (1990) 'The Politics of Professionalism: Consumers or Citizens?' *Leisure Studies*, 9(2): 107–20.

Coalter, F. (1995) 'Compulsory Competitive Tendering for Sport and Leisure Management: A Lost Opportunity', *Managing Leisure: An International Journal*, 1(1): 3–15.

Coalter, F. with Duffield, B. and Long, J. (1987) *The Rationale for Public Sector Investment in Leisure* (London: Sports Council).

Coates, D. (1999) 'Placing New Labour', in B. Jones (ed.), *Political Issues in Britain Today*, 5th edn (Manchester: Manchester University Press).

Cockburn, C. (1977) *The Local State* (London: Pluto Press).

Coghlan, J. and with Webb, I. (1990) *Sport and British Politics Since 1960* (Brighton: Falmer Press).

Collins, M. (1979) *Usage, Management and Planning of Dry Ski Slopes: Three Studies*, Working Paper 14 (London: Sports Council).

Collins, M. and Randolph, L. (1991) *Small Firms in Sport and Recreation*, Working Paper (Loughborough: Department of Physical Education, Sports Science and Recreation Management, Loughborough University).

Conservative Party (1979) *The Arts: The Way Forward* (London: Conservative Political Centre).

Cooke, P. (1989a) *Back to the Future* (London: Unwin Hyman).

Cooke, P. (1989b) *Localities: The Changing Face of Urban Britain* (London: Unwin Hyman).

Critcher, C. (1991) 'Sporting Civic Pride: Sheffield and the World Student Games of 1991', in C. Knox and J. Sugden (eds), *Leisure in the 1990s: Rolling Back the Welfare State* (Brighton: Leisure Studies Association).

Crosland, A. (1956) *The Future of Socialism* (London: Jonathon Cape).

Cunningham, H. (1980) *Leisure in the Industrial Revolution* (London: Croom Helm).

Dahl, R. (1961) *Who Governs? Democracy and Power in an American City* (New Haven: Yale University Press).

Damesick, P. (1986) 'Service Industries, Employment and Regional Development in Britain', *Transactions*, 11(2).

Danziger, J. (1978) *Making Budgets* (Beverly Hills: Sage).

Darke, R. (1992) *Gambling on Sport: Sheffield's Regeneration Strategy for the 90s* (Sheffield University: Unpublished paper).

Deem, R. (1986) *All Work and No Play: The Sociology of Women's Leisure* (Milton Keynes: Open University Press).

Department of Culture Media and Sport (1999a) *Draft Guidance on Regional Cultural Strategies* (London: DCMS).

Department for Education and Employment (1999) *Labour Market Trends* (London: Central Statistical Office).

Department of Culture Media and Sport (1999b) *Local Cultural Strategies – Draft Guidance for Local Authorities* (London: DCMS).

Department of Culture Media and Sport (1999c) *A New Cultural Framework* (London: DCMS). Available: http://www.culture.gov.uk/creative/index_flash.html, 20 February 2000.

Department of Culture Media and Sport (2000a) *Policy Action Team 10 Report on Sport the Arts and Social Exclusion* (London: DCMS). Available: http://www.culture.gov.uk/role/index_flash.html.

Department of Culture Media and Sport (2000b) *A Sporting Future for All* (London: DCMS).

Department of Education and Science (1991) *Sport and Active Recreation* (London: DES).

Department of Environment (1975) *Sport and Recreation* (London: HMSO).

Department of Environment (1977) *A Policy for the Inner Cities* (London: HMSO).

Department of Environment (1990) *Tourism and the Inner City: An Evaluation of Grant Assisted Tourism Projects* (London: HMSO).

Department of National Heritage (1995b) *Sport: Raising the Game* (London: HMSO).

Department of National Heritage (1995a) *Sport: Raising the Game* (London: HMSO).

Department of National Heritage (1995c) *Sport: Raising the Game.*

Department of Trade and Industry, and Sports Industries Federation (1999) *Competitiveness Analysis of the UK Sporting Goods Industry* (London: Department of Trade and Industry/Sports Industries Federation).

Dine, P. (1997) 'Peasants into Sportsmen: Modern Games and the Construction of French National Identity', in P. Dine and I. Henry (eds), *The Symbolism of Sport in France* (Stirling: University of Stirling).

Donaghu, M. T. and Barff, R. (1990) 'Nike Just Did It – International Subcontracting and Flexibility in Athletic Footwear Production', *Regional Studies*, 24(6): 537–52.

Donajgrodsky, A. (1977) *Social Control in Nineteenth Century Britain* (London: Croom Helm).

Dower, M., Rapoport, R., Strelitz, Z. and Kew, S. (1979) *Leisure Provision and People's Needs: Stage II Report* (Dartington: Dartington Amenity Research Trust/Institute for Family and Environmental Research).

Drucker, H. (ed.) (1983) *Developments in British Politics* (London: Macmillan – now Palgrave).

Dulac, C. (1996) *Stratégies d'Acteurs et Changement Social: Trente Ans de Politique Sportive à Grenoble 1965–95* (Université Joseph Fourier – Grenoble 1, Grenoble).

Duncan, J. (1995, 7 December 1995) 'Lottery Sports Boost for Inner Cities', *Guardian*, 7 December: 13.

Duncan, S. and Goodwin, M. (1988) *The Local State and Uneven Development* (London: Polity).

Dunleavy, P. (1980) *Urban Political Analysis* (London: Macmillan – now Palgrave).

Dunleavy, P. (1984) 'The Limits to Local Government', in M. Boddy and C. Fudge (eds), *Local Socialism?* (London: Macmillan – now Palgrave).

Dunleavy, P. and O'Leary, B. (1987) *Theories of the State: The Politics of Liberal Democracy* (London: Macmillan – now Palgrave).

Dunning, E. and Sheard, K. (1976) *Barbarians, Gentlemen and Players* (London: Martin Robertson).

Durkheim, E. (1964) *The Division of Labour in Society* (New York: Free Press).

Eaton, B. (1996) *European Leisure Businesses: Strategies for the Future* (Bury St Edmunds: ELM Publications).

English Sports Council (1998) *The Lottery Sports Fund. The First 3 Years Achievement Report (Jan. 95–Dec. 97)* (London: English Sports Council).

English Sports Council (1999) *Best Value: Case Studies* (London: Sport England, formerly English Sports Council).

English Sports Council (2000) *Best Value: Performance Measurement for Local Authority Sports Halls and Pools* (London: Sport England, formerly English Sports Council).

Erikson, R. and Syms, P. (1986) 'The Effects of Enterprize Zones on Property Prices', *Regional Studies*, 20(1): 1–14.

Escott, K. and Whitfield, D. (1995) *The Gender Impact of CCT in Local Government* (Manchester: Equal Opportunities Commission).

Esland, G. (1980) Professions and Professionalism', in G. Esland and G. Salaman (eds), *The Politics of Work and Occupations* (Milton Keynes: Open University Press).

Etzioni, A. (1993) *The Spirit of Community: Rights, Responsibilities and the Communitarian Agenda* (London: HarperCollins).

Etzioni, A. (1996) *The New Golden Rule: Community and Morality in a Democratic Society* (London: Profile Books).

European Commission (1998) *The European Model of Sport: A Consultation Document* (Brussels: European Commission – DG X).

European Commission (2000) *Low-Wage Employees in EU Countries* (Brussels: Eurostat).

Eurostat. (1998) *Social Portrait of Europe* (Brussels: Statistical Office of the European Communities).

Evans, B. and Taylor, E. (eds) (1997) *From Salisbury to Major* (Manchester: Manchester University Press).

Evans, H. J. (1974) *Service to Sport: The Story of the CCPR 1935–1972* (London: Pelham).

Falconer, P. (1999, May, 1999) *The New Public Management Today: An Overview.* Paper Presented at the ESRC Seminar on Recent Developments in New Public Management, Imperial College, London.

Farnham, D. and Horton, S. (1993) 'The New Public Service Managerialism: An assessment', in D. F. S. Horton (ed.), *Managing the New Public Services* (London: Macmillan – now Palgrave).

Featherstone, M. (1990) *Global Culture: Nationalism, Globalization and Modernity* (London: Sage).

Featherstone, M. (1995) *Undoing Culture: Globalization, Postmodernism and Identity* (London: Sage).

Foley, P. (1991) 'The Impact of the World Student Games On Sheffield', *Environment and Planning C-Government and Policy*, 9(1): 65–78.

Football Task Force (1999) *Football: Commercial Issues* (A Submission to the Minister of Sport) (London: Football Task Force).

Fraser, D. (1984) *The Evolution of the Welfare State*, 2nd edn (London: Macmillan – now Palgrave) .

Friedman, M. (1962) *Capitalism and Freedom* (Chicago: University of Chicago Press).

Friedman, M. (1976) *Unemployment versus Inflation? An Evaluation of the Phillips Curve* (Occasional Papers no. 45) (London: Institute of Economic Affairs).

Fukuyama, F. (1990) 'Are We At the End of History?' *Fortune*, 121(2): 75.

Fukuyama, F. (1993) *The End of History?* (London: Institute of Economic Affairs).

Gamble, A. (1988) *The Free Economy and the Strong State: The Politics of Thatcherism* (London: Macmillan – now Palgrave).

Gamble, A. (1993) 'The Entrails of Thatcherism', *New left Review*, 198: 117.

Garnham, N. (1983) (December 12–13, 1983) *Concepts of Culture, Cultural Policy and the Cultural Industries*. Paper Presented at the Cultural Industries and Cultural Policy in London Conference, 12–13 December (London: Riverside Studios).

Garnham, N. (1987) 'Concepts of Culture: Public Policy and the Cultural Industries', *Cultural Studies*, 1(1).

Geddes, M. (1989) 'The Capitalist State and the Local Economy: "Restructuring for Labour and Beyond" ', *Capital and Class*, 35: 85–120.

Geoghegan, V. (1984) 'Socialism', in R. Eccleshall *et al.* (eds), *Political Ideologies* (London: Hutchinson).

Giddens, A. (1979) *Central Problems in Social Theory* (London: Macmillan – now Palgrave).

Giddens, A. (1990) *The Consequences of Modernity* (Cambridge: Polity Press).

Gilmour, I. (1978) *Inside Right* (London: Quartet Books).

Gilmour, I. (1992) *Dancing with Dogma: Britain under Thatcherism* (London: Simon & Schuster).

Glover, D. (1984) *The Sociology of the Mass Media* (London: Causeway Press).

Golby, J. and Purdue, A. (1984) *The Civilisation of the Crowd* (London: Batsford Press).

Goldsmith, M. (1980) *Politics, Planning and the City* (London: Hutchinson).

González, J. and Urkiola, A. (1993) 'Leisure Policy in Spain', in P. Bramham, I. Henry, H. Mommaas, and H. van der Poel (eds), *Leisure Policies in Europe* (Wallingford: CAB International).

Goodwin, B. (1982) *Using Political Ideas* (London: John Wiley).

Gough, I. (1979) *The Political Economy of the Welfare State* (London: Macmillan – now Palgrave).

Gould, B. (1989) *A Future for Socialism* (London: Cape).

Gramsci, A. (1971) *Selections from the Prison Notebooks* (London: Lawrence & Wishart).

Gratton, C. (1996) 'Work Time and Leisure in Europe: National Differences and European Convergence', in C. Gratton (ed.), *Work, Leisure and the Quality of Life: A Global Perspective* (Sheffield: Leisure Industries Research Centre).

Gratton, C. (1998) *Economic Impact of Major Sports Events: Lessons from the Study of Six World and European Championships.* Paper Presented at the Sport in the City, Sheffield.

Gratton, C. and Henry. I. (eds) (2001) *Sport in the City: The Role of Sport in Economic and Social Regeneration* (London: Routledge).

Gratton, C. and Taylor, P. (1991) 'The Leisure Market in Britain', unpublished manuscript.

Gratton, C. and Taylor, P. (2000) *The Economics of Sport and Recreation* (London: E. & F. N. Spon).

Gray, J. (1996) *After Social Democracy* (London: Demos).

Gray, J. (1997) *Endgames: Questions in late Modern Political Thought* (Cambridge: Polity).

Green, D. (1987) *The New Right: The Counter-Revolution in Political, Economic and Social Thought* (Brighton: Harvester).

Green, E., Hebron, S. and Woodward, D. (1990) *Women's Leisure, What Leisure?* (London: Macmillan – now Palgrave).

Greenleaf, W. (1983) *The British Political Heritage: Vol. 2 The Ideological Heritage* (London: Methuen).

Gregory, S. (1979) *Badminton at Three Sports Centres,* Sports Council Working Paper no. 11 (London: Sports Council).

Griffiths, R. (1995) 'Cultural Strategies and New Modes of Urban Intervention', *Cities,* 12(4): 253–65.

Grimshaw, P. and Prescott-Clarke, S. (1978) *Sport, School and the Community,* Sports Council Working Paper no. 9 (London: Sports Council).

Grundy, N. (1990) 'Attacking Down the Right', unpublished MSc dissertation (Loughborough University, Loughborough).

Gruneau, R. (1975) 'Sport, Social Differentiation and Social Inequality', in D. Ball and J. Loy (eds), *Sport and Social Order* (Reading, MA: Addison-Wesley).

Guardian Editorial (1994) 'Sproat's Changes and Cutbacks/Sport', *Guardian,* 9 July: 21.

Guardian Leader (1997) 'It Needs Cash and Strategy', *Guardian,* 20 December: 18.

Gurr, T. and King, D. (1987) *The City and the State* (London: Macmillan – now Palgrave).

Gyford, J. (1985) *The Politics of Local Socialism* (London: Allen & Unwin).

Hall, C. (1990) 'Private Persons Versus Public Someones: Class, Gender and Politics in England 1780–1850', in T. Lovell (ed.), *British Feminist Thought* (Oxford: Blackwell).

Hall, S. (1982) *Conformity, Consensus and Conflict* (Milton Keynes: Open University).

Hall, S. (1992) 'The Question of Cultural Identity', in S. Hall, D. Held, and T. McGrew (eds), *Modernity and Its Futures* (Cambridge: Polity/Open University Press).

Hall, S. and Jacques, M. (1983) *The Politics of Thatcherism* (London: Lawrence and Wishart).

Hall, S. and Jefferson, T. (eds) (1976) *Resistance through Ritual* (London: Hutchinson).

Hambleton, R. (1988) 'Consumerism, Decentralization and Local Democracy', *Public Administration*, 66(2): 125–47.

Hantrais, L. (1989) 'Central Government Policy in France under the Socialist Administration 1981–6', in P. Bramham, I. Henry, H. Mommaas, and H. van der Poel (eds), *Leisure and Urban Processes: Critical Studies of Leisure Policy in Western European Cities* (London: Routledge).

Hargreaves, J. (1985) 'From Social Democracy to Authoritarian Populism', *Leisure Studies*, 4(2).

Hargreaves, J. (1986) *Sport, Power and Culture: A Social and Historical Analysis of Popular Sports in Britain* (Cambridge: Polity).

Harrison, B. (1967) 'Religion and Recreation in Nineteenth Century England', *Past and Present*, no. 38, December.

Harrison, B. (1971) *Drink and the Victorians: The Temperance Question in England 1815–1872* (London: Faber).

Harvey, D. (1989) *The Condition of Postmodernity* (Oxford: Basil Blackwell).

Hattersley, R. (1987) *Economic Priorities for a Labour Government* (Basingstoke: Macmillan).

Hay, C. (1994) 'Labour's Thatcherite Revisionism: Playing the "Politics of Catch-up" ', *Political studies*, XLII(4): 700–7.

Hay, C. (1997) 'Blaijorism: Towards a One – Vision Polity?' *Political Quarterly*, 68(4): 372–8.

Hayek, F. (1946) *The Road to Serfdom* (London: Routledge).

Hayek, F. (1976) *Law, Legislation and Liberty* (London: Routledge).

Hayes, M. (1994) *The New Right in Britain: An Introduction to Theory and Practice*.

Haynes, R. (1980) *Organisation Theory and Local Government* (London: Allen & Unwin).

Haywood, L. and Henry, I. (1986a) 'Policy Developments in Community Leisure and Recreation: Part 1 – Implications for Management', *Leisure Management*, 6(7).

Haywood, L. and Henry, I. (1986b) 'Policy Developments in Community Leisure and Recreation: Part 2 – Practice, Education and Training', *Leisure Management*, 6(7).

Haywood, L., Kew, F., Bramham, P., Spink, J., Henry, I. and Capenerhurst, J. (1996) *Understanding Leisure*, 2nd edn (Cheltenham: Stanley Thorne).

Hebdige, D. (1988) *Subculture: The Meaning of Style* (London: Routledge).

Held, D. (1980) *Introduction to Critical Theory: Horkheimer to Habermas* (London: Hutchinson).

Heller, A. and Fehér, F. (1991) *The Postmodern Political Condition* (Oxford: Polity Press).

Henley Centre for Forecasting. (1986) *The Economic Impact and Importance of Sport*, study no. 30 (London: Sports Council).

Henry, I. (1984a) 'Conservatism, Socialism and Management of Leisure Services', *Leisure Management*, 4(11).

Henry, I. (1984b) 'Leisure Management and the Politics of the New Right', *Leisure Management*, 4(9).

Henry, I. (1984c) 'Leisure Management and the Social Democratic Tradition', *Leisure Management*, 4(12).

Henry, I. (1984d) 'Urban Deprivation and the Use of Social Indicators for Recreation Planning', in J. Long and R. Hecock (eds), *Leisure, Tourism and Social Change* (Edinburgh: Centre for Leisure Research).

Henry, I. (1987) *The Politics of Leisure and Leisure Policy in Local Government*. Unpublished Doctoral Thesis, Loughborough University, Loughborough.

Henry, I. (1997) 'The Politics of Sport and Symbolism in the City', *Managing Leisure: An International Journal*, 3(2): 65–81.

Henry, I. (1999) 'Globalisation and the Governance of Leisure: The Roles of the Nation-State, the European Union and the City in Leisure Policy in Britain', *Loisir et Societe* [Society and Leisure], 22(2): 355–79.

Henry, I. and Bramham, P. (1986) 'Leisure, the Local State and Social Order', *Leisure Studies*, 5(2).

Henry, I. and Matthews, N. (1998) 'Sport Policy and the European Union: The Post-Maastricht Agenda', *Managing Leisure: An International Journal*, 4(1).

Henry, I. and Paramio Salcines, J. (1999) 'Sport and the Analysis of Symbolic Regimes: An Illustrative Case Study of the City of Sheffield', *Urban Affairs Review*, 34(5): 641–66.

Henry, I. and Paramio-Salcines, J. L. (1998) 'Leisure, Culture and Urban Regimes in Bilbao', in I. Cooper and M. Collins (eds), *Leisure Management: International Perspectives* (Wallingford: CAB International).

Henry, I. and Spink, J. (1990) 'Social Theory, Planning and Management', in I. Henry (ed.), *Management and Planning in the Leisure Industries* (Basingstoke: Macmillan).

Hewison, R. (1994) 'The Arts', in D. Kavanagh and A. Seldon (eds), *The Major Effect* (London: Macmillan – now Palgrave).

Hill, C. (1964) *Society and Puritanism in Pre-Revolutionary England* (Cambridge: Cambridge University Press).

Hirst, P. and Thompson, G. (1995) 'Globalization and the Future of the Nation-State', *Economy and Society*, 24(3): 408–42.

Hobbes, T. (1968) *Leviathan* (Harmondsworth: Penguin).

Hoggett, P. (1987) 'Farewell to Mass Production? Decentralisation as an Emergent Private and Public Sector Paradigm', in P. Hoggett and R.

Hambleton (eds), *Decentralisation and Democracy: Localising Public Services* (Bristol: University of Bristol, School for Advanced Urban Studies, Occasional Paper no. 28).

Hoggett, P. and Bishop, J. (1986) *The Social Organisation of Leisure: A Study of Groups in their Voluntary Sector Context* (London: Sports Council/Economic and Social Research Council).

Holland, P. (1979) *Costing the Quangos* (London: Adam Smith Institute).

Holland, P. (1981) *The Governance of the Quangos* (London: Adam Smith Institute).

Holland, P. (1982) *Quelling the Quangos* (London: Adam Smith Institute).

Holland, S. (1971) *Sovereignty and Multi National Companies* (London: Fabian Society).

Holliday, S. (1996) 'Trends in British Work and Leisure', in C. Gratton (ed.), *Work, Leisure and the Quality of Life: A Global Perspective* (Sheffield: Leisure Industries Research Centre).

Holt, R. (1989) *Sport and the British: A Modern History* (Oxford: Oxford University Press).

Holt, R. and Tomlinson, A. (1994) 'Sport and Leisure', in D. Kavanagh and A. Seldon (eds), *The Major Effect* (London: Macmillan – now Palgrave).

Houlihan, B. (1991) *The Government and Politics of Sport* (London: Routledge).

Houlihan, B. (1997) *Sport, Policy and Politics: An International Comparison* (London: Routledge).

House of Lords Select Committee (1973) *Sport and Leisure (Cobham Report)* (London: HMSO).

Howkins, A. and Lowerson, J. (1979) *Trends in Leisure 1919–1939* (London: Sports Council/Social Sciences Research Council).

Hughes, A. and Witz, A. (1997) 'Feminism and the Matter of Bodies: from de Beauvoir to Butler', *Body and Society*, 3(1): 47–60.

Huizinga, J. (1938) *Homo Ludens: A Study of the Play Element in Culture.* (Vol.???) (1980 Reprint) (London: Routledge & Kegan Paul).

Hutton, W. (1994) *The State We're In* (London: Cape).

Jacques, M. (1997) 'The Great Moving Centre Show', *New Statesman*, 21 November: 26–8.

Jarvie, G. (ed.) (1991) *Sport, Race and Ethnicity* (Brighton: Falmer Press).

Jessop, B. (1988) 'Regulation Theory, Post-Fordism and the State', *Capital and Class*, 34 (Spring).

Jessop, B. (1990a) 'Regulation Theory in Retrospect and Prospect', *Economy and Society*, 19(2).

Jessop, B. (1990c) *State Theory: Putting Capitalist States in their Place* (Oxford: Polity Press).

Jessop, B. (1991) 'Thatcherism and Flexibility – the White Heat of a Post-Fordist Revolution', in (eds) Jessop. B., Kastendiak, H., Nielson, K., Peterson, O. *The Politics of Flexibility* (Aldershot: Edward Elgar) 135–61.

Jessop, B. (1995a) 'The Regulation Approach, Governance and Post-Fordism – Alternative Perspectives on Economic and Political-Change', *Economy and Society*, 24(3): 307–33.

Jessop, B. (1995b) 'Towards a Schumpeterian Workfare Regime in Britain – Reflections on Regulation, Governance, and Welfare-State', *Environment and Planning*, 27(10): 1613–26.

Johnson, T. (1969) *Professions and Power* (London: Macmillan – now Palgrave).

Jones, M. (1998) 'Restructuring the Local State: Economic Governance or Social Regulation?' *Political Geography*, 17(8): 959–88.

Jones, S. (1986) *Workers at Play* (London: Routledge & Kegan Paul).

Jordan, B. (1982) *Mass Unemployment and the Future of Britain* (Oxford: Blackwell).

Kantor, P., Savitch, H. V. and Haddock, S. V. (1997) 'The Political Economy of Urban Regimes – A Comparative Perspective', *Urban Affairs Review*, 32(3): 348–77.

Kaplan, M. (1975) *Leisure: Theory and Policy* (New York: Wiley.

Kavanagh, D. (1994) 'A Major Agenda?' in D. Kavanagh and A. Seldon (eds), *The Major Effect* (London: Macmillan).

Kavanagh, D. (1997) 'The Labour Campaign', *Parliamentary Affairs*, 50(4): 533–41.

Keil, R. (1998) 'Globalization makes States: Perspectives of Local Governance in the Age of the World City', *Review of International Political Economy*, 5(4): 616–46.

Kelly, D. (1999) 'The Strategic Relational View of the State', *Politics*, 19(2): 109–15.

Kelly, O. (1984) *Community, Art and the State* (London: Comedia).

Kerr, H., Ashton, H. and Carless, R. (1959) *The Challenge of Leisure* (London: Conservative Political Centre).

Key Note. (2000) *Key Note Market Review: UK Leisure Trends* 2000 (London: MarketScape Ltd).

Kinnock, N. (1987) 'Kinnock on Leisure', *Leisure Manager*, 7(3).

Klausner, D. (1986) 'Beyond Separate Spheres: Linking Production with Social Reproduction and Consumption', *Environment and Planning D: Society and Space*, 4.

Kronos (1997) *The Economic Impact of Events Staged in Sheffield 1990–1997* (Sheffield: Kronos on behalf of Destination Sheffield, Sheffield City Council's Events Unit and Sheffield International Venues Ltd).

Labour Party (1959) *Leisure for Living* (London: Labour Party).

Labour Party (1977) *The Arts and the People: Labour's Policy towards the Arts* (London: Labour Party).

Labour Party. (1986) *Charter for the Arts* (London: Labour Party).

Labour Party (1997) *Labour's Sporting Nation* (London: Labour Party).

Laffan, B., O'Donnell, R. and Smith, M. (2000) *Europe's Experimental Union: Rethinking Integration* (London: Routledge).

Lane, J.-E. (1995) *The Public Sector: Concepts, Models and Approaches* (London: Sage).

Lansley, S., Goss, S. and Wolmar, C. (1989) *Councils in Conflict: The Rise and Fall of 'Local Socialism'* (London: Macmillan – now Palgrave).

Lash, S. and Urry, J. (1987) *The End of Organised Capitalism* (Cambridge: Polity Press).

Lash, S. and Urry, J. (1994) *Economies of Signs and Space* (London: Sage).

Lawrence, L., Standeven, J. and Tomlinson, A. (1994) *CCT in Leisure Management: An Interim Report* (London: Sports Council and the Sports Council for Wales).

Leach, S., Stewart, J. and Walsh, K. (1994) *The Changing Organisation and Management of Local Government* (London: Macmillan – now Palgrave).

Lefebvre, H. (1971) *Everyday Life in the Modern World* (New York: Harper Torchbooks).

Levitas, R. (1998) *The Inclusive Society? Social Exclusion and New Labour* (London: Routledge).

Lewes, F. and Mennell, S. (1976) *Leisure, Culture and Local Government* (Exeter: University of Exeter).

Limb, M. (1986) 'Community Involvement in Leisure Provision', in F. Coalter (ed.), *The Politics of Leisure* (Brighton: Leisure Studies Association).

Lipietz, A. (1987) *Miracles and Mirages: The Crisis of Global Fordism* (London: Verso).

Lloyd, P. (1985) *Services Administration by Local Authorities* (Cambridge: ICSA Publishing).

Loney, M., Boswell, M. and Clarke, J. (1983) *Social Policy and Social Welfare* (London: Open University Press).

Looseley, D. (1995) *The Politics of Fun: Cultural Policy and Debate in Contemporary France* (Oxford: Berg).

Lowi, T. (1972) From Systems of Policy, Politics and Choice *Public Administration Review*, July–August.

Ludlam, S. and Smith, M. J. (eds) (1996) *Contemporary British Conservatism* (Basingstoke: Macmillan).

MacCormick, N. (1997) 'Democracy, Subsidiarity, and Citizenship in the "European Commonwealth"', *Law and Philosophy*, 16(4): 331–56.

MacEwan, A. and MacEwan, M. (1982) *National Parks: Conservation or Cosmetics?* (London: Allen & Unwin).

Macmillan, H. (1938) *The Middle Way: A Study of the Problems of Economic and Social Progress in a Free and Democratic Society* (London: Conservative Political Centre).

Maguire, J. (1995) 'Sportization Processes: Emergence, Diffusion and Globalization', *Schweizerische Zeitschrift für Soziologie*, 21(3): 577–96.

Maguire, J. (1999) *Global Sport: Identities, Societies, Civilizations* (Oxford: Polity Press).

Major, J. (1995) 'Foreword', in Department of National Heritage (ed.), *Sport: Raising the Game* (London: HMSO).

Malcolmson, R. (1973) *Popular Recreations in English Society 1700–1850* (Cambridge: Cambridge University Press).

Marcuse, H. (1964) *One Dimensional Man* (London: Routledge & Kegan Paul).

Martin, R. (1988) 'Industrial Capitalism in Transition: The Contemporary Reorganisation of the British Space Economy', in D. Massey and J. Allen (eds), *Uneven Redevelopment: Cities and Regions in Transition* (Beverley Hills, CA: Sage).

Martin, W. H. and Mason, S. (1998) *Transforming the Future Quality of Life: Rethinking Free Time and Work* (Sudbury, Suffolk: Leisure Consultants).

Mason, C. and Harrison, R. (1990) 'Small Firms: Pheonix form the Ashes', in D. Pinder (ed.), *Western Europe: Challenge and Change* (London: Belhaven Press).

Mayer, M. (1994) 'Post-Fordist City Politics', in A. Amin (ed.), *Post-Fordism: A Reader* (Oxford: Blackwell).

McCloy, A. (1999) 'Walking: Is this Really a Right to Roam?' *Guardian,* 14 March: 6.

McDowell, L. (1989) 'Labour and Life', in M. Ball, F. Gray, and L. McDowell (eds), *The Transformation of Britain: Contemporary Social and Economic Change* (London: Fontana).

McHardy, A. (1994) 'The Regeneration Game. *Guardian,* 26 October: 29.

McIntosh, P. (1963) *Sport and Society* (Oxford: Brailsford).

Meller, H. (1976) *Leisure and the Changing City 1870–1914* (London: Routledge & Kegan Paul).

Middleton, M. (1991) *Cities in Transition* (London: Michael Joseph).

Miliband, R. (1973) *The State in Capitalist Society* (London: Quartet Books).

Miller, D. (1989) *Market, State and Community: Theoretical Foundations of Market Socialism* (Oxford: Clarendon Press).

Mintel (1994) *Sports Sponsorship* (London: Mintel).

Mintel (1996) *Health and Fitness: Fit for Future Growth* (London: Mintel).

Mintel (1997) *Satellite and Cable Television*, Market Research Report (London: Mintel).

Mintel (1998a) *Leisure Centres and Swimming Pools* (London: Mintel).

Mintel (1998b) *Leisure Trends* (London: Mintel).

Morris, L. (1997) 'Globalization, Migration and the Nation-State: The Path to a Post-National Europe?' *British Journal of Sociology*, 48(2): 192–209.

Moynihan, C. (1987) Open Letter to the Chairman of the Sports Council (November).

Mulgan, G. and Worpole, K. (1986) *Saturday Night or Sunday Morning? From Arts to Industry: New Forms of Cultural Policy* (London: Comedia).

Murphy, J. (1981) *Concepts of Leisure* (Englewood Cliffs, New Jersey: Prentice-Hall).

Myerscough, J. (1974) 'The Recent History of the Use of Leisure Time', in I. Appleton (ed.), *Leisure and Public Policy* (Edinburgh: Scottish Academic Press).

Myerscough, J. (1988) *The Economic Importance of the Arts in Britain* (London: Policy Studies Institute).

Neulinger, J. (1974) *The Psychology of Leisure* (Springfield, Illinois: Charles C. Thomas).

Newton, K. (1976) *Second City Politics* (Oxford: Clarendon Press).

Newton, K. and Karan, T. (1985) *The Politics of Local Government Expenditure* (London: Macmillan – now Palgrave).

Nicholls, G. (1999) 'The Transformation of Local Democracy through the Process of Best Value – the Experience of Pilots in Sport and Leisure Services, unpublished: Sheffield University.

Nicholls, G. and Taylor, P. (1995) 'The Impact on Local Authority Leisure Provision of Compulsory Competitive Tendering, Financial Cuts and Changing Attitudes', *Local Government Studies*, 21(4): 607–22.

Nozick, R. (1974) *Anarchy and the State* (Oxford: Blackwell).

Oakeshott, M. (1976) 'On Being a Conservative', in A. de Crispigny and J. Cronin (eds), *Ideologies of Politics* (London: Open University Press).

O'Connor, J. (1973) *The Fiscal Crisis of the State* (New York: St. James Press).

Office for National Statistics (1996) *Social Trends* (London: HMSO).

Office for National Statistics (1997) *Social Trends* (London: HMSO).

Office for National Statistics (1998) *Social Trends* (London: HMSO).

Office for National Statistics (1999) *Family Spending: A Report on the Family Expenditure Survey* (London: HMSO).

Olson, M. (1982) *The Rise and Decline of Nations* (New Haven: Yale University Press).

Osborne, D. and Gaebler, T. (1992) *Reinventing Government: How the Entrepreneurial Spirit is Transforming the Public Sector* (Reading MA: Addison-Wesley).

Overseas Trade Statistics (1981, 1986, 1991, 1996) *Overseas Trade Statistics of the United Kingdom with the World* (London: Stationery Office).

Owen, D. (1981) *Face the Future* (Harmondsworth: Penguin).

Pahl, R. (1977) 'Managers, Technical Experts and the State', in M. Harloe (ed.), *Captive Cities* (Chichester: John Wiley).

Parker, S. (1971) *The Future of Works and Leisure* (London: MacGibbon & Kee).

Peck, J. and Tickell, A. (1994) 'Searching for a New Institutional Fix: The *After*-Fordist Crisis and the Global-Local Disorder', in A. Amin (ed.), *Post-Fordism: A Reader* (Oxford: Blackwell).

Pendry, T. (1991) 'Letter "Cash Crisis for British Sport" ', *Guardian,* 16 November: 26.

Perlmutter, H. (1991) 'On the Rocky Road to the First Global Civilisation', *Human Relations*, 44(9): 898–906.

Peters, T. (1987) *Thriving on Chaos: Handbook for a Management Revolution* (London: Pan).

Peters, T. (1993) *Liberation Management* (New York: Knopf).

Peters, T. and Austen, N. (1985) *A Passion for Excellence: The Leadership Difference* (London: Collins).

Peters, T. and Waterman, R. (1982) *In Search of Excellence* (London: Harper & Row).

Pieper, J. (1946) *Leisure: The Basis of Culture* (New York: North American Library).

Pierson, C. (1991) *Beyond the Welfare State?: The New Political Economy of Welfare* (Cambridge: Polity Press).

Plant, R. (1983) 'The Resurgence of Ideology', in H. Drucker (ed.), *Developments in British Politics* (London: Macmillan – now Palgrave).

Pond, C. (1989) 'The Changing Distribution of Income, Wealth and Poverty', in C. Hamnett, L. McDowell, and P. Sarre (eds), *The Changing Social Structure* (London: Sage).

Poujol, G. (1993) 'Leisure Policy and Politics in France', in P. Bramham, I. Henry, H. Mommaas, and H. van der Poel (eds), *Leisure Policies in Europe* (Wallingford, Oxon: CAB International).

Public Service Privatisation Unit (1992) 'CCT: The Story So Far', *Leisure Management*, 12(5): 26–8.

Pym, F. (1984) *The Politics of Consent* (London: Hamish Hamilton).

Quinn, J. (1980) *Strategies for Change: Logical Incrementalism* (Homewood, IL: Irwin).

Redcliff-Maud, L. (1969) *Report of he Royal Commission on Local Government in England* (London: HMSO).

Rhodes, M. and van Apeldoorn, B. (1998) 'Capital Unbound? The Transformation of European Corporate Governance', *Journal of European Public Policy*, 5(3): 406–27.

Rhodes, R. A. W. (1996) 'The New Governance: Governing without Government', *Political Studies*, 44(4): 652–67.

Rice, D. (2000) 'It's Not Just a Game – Media Companies Involvement in English Premier League Football Clubs', unpublished undergraduate dissertation Loughborough University, Loughborough.

Ridley, F. (1987) 'Tradition, Change and Crisis in Great Britain', in M. Cumming and R. Katz (eds), *The Patron State: Government and the Arts in Europe, North America and Japan* (Oxford: Oxford University Press).

Riordan, J. (ed.) (1978) *Sport under Communism* (London: Hurst.

Roberts, K. (1978) *Contemporary Society and the Growth of Leisure* (Harlow: Longman).

Robertson, R. (1992) *Globalization: Social Theory and Global Culture* (London: Sage).

Roche, M. (1992) *Problems of Rationality and Democracy in Mega-Event Planning: A Study of Sheffield's World Student Games 1991.* Paper Presented at the Leisure and New Citizenship, the VIIIth European Leisure and Recreation Association Congress, Bilbao, Spain.

Roche, M. (1998) *Sport, Popular Culture and Identity* (Aachen: Meyer & Meyer).

Rodda, J. (1994) 'Sports Politics: Elite to Benefit as Sports Council Goes', *Guardian,* 9 July: 21.

Rojek, C. (1994) *Decentring Leisure: Rethinking Leisure Theory* (London: Sage).

Rosenau, J. (1989) *Interdependence and Conflict in World Politics* (Lexington: D.C. Heath).

Rothbard, M. (1978) *For a New Liberty: The Libertarian Manifesto*, 2nd edn (New York: Collier-Macmillan).

Rubinstein, D. (1997) 'How New is New Labour?', *Political Quarterly*, 68(4): 339–43.

Sarre, P. (1989) 'Recomposition of the Class Structure', in C. Hamnett, L. McDowell and P. Sarre (eds), *The Changing Social Structure* (London: Sage).

Saunders, P. (1981) *Social Theory and the Urban Question* (London: Hutchinson).

Saunders, P. (1984) 'Rethinking Local Politics', in M. Boddy and C. Fudge (eds), *Local Socialism?* (Basingstoke: Macmillan – now Palgrave).

Scarman, L. (1981) *The Brixton Disorders: Report of the Right Honourable Lord Scarman* (London: HMSO).

Scraton, S. (1988) *Feminist Critiques and Reconstructions in the Sociology of Sport.* Paper Presented at the Olympic Scientific Congress, Dankook University, Seoul, South Korea.

Scruton, R. (1980) *The Meaning of Conservatism* (London: Macmillan – now Palgrave).

Selsdon Group. (1978) *A Policy for the Arts: Just Cut Taxes* (London: Selsdon Group).

Seyd, P. (1990) 'Radical Sheffield – From Socialism to Entrepreneurialism', *Political Studies*, 38(2): 335–44.

Seyd, P. (1993) 'The Political Management of Decline 1973–1993', in C. Binfield (ed.), *The History of the City of Sheffield 1843–1993*.Vol. 1, *Politics* (Sheffield: Sheffield Academic Press).

Shaw, M. (1997) 'The State of globalization: Towards a Theory of State Transformation', *Review of international Political Economy*, 4(3): 497–513.

Sheffield City Council (1983) *Employment and Environmental Plan for the Lower Don Valley* (Sheffield: Department of Employment and Economic Development, Sheffield City Council).

Sheffield City Council (1984) *Employment in Sheffield, Yorkshire and Humberside, and Great Britain: Results of the Census of Employment* (Sheffield: Sheffield City Council).

Sheffield City Council Recreation Department (1984) *Leisure Challenge: A Prospect for the Lower Don Valley* (Sheffield: Sheffield City Council).

Sheffield Economic Regeneration Committee (n.d.) *Sheffield 2000: The Development Strategy* (Sheffield: Sheffield City Council).

Shivers, J. (1981) *Leisure and Recreation Concepts: A Critical Analysis* (New York: Allyn and Bacon).

Shoard, M. (1980) *The Theft of the Countryside* (London: Temple Smith).

Shoard, M. (1999) 'Right to Roam: Scots Show the Way', *Guardian,* 26 May: 4.

Shore, C. (1993) 'Inventing the People's Europe – Critical Approaches to European – Community Cultural Policy', *Man*, 28(4): 779–800.

Shutt, J. (1984) 'Tory Enterprize Zones and the Labour Movement', *Capital and Class*, 23.

Skeffington, A. (1969) *Planning and People: Report of the Committee on Public Participation in Planning* (London: HMSO).

Sklair, L. (1991) *Sociology of the Global System* (Brighton: Harvester Wheatsheaf).

Smith, C. (1998a) 'Arts: Why are these People Wrong?' *Guardian,* 12 January: 4.

Smith, M. J. (1998b) 'Reconceptualizing the British State: Theoretical and Empirical Challenges to Central Government', *Public Administration*, 76(1): 45–72.

Sport England. (2000) *Sport England: Sport Action Zones*. Sport England. Available: http://www.english.sports.gov.uk/whatwedo/active_commune/zones.htm.

Sports Council (1979) *Annual Report and Accounts* (London: Sports Council).

Sports Council (1983) *Sport in the Community: The Next Ten Years* (London: Sports Council).

Sports Council (1988) *Sport in the Community: into the 90s. A Strategy for Sport 1988–93* (London: Sports Council).

Stabler, M. (ed.) (1984) *The Economics of Leisure* (Brighton: Leisure Studies Association).

Stoker, G. (1988) *The Politics of Local Government* (London: Macmillan – now Palgrave).

Stoker, G. (1990) 'Regulation Theory, Local Government and the Transition from Fordism', in D. King and J. Pierre (eds) *Challenges to Local Government*, 242–64 (London: Sage).

Stoker, G. (1991) *The Politics of Local Government* (London: Macmillan).

Strange, I. (1993) *Public–Private Partnership and the Politics of Economic Regeneration Policy in Sheffield, c. 1985–1991*. Unpublished PhD, University of Sheffield, Sheffield.

Sullivan, O. (2000) 'The Division of Domestic Labour: Twenty Years of Change?' *Sociology*, 34(3): 437–56.

Summerfield, P. (1981) 'The Effingham Arms and the Empire: Deliberate Selection in the Evolution of the Music Hall in London', in S. Yeo and S. Yeao (eds), *Popular Culture and Class Conflict 1590–1914* (Brighton: Harvester).

Taylor Gooby, P. (1991) 'Welfare State Regimes and Welfare Citizenship', *Journal of European Social Policy*, 1(2): 93–105.

Taylor, J. (1990) 'Sheffield Leisure Services: Compelled to Compete and "Capped" into Contraction. Crisis or Catalyst for Leisure Policy in the City?', paper presented at the Leisure, Culture and the Political Economy of the City Conference, Halkida, Greece: unpublished.

Taylor, P. (1998) *Sports Facility Development and the Role of Forecasting: A Retrospective on Swimming in Sheffield*. Paper Presented at the Sport in the City Conference, Sheffield.

Theakston, K. (1999) 'A Permanent Revolution in Whitehall: The Major Governments and the Civil Service', in P. Dorey (ed.), *The Major Premiership: Politics and Policies under John Major 1990–1997*.

Thompson, E. P. (1963) *The Making of the English Working Class* (London: Gollancz).

Thompson, E. P. (1967) 'Time, Work Discipline and Industrial Capitalism', *Past and Present*, 38.

Thrift, N. (1989) 'Images of Social Change', in C. Hamnett, L. McDowell, and P. Sarre (eds), *The Changing Social Structure* (London: Sage).

Tichlear, M. (1998) 'Impact of TUPE on Compulsory Competitive Tendering: Evidence from Employers', *Local Government Studies*, 24(3): 36–50.

Tomlinson, A. (1979) *Leisure and the Role of Clubs and Voluntary Organisations* (London: Sports Council/ESRC).

Town, S. and King, P. (1985) 'Race and Leisure Policy: Bradford's Race Action Plan', in I. Henry (ed.), *Leisure Policy and Disadvantaged Groups*, September (Brighton: Leisure Studies Quarterly Supplement, Leisure Studies Association).

Trades Union Congress (1976) *The Working Party on the Arts* (London: TUC).

Trades Union Congress (1980) *Sport and Recreation* (London: TUC).

Travis, A. and Veal, A. (1979) *The State and Leisure Provision* (London: Sports Council/Social Sciences Research Council).

Treasury (1981) *The Government's Expenditure Plans 1982/3–1984/5* (London: HMSO).

Treasury (1984) *The Government's Expenditure Plans 1985/6–1987/8* (London: HMSO).

Treasury (1986) *The Government's Expenditure Plans 1987/8–1989/90* (London: HMSO).

Treasury (1987) *The Government's Expenditure Plans 1988/9–1990/1* (London: HMSO).

Treasury (1988) *The Government's Expenditure Plans 1989/90–1991/2* (London: HMSO).

Treasury (1989) *The Government's Expenditure Plans 1990/1–1992/3* (London: HMSO).

Treasury (1990) *The Government's Expenditure Plans 1991/2–1993/4* (London: HMSO).

UK Government (1999) *Modernising Government*. (Vol. CM 4310) (London: HMSO).

Urry, J. (1990) *The Tourist Gaze* (London: Sage).

Vamplew, W. (1988) *Pay Up and Play the Game* (Cambridge: Cambridge University Press).

van der Poel, H. (1993) 'Leisure Policy in the Netherlands', in P. Bramham, I. Henry, H. Mommaas and H. van der Poel (eds), *Leisure Policies in Europe* (Wallingford, Oxon: CAB International).

Veal, A. (1979) 'Special Issue on Leisure Services', *Local Government Studies*, 5(4).

Wachtel, D. (1987) *Cultural Policy in Socialist France* (London: Greenwood).

Walby, S. (1990) *Theorizing Patriarchy* (Oxford: Blackwell).

Wallace, W. (1990) *The Transformation of Western Europe* (London: Pinter).

Wallerstein, I. (1983) *Historical Capitalism* (London: Verso).

Walton, J. (1975) 'Residential Amenity, Respectable Morality and the Rise of the Entertainment Industry: The Case of Blackpool 1860–1914', *Literature and History*, 1: 62–78.

Walvin, J. (1978) *Leisure and Society 1830–1950* (London: Longman).

Waters, C. (1990) *British Socialism and the Politics of Popular Culture* (Manchester: Manchester University Press).

Whannel, G. (1983) *Blowing the Whistle: The Politics of Sport* (London: Pluto Press).

White, J. (1988) 'Women in Leisure Services Management', in E. Wimbush and M. Talbot (eds), *Relative Freedoms* (London: Open University Press).

Whitsun, D. (1984) *Leisure and the State: Theorising Struggles over Everyday Life*. Paper Presented at the Leisure, Planning, Politics and People: First International Conference of the Leisure Studies Association, Sussex University.

Wilding, P. (1992) 'The British Welfare State – Thatcherism's Enduring Legacy', *Policy and Politics*, 20(3): 201–12.

Wilding, R. (1989) *Supporting the Arts: A Review of the Structure of Arts Funding* (London: Office of Arts and Libraries).

Williams, A., Shore, G. and Huber, M. (1995) 'The Arts and Economic Development: Regional and Urban–Rural Contrast in UK Local Authority Policies for Sport', *Regional Studies*, 29(1): 73–80.

Williams, C. (1999) *Best Value in Leisure Services: A Philosophy or a Quality System*. Paper Presented at the Leisure Studies Association Annual Conference, Cheltenham.

Williams, R. (1981a) *Culture* (London: Fontana).

Williams, S. (1981b) *Politics is for People* (Harmondsworth: Penguin).

Willis, P. (1982) 'Women in Sport in Ideology', in J. Hargreaves (ed.), *Sport, Culture and Ideology* (London: Routledge & Kegan Paul).

Wimbush, E. and Talbot, M. (eds) (1988) *Relative Freedoms* (London: Open University Press).

Wittgenstein, L. (1970) *Philosophical Investigations* (Oxford: Blackwell).

Witts, R. (1998) *Artist Unknown. An Alternative History of the AAs Council* (London: Little, Brown).

Wolff, J. (1993) *Aesthetics and the Sociology of Art* (London: Macmillan – now Palgrave).

Wright, T. (1996) *Socialisms Old and New* (London: Routledge).

Wynne, D. (1992) *The Culture Industry – the Arts in Urban Regeneration* (Aldershot: Avebury).

Young, H. (1998) 'Comment: Culture? No These People Would Prefer to be Seen with Noel Galagher', *Guardian*, 21 May: 20.

Young, K. (1994) 'Local Government', in D. Kavanagh and A. Seldon (eds), *The Major Effect* (London: Macmillan).

Yule, J. (1992) 'Gender and Leisure Policy', *Leisure Studies*, 11(2).

Yule, J. (1997) 'Engendered Ideologies and Leisure Policy in the UK. Part 1: Gender Ideologies', *Leisure Studies*, 16(2): 61–84.

Index

278   *Index*